Colección Támesis

SERIE A: MONOGRAFÍAS, 230

A COMPANION TO MEXICAN STUDIES

This most recent of the Tamesis Companion series traces the evolution of the major creative aspects of Mexican culture from pre-Columbian times to the present. Dealing in turn with the cultures of Mesoamerica, the colonial period, the onset of independence, and the modern era, the author explores Aztec arts, the role of the performing arts in the process of evangelisation, manifestations of cultural dependence, of the search for national identity, and the struggle for modernity, drawing examples from such diverse activities as architecture, painting, music, dance, literature, film and media. There is also a brief account of the distinctive characteristics of Mexican Spanish. Maps, a chronology, a bibliographical essay and a lengthy bibliography round off this comprehensive guide, making it an indispensable research tool for those seriously interested in Mexican culture.

PETER STANDISH is Professor of Spanish at one of the divisions of the University of North Carolina system.

PETER STANDISH

A COMPANION TO MEXICAN STUDIES

TAMESIS

First published 2006
by Tamesis, Woodbridge
Paperback edition 2010

Transferred to digital printing

ISBN 978-1-85566-134-9 hardback
ISBN 978-1-85566-214-8 paperback

Tamesis is an imprint of Boydell & Brewer Ltd
PO Box 9, Woodbridge, Suffolk IP12 3DF, UK
and of Boydell & Brewer Inc.
668 Mt Hope Avenue, Rochester, NY 14620, USA
website: www.boydellandbrewer.com

A CiP catalogue record for this book is available from the British Library

This publication is printed on acid-free paper

CONTENTS

ILLUSTRATIONS

Jacket: The church at Tonantzintla, near Puebla, showing evidence of the fusion of Indian traits with Christian/Spanish ones

Illustrations

Maps

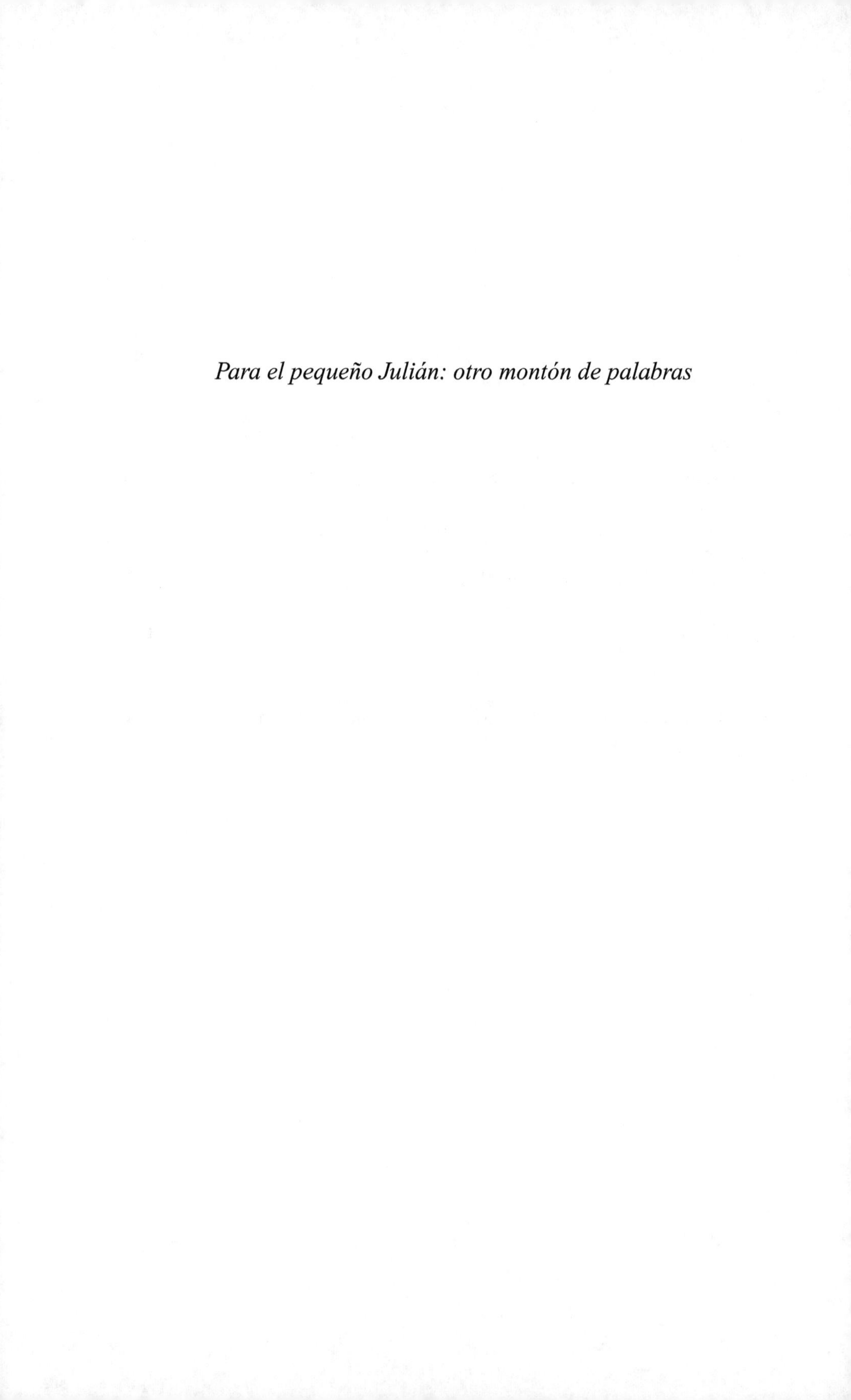

Para el pequeño Julián: otro montón de palabras

ACKNOWLEDGEMENTS

I am grateful to my colleagues Paul Fallon and Juan José Daneri for their help; the former made some bibliographical suggestions relating to the border culture, the latter made others relating to the colonial period and cast a friendly critical eye over the early chapters of the manuscript. The black and white illustrations are from photographs taken by myself; others in colour are reproduced by permission. Thanks are due to the Graduate School and the Thomas Harriot College of Arts and Sciences, both of East Carolina University; their financial support made possible the inclusion of colour illustrations.

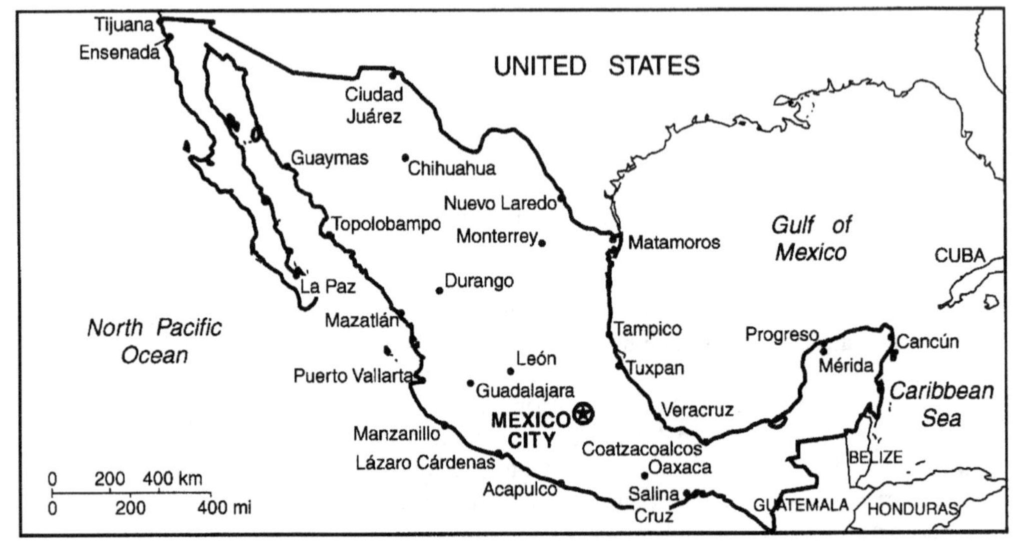

Major Towns

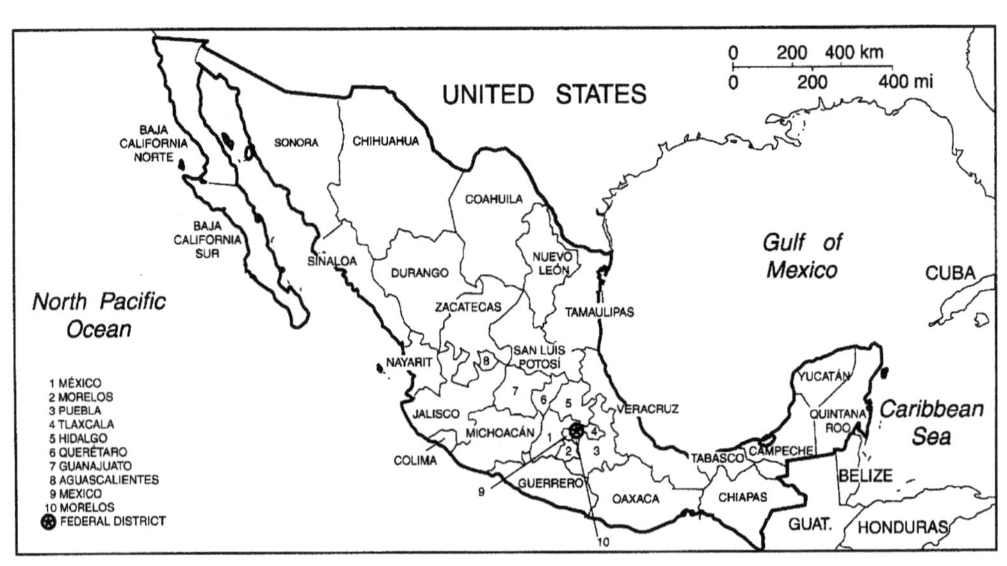

States

Introduction: Limits, Definitions

Mexico is a strikingly unusual and contradictory place. Its modern culture is built upon underlying Indian civilizations, impositions from Spain and successive infusions from Europe and North America: it is a country where the ancient and the modern now coexist, sometimes in hybridized forms and sometimes awkwardly juxtaposed with one another.

Like most other Spanish-American countries, Mexico became independent from Spain in the early nineteenth century and then began to tackle the process of establishing its own institutions and showing how it was different from other countries. Ever since then Mexico has gone out of its way to build a shared idea of nationhood and to project a unified national image; and yet one can see signs of difference and inequality all around. One might also say that the country's character, a strange marriage of dynamism and inertia, is epitomized by the oxymoronic name of the political party that ruled the country for some seventy years in the twentieth century, the Partido Revolucionario Institucional.

Mexico is, and has been, an important country. In our own day it is populous and linguistically significant, boasting more Spanish speakers than any other nation in the world, about twice as many as Spain.[1] Moreover, despite the loss of more than half of its territory to the United States during the nineteenth century, Mexico is still a big country. Its role in the wider ambit of the Americas has been a crucial one, a role that began when Mexico became the main hub from which the Americas were explored and conquered during the sixteenth century. In fact at that time it was even called 'Nueva España', and in a sense it came to stand for the New World. Since the initial break from Spain (which proved, in any case, never to be a total one) the country has been periodically influenced by Europe, in addition to which it has had a close, if sometimes fraught, relationship with United States. If the estimates prove to be accurate, by 2025 Mexico will lose its position as the country with most speakers of Spanish to, ironically, that old rival, the United States, and largely because of the number of Mexican nationals who are crossing the northern border to live there.

In view of all this, it is hardly surprising that an enormous amount has been written about this country, by Mexicans and foreigners alike, and especially by North Americans. Unlike some countries in Latin America, Mexico has not

1 At the time of writing, estimates of the population of Mexico range from 90 to 100 million.

been forgotten. As for the present book, I shall attempt to map out the core elements of the past that have led to the creation of modern Mexico – not just the political history but also the cultural factors that have helped make the country what it is. Its history falls quite conveniently into a number of periods: the pre-Hispanic, the colonial, the post-independence period and the post-revolutionary one. We shall look at each of these periods in turn and at some of their cultural products – art, literature, music and so forth. It is largely by means of cultural products like these, in other words through the conscious creation of culture, that peoples and nations actively identify themselves. Obviously enough, all works of art, all creative endeavours, are personal; they all have their own characteristics, their own structure and language. And yet they are also products of time, tradition and social context. It is the less deliberately contrived aspects of culture, such as customs, forms of social organization and belief systems, that provide the context and help shape identity.

My survey of the modern era is far more comprehensive than those of earlier periods, not least because one has to take into account new cultural inventions that grew to such importance during the twentieth century, such as non-print media and cinema. Moreover, we now live in an era in which the volume of cultural productivity is at an unprecedented level, an era whose technologies allow us to conserve and access an immense part of that volume. Following the chapter on the post-revolutionary period, which is the last in the historical survey, I have included a brief chapter dealing with language varieties. Additional material includes some colour reproductions of artworks; given that on the one hand the Mesoamerican artifacts and on the other the works of the muralists and some later artists have been widely reproduced and discussed both inside and outside Mexico, I have preferred to include here some illustrative images of colonial architecture and some art reproductions of less widely accessible but no less distinctively Mexican works.[2] There are also maps, a glossary, a chronology, some suggestions for further reading and a lengthy but far from exhaustive bibliography.[3]

I assume an intelligent and sophisticated readership, if not of specialists then at least of people who are taking a real interest in the study of Mexico; the aim is to offer the reader an informative, critical overview and a basis for serious work on Mexican culture. In a book that tackles so vast a field as this, compromises have to be made: I have had to be ruthlessly selective and there will inevitably be those who find fault with my choices. I have tried to give the essentials, to exemplify and synthesize, to widen perspectives, raise some issues and occasionally to be provocative.

Before we proceed, a moment must be taken to gloss the term 'New World'. Although accepted without question for so long, by 1992, the five-hundredth

2 The border culture is referred to at a number of points but for reasons of space there has been no attempt to cover Mexican culture as found within the United States.

3 Throughout this book the translations are my own unless otherwise specified.

anniversary of Columbus' first voyage, the use of that term had become politically incorrect. At about that time people began to speak of the 'encounter' rather than the 'conquest', even though a conquest it undoubtedly had been. Back in Madrid, the Plaza de Colón was diplomatically renamed 'Plaza de la Hispanidad', and alongside Columbus' statue was placed a series of monoliths with inscriptions drawn from the major texts documenting the discovery and others from the indigenous civilizations that were conquered. Yet what the Spaniards encountered was certainly a 'New World' to them, and in that sense they did discover it; they learned from it and it transformed their lives, the lives of others in Europe and the understanding of what the world was. In fact the whole business of looking at other cultures, the discipline of anthropology, grew as a result.

The story of Mexico, like any story, can be recounted in a number of ways. The custom was once to start with the arrival of the Spaniards and to tell what they discovered, and until late in the twentieth century no-one felt the need to approach the subject any differently. However, with changes in sensibilities and perceptions it then became *de rigueur* to begin with the ancient civilizations (even if – or perhaps especially if – those telling the story were scholars from Europe or the United States). So it is that to see 'el encuentro' as a process of discovery by Spaniards and fellow Europeans is now viewed as 'eurocentric'. The alternative way of looking at it all, the more politically correct view, is as the exercise of imperial power, as the imposition of one worldview upon others; accordingly, from the American standpoint the arrival of the Spaniards was an unwelcome surprise, a quite different sort of discovery, one that brought them hardship. A new lifestyle and a new set of beliefs were thrust upon them. Violence apart, perhaps the most lamentable aspect of it was that there were ways in which the principal indigenous civilizations were more advanced than their European counterparts, so that in those respects the invasion represented a step backwards for the former.

An interestingly new angle on the history of Latin America was provided in the mid-1980s by the Uruguayan writer Eduardo Galeano. In his *Memoria de fuego* Galeano brought together a collection of 'alternative texts', that is to say documents that he hoped might redress the balance by telling history from the point of view of the underdogs. Whatever the effectiveness of his alternative version of history, Galeano's efforts do make it clear that studying the early history of Latin America is awash with problems. Chief among them is the fact that our main sources of information, the published historical accounts, were on the whole written by Spaniards, for Spaniards (or at least for those who felt 'Spanish'). Evidence from the Indian civilizations themselves often did not survive conquest: texts and artifacts were destroyed in the fervour of the Christian crusade, or because they were thought by the Spaniards to be subversive. Witness the case of Diego de Landa, a bishop who in 1562 presided over the burning of Maya hieroglyphs, on the grounds that 'no tenían cosa en que no hubiese superstición y falsedades del demonio' (they consisted of nothing but superstition and devilish lies). He made some amends by also recording information about their culture in his *Relación de las cosas de Yucatán*, but real damage had been done. Moreover, in general much of the evidence that has survived into the present day has been unintelligible to foreigners, at least until recently, when great advances have been made in deciphering codes of communication. In any case, a good part of the indigenous tradition was oral, and ephemeral because of it.[4] Finally, perhaps the most important consideration of all is that even when documents are available they invariably come down to us translated, transformed or interpreted, mediated by foreign eyes and hands.

This brings us to another issue that must be addressed here: the question of where, from a historical point of view, Mexico begins. At the time of colonial rule, the lands that Spain ruled and that ran from present-day Panama to well into the US were, as has been noted, officially known as 'New Spain'. Though even then the name 'Mexico' was in everyday use, it only acquired *de jure* status in the early nineteenth century, after independence from Spain. Furthermore, as has also been noted, the Mexico we now know is a country whose borders were defined only towards the end of that century, after significant territories had been lost in the war with the United States. One might conclude that Mexican Studies should properly deal only with the post-independence era;[5] yet it would be impossible to give anything approaching a balanced account, even of that era alone, without reference to the colonial and pre-colonial heritages. To elide the colonial era is to turn a blind eye to such things as the underlying causes of social structure and cultural dependence. To deliberately sideline the Indian cultural contribution is to distort the picture, not to say to insult the Indians. The very name 'Mexico' derives from the pre-colonial heritage, from the Mexica peoples who had become dominant in the central valley by the time the Spaniards began their conquest. So within the limits of the material one can access, and despite the fact that in a single volume addressing so broad a subject one has to make compromises, an attempt must be made to do some justice to the colonial and Indian heritages. When all is said and done, it is curiously appropriate that the contradictory nation that Mexico now is, that strange amalgam of the ancient and the modern, should bear such an ancient name.

In reference to the question of breadth, a final word should be said about that catch-all term 'studies'. Although its use is quite commonplace these days, it is a relatively new term in university curricula, one that spread across the academic landscape during the second half of the twentieth century. At first, its attraction lay in that it seemed to signal that traditional subject divisions were breaking down; in the view of some people, however, the use of the term

4 'Mesoamerica' is a term invented by an anthropologist. It refers to the areas of present day Central America and Mexico that were once dominated by indigenous peoples. Some of the peoples of Mesoamerica had sophisticated writing systems, but those of the Caribbean and South America did not.

5 For example, González Peña, the author of one of the standard histories of Mexican literature, assumes just that.

'studies' heralded a loss of focus, even a loss of intellectual rigour. Be that as it may, the word is now firmly entrenched in the academic vocabulary. In recent years, and perhaps especially with regard to the subjects that concern us most here, the use of 'studies' can also be seen as a way of reacting against hermeticism, in other words against the tendency of academic subjects to close themselves off in their own worlds, sometimes obscured by walls of jargon. There is no doubt that as our academic horizons widen the focus can become less sharp, but it is no less clear that benefits also accrue: a wider angle can help us to see the workings of society and culture not in isolation but in relation to each other. It is in this spirit that this book was written.

1
Mesoamerica

As early as the late sixteenth century, José de Acosta, a prescient Jesuit priest who had come to New Spain, speculated that the first inhabitants of the Americas might have migrated there from Asia across the Bering Strait, which was once a bridge between continents. It was an idea that took another three centuries to become commonplace. Nowadays, though there remains some uncertainty as to precise dates, it is widely thought that such migrations began about 50,000 years ago. It is believed that the migrants travelled south, dispersing over the great plains of the American Midwest, and reaching as far as South America. In the area that is now Mexico, they settled and developed primarily in the flat band of land that runs from Texas around the Gulf coast to the Yucatán peninsula, and also in the south and in the central basin where modern Mexico City now sits. It is important to stress that the boundaries of indigenous civilizations and settlements did not neatly coincide with those of present-day countries or provinces; the most notable illustration of this is the case of the Mayas, whose great civilization occupied significant parts of what is now Mexico, but also areas of Guatemala, Honduras, Belize and El Salvador. For that reason there is clearly a need for a term to refer to such areas without falling back on qualified references to modern nations, as I have just done; in 1943 a US anthropologist called Paul Kirchoff coined the term 'Mesoamerica'.

There is evidence of agricultural activity and simple village life in Mesoamerica dating from about 1800 BC, while the earliest human remains found there date from approximately 12,000 BC. Thereafter, a number of civilizations grew, some more complex than others, the two most sophisticated being those of the Mayas and the Aztecs. These civilizations were based on agriculture, and had progressed beyond hunting and gathering. As the anthropologist Eric Wolf points out, however, 'as soon as the basic need is met, [every human society] raises its sights and tries to transcend its earthbound limitations'.[1] In other words, they also developed spiritually, intellectually and artistically.

It has become customary to classify the indigenous civilizations into three main periods, though it must be said that these divisions, and particularly the labels applied to them, have sometimes been contested; the labels are best thought of as simply chronological rather than evaluative, and the dates as approximate. The first period, known as the Pre-Classic or Formative Period,

1 *Sons of the Shaking Earth* (1972 edn), p. 69.

covers 15,000 BC to AD 150; the second, the Classic, is from AD 150 to AD 900; the Post-Classic runs on to the time of the Spanish invasion (1519).

Strikingly, the civilizations of Mesoamerica share a number of characteristics that are generally not found elsewhere in the Americas. They had a sophisticated knowledge of astronomy, and resulting from it a calendar that was based on the solar cycle but also on a shorter sacred cycle; they shared common deities; they had forms of confession and penance; they practised human sacrifice; they had hieroglyphic writing systems and written records; there was a ball game somewhat similar to basketball; and there were well-organized forms of trade, with cacao beans serving as a form of currency. Other customs, such as the use of tobacco, and a diet in which maize was the staple, were shared by peoples in other parts of the Americas. There were no beasts of burden in Mesoamerica, and the only known domesticated animals, prior to the advent of the Spaniards, were the turkey and the dog. One curiosity is the absence of the exploitation of the wheel for transport, and this despite the fact that the wheel is known to have been used in Mesoamerican toys. It is worth noting that a great many buildings and artifacts made by these peoples were produced without the use of metal, which remained unknown until late in the Classic Period.

The major civilization of the Formative Period was that of the Olmecs, whose heartland was in the southeastern coastal area, first at a place now called San Lorenzo and then at La Venta, which is on the Gulf coast, to the south of Veracruz; they were also in Tabasco. It was only relatively recently, in the 1930s and 1940s, that Matthew Stirling discovered and excavated sites in that area; he maintained (and eventually won acceptance for) the view that here was a major civilization that pre-dated the Maya. Possibly the Olmecs were Maya-speaking, but an alternative theory that commands much respect holds that they spoke a language of the Mixe-Zoquean family. At any rate, the name 'Olmec', baseless though it may be, has stuck. We now know that other peoples of Mesoamerica inherited much from the Olmecs, so that theirs is often referred to as the 'mother' civilization of Mesoamerica. The Olmecs had advanced social and economic systems, and they traded widely, but they were not a peaceful people. Many mysteries still surround them. Despite these and the conflicting speculations about the origins and the spread of Olmec civilization (there are, after all, no extant documents to help us) there is a consensus that during the Formative Period there was a dominant ideology that is reflected throughout artworks of the time.

The art of the Olmecs suggests that they believed that the union of a woman with a jaguar had given rise to 'were-jaguar' offspring, to humans with cat-like features. The ravages of climate in the Gulf region, not to mention deliberate destruction, have limited what has survived into present times. There are huge, very three-dimensional basalt heads, some with feline characteristics, and some, perhaps more strikingly, of human types whose heavy features do not seem to match those found among any of the peoples of Mesoamerica. About ten such heads have been found at San Lorenzo. Among important surviving artifacts is the famous jade Kunz Axe, now in the American Museum of Natural History, in New York; this exemplary piece portrays a were-jaguar – slanting eyes, a howling, toothless mouth – holding a miniature axe. Although jaguar imagery is quite frequent in Olmec art, so too is imagery of other tropical animals, and such images may be associated with deities.

Archaeologists excavating San Lorenzo found that the whole site was man-made, that it had a sophisticated drainage system, and that it appeared to have been designed following a zoomorphic pattern. It seems that in about 900 BC whatever structures were standing were then buried or perhaps ritually destroyed, monuments were defaced or broken, sculptures of humans beheaded. It has been suggested that some monuments were recarved into heads, and that this was done to represent the transition from active power to memorialization.

The Olmecs were aware of the properties of reflective and magnetic substances; the former, for example, were used not only to reflect images but also to cast light. La Venta, which is now in an area dotted with oilrigs, was laid out according to astronomically determined lines, its structures designed to be interred rather than fully seen. The most imposing structure is a pyramid of sorts, perhaps shaped in imitation of a volcano, perhaps simply eroded into its fluted contours, and perhaps a burial site: other burial sites are nearby. The Olmecs were also great stone workers – carving, drilling and cutting – who not only made monuments, but also small, portable objects, examples of which have been found all over Mexico, especially in the state of Guerrero. At Teopantecuanitlan, in the highlands of that state, the Olmecs also had a sacred site where, thanks to a drier climate, their ceramics fared better than in the Gulf settlements. The discovery, only in 1983, of the Teopantecuanitlan connexion, brought to light the existence of expressive and lifelike ceramic human figures as fine as any in the ancient New World, together with bowls and even wood carvings. Among surviving Olmec objects some have been found that were carved from jade and inscribed with hieroglyphs, perhaps dating from the middle of the Formative Period; this may be the earliest evidence of writing systems in Mesoamerica.

From Tres Zapotes, an Olmec settlement that survived after the demise of La Venta, comes one of the oldest dated fragments in the New World, known as Stela C. It is part of a basalt monument that has a representation of a were-jaguar on one side, and more importantly, on the other side an inscription from the Long Count, which was a system of dating that started from a fixed time (13 August 3114 BC, by our own calendar). No-one knows quite why that particular starting date was chosen. The numerical language used for expressing such dates was one of bars and dots, each of the former having a value of five and each of the latter, one.

The Classic Period, coinciding approximately with the Christian first millennium, saw the rise of the major Mesoamerican civilizations, widespread literacy, the use of sophisticated numerical and writing systems, a complete pantheon of deities, and the emergence of ruling religious élites. Major societies developed in three areas, though not all at the same time: in the Valley of Mexico, around Oaxaca, and in the lowlands of the south. The city of Teotihuacan was the centre of one of the earliest of these societies and it dominated the Valley of Mexico, being located in a part of it that had an abundant water supply and good sources of obsidian, which was a much-valued commodity. A canal system was developed, and the city itself came to cover more land than imperial Rome. It boasted impressive civic and ceremonial buildings, serving a population that rose to between 125,000 and 200,000 (depending on estimates). Even at 125,000, Teotihuacan would have been the sixth largest city in the world by the middle of the millennium. Teotihuacan's influence extended well beyond the Valley of Mexico. In fact about 700 miles south of it is to be found an outpost at Kaminajuyú, where architectural features and other evidence indicate a close association with Teotihuacan; and even in Mayan areas evidence of Teotihuacan's influence has been found. It seems that Teotihuacan's artifacts were widely valued; perhaps their ubiquitousness is evidence that the Teotihuacanos not only traded but invaded.

Teotihuacan was a major commercial, manufacturing and religious centre. Apart from obsidian, it traded in clay and ceramic products, perhaps in textiles and timber. It imported materials such as feathers, cotton and rubber from lowland societies. It is a rare example of a carefully planned city, laid out on a grid pattern, at the heart of which is an immense thoroughfare known as the Avenue of the Dead, long thought to have been 3 km long but now known to have been twice that length, and crossed by another of similar length. Two pyramids dominate the scene, one dedicated to the Sun, the other to the Moon. The larger of the two is the Pyramid of the Sun, at some 60 metres, but the more commanding view is from that of the Moon, which looks down the full length of the avenue. Both are filled with adobe brick and stones, and both were once crowned with wooden temples. The many palaces are built in a fashion known as *talud-tablero*, with vertical, flanged façades placed on an angled base. The city was zoned by walls, these zones perhaps demarcating commercial, regional or family groupings. It was a cosmopolitan city: there was, for example, an Oaxacan zone, where the customs of that area predominated, while another was devoted to peoples from eastern Mayan areas. The palaces of the lords were typically single-storey, but had many rooms and several courtyards.[2]

For the most part, the Teotihuacano murals reflect religious beliefs and they are frequently didactic in style. Many have repeated animal imagery. In the most famous of the murals, at Tepantitla, the dominant deity is a spider woman figure, mother of the universe and supreme deity for the Teotihuacanos. Other deities that appear prominently in Teotihuacan are the rain god (who would become Tlaloc for the Aztecs) and the plumed serpent (Quetzalcoatl). Another pyramidal structure known commonly as the Temple of Quetzalcoatl, according to Coe (1994: 98) offers an alternative view of the creation myth, with opposing

2 In his poem 'Himno entre ruinas' Octavio Paz tries to reconcile the rituals of ancient times with those of modern young visitors to Teotihuacan. Like many other sites, though perhaps more than most, given the proximity of Mexico City, Teotihuacan suffers from the effects of busloads of tourists and ugly commercialism.

images of serpents, 'one representing life, greenness, and peace, and the other heat, the desert regions, and war'. This temple also provides evidence of mass human sacrifice, for the skeletons of groups of eighteen victims, representing the number of months in a year, have been found there, as have those of single victims, one at each of the four corners of the pyramid.

Teotihuacano art is generally refined, stylized and elegant. It is often polychromatic, with colours that remind one of those of medieval Europe. It is also repetitive, and lacks the three-dimensionality of Olmec artworks. Some of the best sculpted works from Teotihuacan are masks made of serpentine, onyx, or granite, representing genderless and ageless human faces. A similar anonymity is found in the early ceramic figurines; many of these have been found, and in fact, like other ceramic products, they were mass-produced. Obsidian and shells were used to make objects to accompany burials, such as those of the victims referred to above, whose remains were accompanied by necklaces of jawbones and teeth, some of them fashioned from shell. Characteristic are jars or pots set on three block-like feet, often with lids. 'Thin Orange' is the name used to refer to a fine style of earthenware from Puebla, which was under Teotihuacan's control.

The origins of the Teotihuacanos are unclear. Perhaps affinities with the Toltecs and Aztecs point to a common Nahua heritage; certainly it is known that centuries after the fall of Teotihuacan it was a mythical place, a place of pilgrimage for the Aztecs. What is clear is that the city was deliberately destroyed in about AD 700, by unidentified forces. In any case, there is evidence that its influence had been on the wane for some years prior to that time, and that the influence of the Mayas was on the increase. With the unifying effect of Teotihuacan gone, there came both a decline of interregional trade and increasing fragmentation, with cultures developing in relative isolation from one another.

During the Classic era other significant developments occurred in the region of Veracruz and especially among the Zapotecs at Monte Albán close to Oaxaca. Monte Albán was inhabited by people who had independently developed their own writing system. Although influenced by the contemporary Teotihuacan (for example, the gods of Monte Albán were similar to those of Teotihuacan, but had Zapotec names, and its buildings were similarly constructed), Monte Albán was somewhat off the beaten track, able to develop with a degree of independence and probably less subject to the sort of disruptions that marked the closing years of the Classic era elsewhere. Monte Albán had rich ceramics, lavish tombs, murals and hieroglyphs that have not been fully studied. The Zapotecs established a powerful political alliance with the Mixtecs, cemented by intermarriage among the noble classes, and Mitla became a major centre for them. The authority of their rulers derived from their sacred texts, as was the case with the Mayas.[3]

3 Knight (79–81) notes that while general histories of Latin America tend to mention the Zapotec civilization at Monte Albán only *en passant*, seeing it as local rather than imperial,

The Mayas

Early Maya centres, further south, date from about a hundred years after the rise of Teotihuacan; the main ones are at Tikal and Uaxactún. Both of these were invaded and much influenced by Teotihuacan, but with the fall of the latter other Maya states rose in prominence, and so did rivalries between them all. Indeed, though for a long time it was argued that the Mayas were the peace-lovers of Mesoamerica, 'the earlier, idyllic view of the classic Maya as the peace-loving flower children of Mesoamerica has been largely discredited' (Fariss: 140). Decorative friezes at Bonampak and at Palenque show scenes of war and captivity; stones bear records of warring dynasties and the sacrifice of prisoners, suggesting that the powerful élites were somewhat belligerent; Knight (100) describes it as 'a Mesoamerican version of Machiavelli's Italy'.

By late Classic times, Tikal (in the northern part of modern Guatemala) was only one of several important centres, ranging from Palenque to the west of it, to Uxmal in the northeast, to Copán in the south. It is estimated that at its peak Tikal may have had 50,000 inhabitants. Excavations have shown that Tikal was laid out to contrast open spaces with massive stone structures, initially on a north–south axis. It had a typical radial pyramid, a grand plaza and an acropolis surrounded by temples housing tombs. Such memorials and religious monuments, and their accompanying chronological markers, would be found in other, later Maya sites. It is interesting to note that different architectural styles are not used to contrast the religious and civic functions of the structures concerned, and that while the precise configurations vary, all Maya buildings use raised platforms and vaulted chambers.

Generally, the Mayas occupied verdant lands with friendly topographies and climates; they were not as limited by natural resources and barriers as were the peoples of the central valley, nor did they have to trade in order to meet their needs. Not surprisingly, the Mayas spread across the surrounding countryside, and so urbanization in their case never reached the level of concentration that one finds at Teotihuacan. Tikal, for example, is thought to have had jurisdiction over settlements covering about 120 well-communicated square kilometres. What gave strength to the main cities was neither their size nor location but their religious function.

Maya society has a number of interesting features. At the top of the Maya class structure was a secular and religious élite; below that came the workers, who presumably paid tributes to the state in the form of the products of their labours, which were then redistributed among the community, though ultimately benefiting the élite. Each class was subdivided into specialisms, and each of these had its status in the hierarchy; for example, some priests special-

its localness in fact provides 'an instructive example of a maize-based, highland culture whose evolution can be traced, in continuous fashion, from its agrarian origins . . . down to historical times. It can therefore be particularly suggestive of the forces shaping highland Mesoamerican society.'

ized in astronomy, others in mathematics. The Maya ideal of physical beauty led to the heads of babies being bound to boards, so that they grew flat, and beads being dangled before their noses so that they might become cross-eyed, a characteristic that was particularly valued in women. Prosperous adults would have jade inlays in their teeth. They would also have themselves commemorated in artworks. A representative sculpture of a Tikal Maya lord shows his curled right hand holding a bar or rod and his left hand supporting a supernatural image (the jaguar god of the underworld), thought to represent the patron of the city.

The Mayas may not have urbanized on the scale of the Teotihuacanos, but they outdid them on the cultural front, with finer, more profusely and inventively decorated buildings, more freely decorated ceramics and more imagination applied to ceremonial and recreational areas. One might almost say that their decorative instinct was baroque. Buildings were often decorated inside and out. Among surviving wall-paintings, the one for a tomb at Río Azul, in northeast Petén (Guatemala), is among the most impressive, portraying the sun god and the watery entrance to the underworld and the afterlife. Some of the best wall-paintings are at Bonampak; these depict, for example, masked performers at a religious ceremony and a scene at the court of the king, with captives being tortured. Exterior stonework is no less impressive for its intricacy and style, which sometimes seems geometric, often somehow oriental, though with naturalistic and sometimes narrative elements. Maya buildings have a number of striking features, structural as well as decorative, as can be seen in the temples at Palenque, with their vaulted roofs. Pyramids (temple 1 at Tikal would be the prime example) can be precipitous structures with shallow steps that oblige one to climb in a zig-zag manner, no doubt as a sign of deference to those on high. A real Maya forte was *bas-relief* stone carving, of which there are notable examples at Bonampak and Palenque, but at Copan the sculptures are more three-dimensional.

As to pottery, that ranges from ordinary, mass-produced items to items of real sophistication, such as ceremonial incense burners. Delicate, hollow figurines that also serve as whistles come from the burial site at Jaina, a small island off the coast of Campeche. On some of these a brilliant blue pigment is evident, the 'Maya blue', which was made with indigo. Some late-Classic bowls and dishes are painted in several colours and with the same degree of complexity as the wall-paintings; being fired at low temperatures, however, these were not the most durable pieces of pottery. And then there are the jade and marble carvings; the former was the most precious substance to the Mayas, the latter less commonly used. Surely there were also many artworks made of less durable materials, like wood and cloth, that did not survive the ravages of time and climate, let alone the cataclysm that put paid to the Maya's southern settlements.

Traumatic events affected many states across Mesoamerica as the Classic era drew to a close. The fall of Teotihuacan made way, eventually, for the rise of the Toltecs and later the Aztecs. But the most intriguing case is that of the Mayas, whose southern lowland cities seem to have collapsed or been abandoned quite suddenly, and at their peak, while parts of Belize and Yucatán grew in importance. The causes of the collapse remain a matter of speculation: natural disasters, supernatural signs, crop failures, diseases and wars (whether between rival Mayans or involving outsiders) have all been advanced as possible causes. Certainly there were wars, and it is thought probable that by the end of the eighth century there were problems of both overpopulation and environmental degradation.

In the Yucatán peninsula, Chichen-Itzá and Uxmal now became the principal Maya cities. Uxmal, whose buildings are of cement and rubble faced with limestone, is one of the finest Maya cities. There are two huge pyramids, one of which can be entered through a monster-mask doorway, several palaces with large courtyards and a 'nunnery' with façades decorated with mosaics. The finest building is beside the largest pyramid: it is the 'Palace of the Governor', with its long frieze of stone mosaic that melds latticework with monster motifs. Chichen-Itzá shows more signs of Toltec influence. It is dominated by the pyramid called the 'Castle' and across from that by the 'Temple of the Warriors', with its huge sculpture of the reclining rain god Chac Mool. Here in Chichen-Itzá is Mesoamerica's largest ballcourt (with walls over 8 metres high) and near that a long platform carved with human skulls set on stakes, evidence that human sacrifice was practised in this place, perhaps upon the losing team of ballplayers. Sacrifices were also made to the rain god, the victims being tossed into huge natural wells known as *cenotes*. In addition to bones, Toltec artifacts have been recovered from the *cenotes*; these include objects of jade and gold, showing that metals were now being worked.

The ballgame itself, which had long roots in Mesoamerica, was a ceremony that combined ritual, sport and entertainment. In its Maya version it was played with a hard rubber ball on a court that was wider at the ends than in the middle, and the object was to make the ball pass through a stone hoop, mounted vertically at some height. Since players could only hit the ball with their hips and knees, a 'goal' was an infrequent occurrence, though it would be enough to win the game outright. Otherwise, it seems that games were won on a points system based on the execution of particular moves. The players wore protective deerskin suits, sometimes playing in teams, sometimes individually. One use of the ballgame was to settle disputes but it also had a sacred function, the ball itself being viewed as the sun following its course through the darkness of the underworld, and the game as a holy battle between the sun and the moon, the sun and the planet Venus, or the gods of youth and those of old age. In sacrificial terms, the ball could represent a human head. Priests would sometimes use the matches as a means of divining the future. The ballgame was also a social event, sometimes played against teams from rival communities, with participants from the nobility as well as from the ranks of the commoners, and there was a great deal of gambling associated with it.

By the time the Spaniards came, the glories of the Maya were a thing of the past, any unity was gone and there were warring factions, as there had been centuries before. Partly because there was no single focus of power, however, and also due to the Mayas' guerrilla tactics, it took the Spaniards till 1542 to gain control of Yucatán and establish Mérida as its capital. The Mayas continued to be rebellious throughout the sixteenth century, and even thereafter. In the mid-nineteenth century they rose up again against the white oppressors, even coming close to taking back the Yucatán peninsula; in 1910 the Maya of Quintana Roo rebelled against the regime of the dictatorial President Porfirio Díaz. Nor was the widely reported Zapatista rebellion of 1994 in Chiapas the first there; the core of that rebellion was made up of highland groups of Tzotzil and Tzeltal Mayas. These days, there are about seven and a half million Mayas in all, many of them living in relative isolation, clinging to their traditions as best they can.[4]

Maya documents

The Mayas had codices ('books') whose paper was made of bark, which was folded like a screen and coated with a preservative chalky substance. These were read starting from the right and in a zig-zag manner, and their language was partly iconic, partly pictographic. Maya pottery shows us that in Classic times their codices had jaguar-skin covers and were painted with quills dipped in shells containing red and black paints. Thousands of such codices are believed to have existed, covering history, prophesies, genealogies and scientific knowledge, not to mention creative works, but few have survived into our own times. Those that have are from the post-Classic era and from the northern Mayan territories. The one known as the Dresden Codex is nearly 4 metres long; it is thought to be Aztec-influenced and to date from shortly before the conquest, as are the less important Madrid Codex and the Paris Codex, the latter being very fragmentary. A fourth is known as the Grolier Codex; its surviving portion consists of half of a cosmological table. Though its authenticity was once in doubt, this codex is now believed to be genuine and also the earliest of the four, dating from 1230.

Some records that were written in Maya script have come down to us as Spanish transcriptions. The *Popol Vuh* is sometimes called the Sacred Book of the Maya, though its name really means 'Record of the Community'. It was written following the massacre ordered by the infamous Pedro de Alvarado, the 'sun', as the *Popol Vuh* itself describes him, which burned the Maya kings and ended the Maya community. The original Quiché manuscript, probably transcribed into Spanish during the middle of the sixteenth century, was discovered a century and a half later in highland Guatemala, by a parish priest. After he had copied it (in both Quiché and Spanish) it then lay forgotten until rediscovered and published in Vienna, in Spanish, in 1857. A later version was published in Paris. Inevitably, the *Popol Vuh* has suffered transformation in the

4 Some 60 percent of the population of present-day Guatemala is Mayan.

process. With imaginative stories interspersed throughout, it begins by recounting the myth of creation (following failed attempts with mud and wood, the gods succeed in their third, with maize), then it goes on to tell of the struggles between the false and the true gods, finally turning to details of Quiché genealogy.

The other major survival is the series of Books of Chilam Balam, eighteen in all, according to León-Portilla; of these, the three that have been most carefully studied are the *Chilam Balam de Chumayel*, the *Chilam Balam de Tizimín* and the *Chilam Balam de Maní*. These complex works were written by the high priests of Yucatán and they consist of symbolic recreations of myths, together with historical and prophetic tales.

Though we know from Diego de Landa and others that there was a resilient tradition of Mayan drama, and that some of it was even independent of religious ritual, only one play survives from that pre-conquest tradition, *Rabinal Achí*. This spectacle, originally in the Quiché language, was copied in the mid nineteenth century from a manuscript that was in the hands of a native elder. It tells of the struggle between the title figure and another warrior, Quiché Achí; the latter is vanquished and brought before the king, whereupon a verbal duel ensues, leading to the death of the captive.[5] *Rabinal Achí* is didactic, full of formulas and standard forms of courtesy, and repetitive, though alleviated by music and dance interludes.

The rise of the Aztecs

The Toltecs, who were prestigious and highly influential on other cultures, dispersed from their capital Tula throughout the central valley and beyond, but eventually lost power to warring peoples who had migrated from the north. In time one nation, the Mexicas (more commonly known as the Aztecs) became dominant in the central valley. The Aztecs had come there in search of a promised land which, according to Aztec legend, would be recognizable by the presence of an eagle perched on a cactus, with a serpent in its beak (see colour plate 1). Driven by that legend, and with its prophecy realized, in 1325 the Aztecs founded the city of Tenochtitlan on land they reclaimed, by means of the raised- garden or *chinampa* system, from Lake Texcoco. By 1428, thanks to a triple alliance, the Aztecs had consolidated their authority, their operations were centralized and Tenochtitlan had become a showplace. Its fate, however, was to be destroyed two centuries later and then submerged once again, by Mexico City.

The Aztecs, though notorious for the scale of their human sacrifices, were a principled people who behaved in consonance with the instructions of their god,

[5] León-Portilla gives a full account of the spectacle in his *Pre-Columbian Literatures* . . . (1969), pp. 103–6. The text itself can be read in Monterde's *Rabinal Achí: teatro indígena prehispánico*. A recent translation into English is provided by Tedlock (2003), who also supplies a highly informative introductory essay.

Huizilopochtli. They believed that provided there was human sacrifice the sun would rise, the world would continue to be, and life-giving rain would come only in response to the tears of child victims. The Aztecs found many victims by undertaking *xochiyaoyotl* ('guerras floridas' in Spanish), the Wars of the Flowers, whose purpose was to take live prisoners from other nations. Some of these nations came under direct Aztec rule, while others, especially the distant ones, were allowed a degree of autonomy on condition that they paid tribute to their masters. Discontent among the subjugated peoples was therefore rife; it would lead to their making alliances with the invading Spaniards, and contribute towards the eventual defeat of the Aztecs.

In contrast with this gruesome picture of sacrifice, the Aztecs had developed a society that was disciplined, well-organized and culturally quite sophisticated. Tenochtitlan itself impressed the Spaniards with its size, its orderliness and its cleanliness. It was a planned city built on reclaimed land in the middle of the shallow lake and connected to the mainland by causeways. A large monumental centre of some eighty stone buildings and many squares was presided over by a main temple and an imperial palace. Within the city there was a sacred precinct. Around the centre stood the houses of the nobility, and beyond those there lay the adobe dwellings of the commoners, the whole place being punctuated by cultivated areas. At the top of the social hierarchy was a privileged class of nobles and priests the *pilli* and the *tatloani*; the designation *huey tatloani* ('Great Lord') was reserved for the supreme authority. The commoners (*macehuales*) were above the classes of servants and slaves. Certain individuals were granted élite status in commerce or politics, while a distinguished record in battle was one of few ways of bettering oneself socially. The offspring of the nobility were educated for leadership, but those of the commoners were taught trades and then assigned to communities where they would spend the rest of their working days. The life of the commoner was thus regulated and routine, but secure. Those who survived to the age of 52, which was a significant number in the Aztec time cycle, were allowed to retire. The fruits of the commoners' labours were destined primarily for community support, but part went to benefit the nobility.

Aztec arts

Stone sculpture was a major form of Aztec expression, a means of recording their history, and they worked in stone with greater sophistication than did their ancestors. Animals, and particularly snakes, are often portrayed, sometimes realistically and sometimes in a stylized fashion, for example in images of Quetzalcoatl, the plumed serpent. Powerful representations of jaguars reflect the fact that the élite troops were conceived of as jaguar warriors. Smith notes: 'The basic themes or messages of Mexica imperial sculpture were that the Mexica possessed the religious and political right to rule the world, that they had inherited this right from the ancient civilizations of Teotihuacan and the

Toltecs, and that the empire enjoyed a cosmic significance beyond mere politics' (Michael E. Smith: 260). The famous calendar stone, nearly 4 metres in diameter and now in the Museo Nacional de Antropología, reflects this worldview, indicating that Aztec rule extended in all four directions and that it was based on sacred principles, in accordance with the wishes of the gods.

Poetry, narration and oratory were highly valued oral skills, closely associated with religious ceremony and practised by the nobles and priests. Similarly, music and dance were holy arts. Musicians were trained in special schools (*cuicacalli*) and once qualified wore a distinctive cord dangling from their heads. Their wind instruments included clay and bone pipes and trumpet shells, and percussion instruments ranged from gongs and drums through rattles and scrapers, for example made of tortoise shells. The music itself is thought to have been pentatonic, and monodic in style, that is to say composed for a single voice; there is also evidence that some was antiphonal. Much of this can be deduced from illustrations in the codices, which also show dancers of both sexes moving in circles around the musicians.

Aztec poetry is especially rich, and remarkably 'modern' in some respects. Indicatively, the Nahuatl expression that is equivalent in meaning to 'poetry' is 'in xóchitl in cuícatl', which literally means 'flower and song'. It is a poetry that makes much use of repetition, its syntactic structure reflecting the Aztec worldview. Associations between images are exploited, creating a playful web of meaning, sometimes to erotic effect, as in 'The Song of the Women of Chalco', written in the second half of the fifteenth century by Aquiauhtzin of Ayapanco and curiously similar in some respects to the biblical 'Song of Songs'. Aztec poetry employs coupled nouns or phrases to convey other concepts by association; thus, 'jade, fine feathers' equates with 'beauty', 'skirt, blouse' means 'woman', 'dust, filth' is 'evil' and (more obscurely, but perhaps to indicate their distance from the centre of power) 'tail, wing' means 'commoners'. There are several categories of poetry, of which the most important are: *Yaocuícatl* – sung in praise of warlike prowess; *Teocuícatl* – sung in praise of the gods; *Xochicuícatl* – sung in reference to flowers, which to the Aztecs were symbols of words and of poetry itself, as well as of divine works; and *Icnocuícatl* – sung to express sadness or introspection. Some of the *Icnocuícatl* poetry tells of the fall of Tenochtitlan. The work of a famous poet-king called Nezahualcóyotl (1402–72) provides fine examples of *Icnocuícatl*: for instance, regarding the transience of life he writes (León-Portilla, *Cantos y crónicas*: 169):

> I, Nezahualcóyotl, wonder
> Do we truly live rooted on earth?
> Not on earth forever
> only briefly here.
> Though it be of jade, it cracks,
> though it be of gold, it breaks,
> though it be of Quetzal feathers, it tears.

Not on earth forever:
only briefly here.

Prose works are of two types, one (*teotlahtolli*) telling stories of the gods and the origins of mankind, the other (*huehuetlahtolli*) consisting of the words of the old and wise, for example their advice to the young. Bernardino de Sahagún's *Historia general de las cosas de Nueva España* (otherwise known as the *Códice florentino*, because there is a copy of it in Florence) is an important source of both prose and poetry. Other samples of poetry can be found in *Cantares mexicanos* and in the *Romances de los señores de Nueva España*, but for most readers the most convenient sources both of poetry and of information about Aztec culture in general are to be found in the works of the pioneer scholar in this field, Miguel León-Portilla.

2

Cultures and Conquest

The arrival of Hernán Cortés in Mexican territory was no chance matter. Previous Spanish explorations along the Gulf and Caribbean coasts had generated rumours of fabulous civilizations and whetted the Spanish appetite for conquest. Cortés himself was an educated man from a comfortable background who had attended the University of Salamanca, though he abandoned his studies at the age of nineteen in order to seek a fortune in the New World. He began his colonial life as a settler in La Española (Hispaniola) and while there ingratiated himself with the future governor of Cuba, Diego Velázquez. Once in Cuba, the two men together planned the expedition to Mexico until Velázquez grew uneasy about Cortés' ambitions, and ordered him not to set sail; but Cortés defiantly set out in 1519, with 800 men and 16 horses. In Yucatán, Cortés joined company with one Jerónimo de Aguilar, who had been shipwrecked there during a previous Spanish expedition and had learned to speak Mayan. Following the meeting between Cortés and Aguilar a local chieftain gave Cortés twenty slaves, among them a princess who spoke Maya and Nahuatl. She and Aguilar were to serve as the interpreters through whom Cortés communicated with the indigenous peoples, but Malintzín, the Indian woman, was to become by far the more significant of the two in the Mexican psyche, for she also became Cortés' mistress and bore him a son who came to symbolize the start of a new 'Mexican' *mestizo* race. She was Malintzín to the Indians, Doña Marina to the Spaniards, or Malinche, the popular name by which she is now generally known. In one of his *Cartas de relación*, the letters he sent back to Carlos V, Cortés said that after God, Spain owed the conquest to Malinche. However, from the point of view of many of the Indians, she was a traitor, and their demise was attributable in part to her collusion with the invaders. These negative associations are the ones that have lasted in the Mexican mind: nowadays the term 'malinchismo' has come to refer to betrayal in general, and particularly to the betrayal of one's culture, such as can be seen in the behaviour of those who admire all that is foreign, and especially those who 'sell out' to the United States.

By all accounts Cortés was a determined and daring man. At one point his soldiers, seeing the overwhelming odds against them, lost heart and wanted to sail back to safety, to which Cortés responded by scuttling the ships, thus forcing everyone, including himself, to face the enemy. How did so meagre a force of Spaniards overthrow a whole empire? The answer is that a surprising number of things worked in Cortés' favour. The Indians knew neither firearms nor horses and they were overawed by them. Their custom was to exact tribute from other peoples, and failing that to use force to subjugate them. More significantly for the present story, they engaged in ritual wars whose tactics were designed not to kill but to take captives for subsequent sacrifice: they thought killing them in action a waste. But in any case they did not expect conquest and violence from the visitors, for Cortés' arrival coincided with certain signs that the Aztecs took as supernatural; as legend had it the banished, benign god Quetzalcoatl was due to return at that time, and would do so in a physical guise that by chance matched that of the Spaniard.[1] Futhermore, it must be borne in mind that there was discontent among the many peoples from whom the Aztecs were demanding tribute, and whom they had been raiding in order to capture candidates for sacrifice; these were factors that encouraged the aggrieved Indians to forge alliances with the Spaniards. Finally, the Spaniards had a more insidious and unconscious weapon in the smallpox that they inadvertently carried over from Europe and spread among people who had developed no resistance to the disease.

This is not the place to give a detailed account of the dramatic events that sealed the Spanish victory. Suffice it to say that having been welcomed into Tenochtitlan, the Aztec capital, by its *Huey Tatloani* Montezuma, the Spaniards abused their welcome, making their host a virtual prisoner. There then came a point when Cortés had to leave the city and go back to the coast to deal with a force sent by Velázquez to stop him, and in his absence things in Tenochtitlan got out of hand. On his return to the city Cortés placed Montezuma before his rebellious subjects in the hope of re-establishing order. According to the account of events by Bernal Díaz del Castillo, a soldier who chronicled the conquest, Montezuma was then stoned to death by his own subjects, and Cortés wept at his death; but the Aztec version holds that Cortés stabbed Montezuma in the back. In the ensuing riot the Spaniards fought to escape from the city, suffering many losses; it became known as the 'Noche Triste'. Some of the Spaniards drowned beneath the weight of the gold they were trying to take with them as they retreated; their greed for it was incomprehensible to the Aztecs, who regarded gold as the excrement of the gods, and thought that the Spaniards lusted after it like pigs. Later, the Spaniards regrouped, joined their Indian allies and laid siege to the city, until its inhabitants starved or died from smallpox. And then Tenochtitlan, larger, cleaner and better organized than any European city of the time, was razed to the ground.

Thus began the confluence of cultures that gives us modern Mexico. The Spaniards, in their zeal not only to subjugate but also to convert, superimposed buildings, and tried to do the same with social structures and beliefs; to this there was some resistance and a certain amount of accommodation also took place. Life changed radically for the Indian nobility, but in the early years the lives of the commoners, who were accustomed to being governed by others,

[1] Some analysts have suggested that this is a post-conquest legend.

went on much as usual. Ever since those days of conquest, Mexicans, even those of the minority white, Europeanized, prosperous variety, have tended to turn to the Indian heritage when trying to define national identity. The same goes for official projections of Mexican culture, which have sometimes smacked of hypocrisy, given the fact that the Indians have tended to be left to live marginalized, underprivileged lives. It is understandable that modern Mexicans should make much of their Indian heritage when trying to impress outsiders, but the fact is that for everyday purposes at home in Mexico, things 'Indian' are commonly considered inferior.

Spanish accounts of the conquest

Cortés' *Cartas de relación*, of which there were five, were reports to the Emperor Carlos V but also attempts at self-justification, since Cortés had acted in defiance of the authority of the emperor's representative, the governor of Cuba. The *Cartas* are symptomatic of a problem that clouds the work of a number of writers in early colonial times, namely that they wrote in a manner calculated to please their patrons and protectors, saying what the latter might want to hear. In his *Diario de navegación* Columbus had done exactly this, no doubt carried away by his enthusiasm but equally clearly writing to please the Catholic Monarchs; sceptics dubbed him the 'almirante de los mosquitos' because of it, ironically alluding to the absence of nasty details in his accounts. Seen in this context, the *Historia verdadera de la conquista de la Nueva España* (True History of the Conquest of New Spain) by Bernal Díaz del Castillo is refreshing and revealing. He claimed to have written his account of the conquest of Mexico in an effort to set the facts straight, particularly as misrepresented in the writings of another chronicler, Francisco López de Gómara: hence the 'verdadera' of Díaz's title. López de Gómara, in *Historia general de las Indias* (1552), had written favouring the *conquistadores* and basing his account on second-hand information: he may have been close to Cortés, but López de Gómara never set foot in the New World. Bernal Díaz, at one point in his own account (end of Chapter XXIX), corrects some of López de Gómara's misinformation and adds 'y no me maravillo, pues lo que dice es por nuevas' (and I am not surprised, since what he is saying, he knows second-hand).

One problem with the storytelling was that the Spaniards liked to think of themselves as knights in shining armour, like the heroes of the medieval tales of chivalry. Díaz, who describes himself as an 'idiota sin letras' (uneducated and ignorant), was perhaps less so than he claims. Nor was he beyond making grand comparisons; for example, in describing the impressiveness of Tenochtitlan he writes 'parecía a las cosas de encantamiento en el libro de Amadís' (it seemed like the enchantments in *Amadis of Gaul*). Yet on balance he is clearly an ordinary soldier, an unpretentious man. His book was finished in Guatemala about fifty years after the events described, and published in Madrid a further sixty years later, in 1632. It offers an engagingly direct account, insistently based on personal experience (even though filtered by memory), one that marvels at the discoveries but also acknowledges the costs on both sides. Here is part of Bernal's account of the first meeting of Cortés and Montezuma:

> Ya que llegábamos cerca de México, adonde estaban otras torrecillas, se apeó el gran Montezuma de las andas, y traíanle de brazo aquellos grandes caciques, debajo de un palio muy riquísimo a maravilla, y el color de plumas verdes con grandes labores de oro, con mucha argentería y perlas y piedras chalchiuis, que colgaban de unas como bordaduras, que hubo mucho que mirar en ello. Y el gran Montezuma venía muy ricamente ataviado, según su usanza, y traía calzados unos como cotaras, que así se dice lo que se calzan; las suelas de oro y muy preciada pedrería por encima de ellas; y los cuatro señores que le traían de brazo venían con rica manera de vestidos a su usanza, que parece ser se los tenían aparejados en el camino para entrar con su señor, que no traían los vestidos con los que nos fueron a recibir, y venían, sin aquellos cuatro señores, otros cuatro grandes caciques que traían el palio sobre sus cabezas, y otros muchos señores que venían delante del gran Montezuma, barriendo el suelo por donde había de pisar, y le ponían mantas por que no pisase la tierra. Todos estos señores ni por pensamiento le miraban en la cara, sino los ojos bajos y con mucho acato, excepto aquellos cuatro deudos y sobrinos suyos que lo llevaban de brazo. Y como Cortés vió y entendió y le dijeron que venía el gran Montezuma, se apeó del caballo, y desde que llegó cerca de Montezuma, a una se hicieron grandes acatos. [. . .] Y entonces sacó Cortés un collar que traía muy a mano de unas piedras de vidrio, que ya he dicho que se dicen margaritas, que tienen dentro de sí muchas labores y diversidad de colores y venía ensartado en unos cordones de oro con almizque por que diesen buen olor, y se le echó al cuello al gran Montezuma, y cuando se le puso le iba a abrazar, y aquellos grandes señores que iban con Montezuma detuvieron el brazo de Cortés que no lo abrazase, porque lo tenían por menosprecio.
>
> [. . .]
>
> Quiero ahora decir la multitud de hombres y mujeres y muchachos que estaban en las calles y azoteas y en canoas en aquellas acequias que nos salían a mirar. Era cosa de notar, que ahora que lo estoy escribiendo se me representa todo delante de mis ojos como si ayer fuera cuando esto pasó, y considerada la cosa, es gran merced que Nuestro Señor Jesucristo fue servido darnos gracia y esfuerso para osar entrar en tal ciudad y me haber guardado de muchos peligros de muerte, como adelante verán. Doile muchas gracias por ello, que a tal tiempo me ha traído para poderlo escribir, y aunque no tan cumplidamente como convenía y se requiere.
>
> (As we approached Mexico, where there were more turrets, the great Montezuma came down from the dais, escorted by the high chieftains, beneath a most wondrous canopy, the colour of green feathers, with fine gold-work, and much silver, and pearls and emeralds hanging from something like embroidery, all of it wondrous to behold. And the great Montezuma was most richly attired, according to his style, with sandals of the kind that they call *cotaras* here; the soles were of gold encrusted with precious stones; and the four lords who were escorting him were richly dressed in their own style, for it seems

that on the way they had decked themselves out in preparation for entering with their master, for they were no longer wearing the clothes that they had received us in, and apart from those four gentlemen there came four more chieftains who were carrying the canopy over their heads, and many other gentlemen went before Montezuma, sweeping the ground where he would tread, and laying down blankets so that his feet should not touch the earth. All these lords never once raised their eyes to look him in the face, but instead looked down and showed the greatest respect, save for the four relatives or nephews who were leading him by the arm. And as Cortés saw and understood that they were saying that the great Montezuma was approaching, he dismounted and once he was close to Montezuma the two of them treated each other with the utmost respect. [. . .] And then Cortés took out a necklace that he had with him, made of glass-like stones, of the sort that as I have said are known as *margaritas*, with much fine handiwork and many colours and threaded onto gold thread, with to give it a fine scent, and he placed it around the neck of Montezuma, and when he did so he made as if to embrace him, and the chieftains who were accompanying Montezuma held back Cortés' arm, for they saw this as a sign of disrespect.

[. . .]

I would now like to tell of the multitude of men and women and children who were in the streets and on the roofs and in canoes on the canals, who had come out to see. It was a sight to behold, and now that I am writing about it it all comes back to me as if it had happened yesterday, and all things considered it is a great mercy that Our Lord saw fit to give us the grace and strength to dare enter that city and that he should have kept me from danger of death, as shall be seen anon. I give him great thanks for it, for He has brought me to the point where I may write about it all, albeit not with the polish that the task deserves and demands.)

The view that the culture of the Indians was the work of the devil was expressed in one way or another by many of the chroniclers, among them Toribio de Benavente (alias Motolinía), Diego de Landa and José de Acosta, respectively in *Historia de los indios de la Nueva España* (1541), *Relación de las cosas de Yucatán* (written c. 1570 but not published until 1864), and *Historia natural y moral de las Indias* (1590). Interestingly, Acosta's work also raises some doubts regarding certain Christian assumptions, such as the idea that the biblical story of Noah's ark might account for the diversity of species. In *Historia de los indios de la Nueva España* Diego de Landa, who had become notorious for presiding over the destruction of many indigenous documents, and inquisitorial interrogations leading to numerous mutilations and deaths among the Mayas, partially atones for his destructiveness by providing essential information about them.

Much to the chagrin of official Spain, not all the accounts of conquest written by Spaniards were favourable to the Spanish image. Fray Bartolomé de las Casas, the first priest to be ordained in the New World, had heard a sermon given in Santo Domingo by a Dominican friar, Antonio de Montesinos, in which the Spaniards were castigated for their cruel treatment of the island's natives;

inspired by that sermon, Las Casas renounced his colonial privileges and joined the Dominican Order, thereafter dedicating his life to the goal of persuading the Crown to put an end to the injustices and cruelty. The upshot was lawsuits and controversy that lasted for years, for many interested parties were benefiting from the colonial practices, including Spain itself. A fierce debate took place concerning whether the conquest was just. Some, like Juan Ginés de Sepúlveda, argued forcefully that it was, that the faithless Indians were savages being duly punished for their errant ways and that slavery was their rightful condition. For all his energetic advocacy of the Indian cause, Las Casas saw that the argument was not being won; in his desperation to save the Indian population from decimation, he resorted to the draconian solution of advocating the importation of slaves from Africa. He also resolved in 1552 to publish his writings about the conquest. In his *Historia general de las Indias* he attacks the very notion of slavery. His most controversial work, however, has been the *Brevísima relación de la destrucción de Indias*, for this was the work that sowed the seeds of the *leyenda negra*, Spain's reputation for cruelty, which the country's European adversaries were pleased to exploit for propaganda purposes in later years. An English translation dated 1689, for example, glossed itself as 'Popery truly display'd in its bloody colours: or, a faithful narrative of the horrid and unexampled massacres, butcheries and all manner of cruelties, that hell and malice could invent, committed by the popish Spanish party on the inhabitants of West-India'. In the following extract from the *Brevísima relación . . .*, having dealt with the Caribbean, Las Casas is turning his attention to Nueva España:

> Entre otras matanzas hicieron ésta en una ciudad grande de más de treinta mil vecinos, que se llama Cholula: que saliendo a recebir todos los señores de la tierra y comarca, y primero todos los sacerdotes con el sacerdote mayor, a los cristianos en procesión y con grande acatamiento y reverencia, y llevándolos en medio a aposentar a la ciudad y a las casas de aposentos del señor o señores della principales, acordaron los españoles de hacer allí una matanza o castigo (como ellos dicen) para poner y sembrar su temor y braveza en todos los rincones de aquellas tierras. Porque siempre fue ésta su determinación en todas las tierras que los españoles han entrado, conviene a saber, hacer una cruel y señalada matanza, porque tiemblen dellos aquellas ovejas mansas. Así que enviaron para esto primero a llamar todos los señores y nobles de la ciudad y de todos los lugares a ella subjetos, con el señor principal. Y así como venían y entraban a hablar al capitán de los españoles, luego eran presos sin que nadie los sintiese, que pudiese llevar las nuevas. Habíanles pedido cinco o seis mil indios que les llevasen las cargas: vinieron todos luego y metenlos en el patio de las casas. Ver a estos indios cuanto se aparejan para llevar las cargas de los españoles es haber dellos una gran compasión y lástima, porque vienen desnudos en cueros, solamente cubiertas sus vergüenzas y con unas redecillas en el hombro con su pobre comida: ponense todos en cuclillas, como unos corderos muy mansos. Todos ayuntados y juntos en el patio con otras gentes que a vueltas estaban, ponense a las puertas del patio españoles armados que guardasen, y todos los demás echan mano a sus espadas y meten a espada y a lanzadas todas aquellas ovejas, que uno ni

> ninguno pudo escaparse que no fuese trucidado. A cabo de dos o tres días saltan muchos indios vivos llenos de sangre, que se habían escondido y amparado debajo de los muertos (como eran tantos); iban llorando ante los españoles pidiendo misericordia, que no los matasen. De los cuales ninguna misericordia ni compasión hubieron, antes así como salían los hacían pedazos.
>
> [. . .]
>
> Otra gran matanza hicieron en la ciudad de Tepeaca, que era mucho mayor y de más vecinos y gente que la dicha, donde mataron a espada infinita gente, con grandes particularidades de crueldad.
>
> (Together with other massacres they indulged in this one at a city of over thirty thousand inhabitants that is called Cholula: as all the lords of that region came out, led by the priests and the high priest, in a great a highly respectful procession, to welcome the Christians, accompanying them to their lodgings in the city, and to those of the chief lords and ladies, the Spaniards decided to carry out a massacre or to chastise them (as they describe it) in order to sow fear of their might in every corner of those lands. For it should be made clear that this was always the purpose of the Spaniards, in all the lands they occupied: to carry out a cruel and decisive massacre, so that those gentle lambs should fear them. So their first step was to summon all the lords and nobles of the city and of all adjacent lands that were subject to it, together with the man of highest authority. And as they arrived and entered in order to speak with the Captain of the Spaniards, they were taken prisoner without anyone knowing or being able to spread the news. They had asked for five or six thousand Indians to serve as bearers: these then came and were confined to the central patio. To see these Indians arriving to carry the Spaniards' loads was to feel great pity and compassion for them, for they came naked, save for their private parts, and with string bags over their shoulders carrying their meagre food: they all crouched down like the gentlest lambs. Once they were all assembled in the patio together with other people who were nearby, the Spaniards put armed guards at the entrances to keep them in, and the rest of them grasped their swords and set about hacking and running through those lambs so that none could escape being killed. After two or three days many Indians who were still alive and had hidden and shielded themselves beneath the bodies (that were so many) got up, covered in blood; they implored the Spaniards for mercy, that they might not be killed. But mercy there was none, nor pity, and instead they cut them to pieces as they appeared.
>
> [. . .]
>
> They carried out another great massacre at the city of Tepeaca, which was much larger and had more people than the one just mentioned, and there they put countless people to death by the sword, and indulged in extreme cruelty.)

All this occurred on the way to Tenochtitlan, and the 'capitán' responsible, though Las Casas never names him, must have been Cortés. At one point during the account of the massacre at Cholula Cortés is said to have been triumphantly reciting lines from a *romance* about the fall of Rome, as he helped put paid to more Indians. Las Casas goes on to describe the events at Tenochtitlan, the imprisonment of Montezuma and the taking of the Aztec capital, an account that makes for an interesting comparison with Díaz del Castillo's.

Even these days, Las Casas is a controversial figure and is accused of exaggeration. His style can certainly be lurid: his Indians are always going like lambs to the slaughter, his Spaniards are voracious lions ready to prey upon them; but was this style unusual in a passionate preacher? In one episode Las Casas tells a story of a plague of ants, which he says was sent by God as just punishment to destroy the profitable crops of the settlers who had so abused the natives (among other things by bringing their own plague – smallpox – upon them). André Saint-Lu, in the introduction to his edition of the *Brevísima relación* . . ., says that the exaggerations and the florid metaphors are merely rhetorical devices designed to reinforce the message, even if Las Casas uses them a little ineptly at times. Others bear out the factual basis for Las Casas' assertions, in the sense that there has been general agreement among historians down the ages that the Indians suffered and the population declined dramatically. Motolinía, who was a contemporary and one of those who believed that such things were the will of God and a just retribution for unchristian ways, counts the violence of conquest and the mistreatment of Indians by settlers as major causes of the population decline, together with disease and other hardships. Quite how large-scale that decline was is a matter of intense debate; estimates as to how many natives there were at the time of the Spaniards' arrival vary from as few as 2 million to as many as 25 million, and even estimates of the proportional drop vary from 50 to 90 percent. As Melville notes (Meyer and Beezley: 226), 'given the nature of documentation of 16th century populations, the debate between the "maximalists", who argue for a large contact population and a truly appalling drop in numbers, and the "minimalists", who argue for a smaller population and a less dramatic collapse, probably can never be resolved'. Cook and Borah's figures suggest that Central Mexico had something over 23 million people in 1519, when the Spaniards arrived, and that within four years the number had dropped to below 17 million; by 1570 only 30 percent of the 23 million remained.

We owe an immense amount to the initiative of Fray Bernardino de Sahagún, who compiled *Historia general de las cosas de Nueva España* (completed in 1577 but not published until 1830, two hundred and forty years after his death in 1590). Sahagún was in Mexico for about sixty years and spent much of that time gathering the information that eventually led to this substantial, four-volume work. The methodology Sahagún employed in compiling it is of no less interest than the information itself, for he acted rather as might a modern anthropologist, sending out trained interviewers to seek information from a large number of informants, and then producing a digest. Initially the information was in Nahuatl, then it was translated into Spanish. Sahagún's dedication to the task of recording the native culture was rewarded with suspicion on the part of the Church, his material was confiscated as part of a general attempt at damage control, and he died believing that it would never be published. Yet history has vindicated him by recognizing the immense importance of his work, not least because it allows us to glimpse the conquest from the standpoint of some of the Indians, in particular those of Tlatelolco. On the instructions of Philip II, Sahagún's original material was taken to Spain, where it is now in the Real Academia de Historia and the Palacio Nacional.

Here is a sample from one of Sahagún's informants, describing a real turning point in relations between the Spaniards and the Aztecs of Tenochtitlan: it is the point at which the latter were celebrating a major event in their calendar, while Cortés was away dealing with forces sent by Velázquez, and the hot-headed Pedro de Alvarado was in charge:

> Pues así las cosas, mientras se está gozando de la fiesta, ya es el baile, ya es el canto, ya se enlaza un canto con otro, y los cantos son como un estruendo de olas, en ese preciso momento los españoles toman la determinaci6n de matar a la gente. Luego vienen hacia acá, todos vienen en armas de guerra.
>
> Vienen a cerrar las salidas, los pasos, las entradas . . . Y luego que hubieron cerrado en todas ellas se apostaron: ya nadie pudo salir.
>
> [. . .]
>
> Inmediatamente cercan a los que bailan, se lanzan al lugar de los atabales: dieron un tajo al que estaba tañendo: le cortaron ambos brazos. Luego lo decapitaron: lejos fue a caer su cabeza cercenada. Al momento todos acuchillan, alancean a la gente y les dan tajos, con las espadas los hieren. . . . A algunos les acometieron por detrás; inmediatamente cayeron por tierra dispersas sus entrañas. A otros les desgarraron la cabeza: les rebanaron la cabeza, enteramente hecha trizas quedó su cabeza.
>
> Pero a otros les dieron tajos en los hombros: hechos grietas, desgarrados quedaron sus cuerpos. A aquéllos hieren en los muslos, a éstos en las pantorrillas, a los de más allá en pleno abdomen. Todas las entrañas cayeron por tierra. Y había algunos que aún en vano corrían: iban arrastrando los intestinos y parecían enredarse los pies en ellos. Anhelosos de ponerse en salvo, no hallaban a donde dirigirse.
>
> (So with things as they were, with people enjoying the festivities, and the dances in progress and the singing going on, with one song leading to another as if in waves of noise, at precisely that time the Spaniards decide to start killing people. They rush over bearing their weapons. They close off the exits, the passages and the entrances . . . And once they had closed them all they stood guard: now no-one could leave. Immediately they surround the people who are dancing, they rush over to the place where the drums are: they wounded the man who was playing: they cut off both his arms. Then they decapitated him: his head rolled a long way away. Then they all start slashing, they run people through and cut them up, wounding them with their sword . . . Some they attacked from behind; their entrails spilled immediately out onto the ground. Others they attacked in the head: they trimmed it off, left the head chopped to bits. But others they struck in the shoulder: they cut deeply, tearing the body to pieces. Some were struck in the thigh, others in the calf, still others in the belly. All their guts spilled onto the ground. And some people tried to run away: they dragged their intestines with them and seemed to get their feet tangled up in them. They were desperate to get to safety, and there was nowhere to turn.)

Apart from the work of Sahagún, our principal sources of information regarding the Indian view of the conquest are the poems of the *cantares* (whose manuscript is in the Biblioteca Nacional in Mexico City), some anonymous eyewitness accounts given by Indians from Tlatelolco around 1528 (a manuscript now in Paris), and those of other Indians who were allies of Cortés or had otherwise assimilated to the new society. For this last category the main sources are the *Historia de Tlaxcala* by Diego Muñoz Camargo, a *mestizo*, the writings of Fernando de Alva Ixtilxóchitl, a relative of the celebrated poet-king Nezahualcóyotl, and those of Alvarado Tezozomoc. A number of sources are pictographic, an important example being the *Lienzo de Tlaxcala*, which dates from the mid-sixteenth century and has some eighty illustrations. Also important is Fray Diego de Durán's *Historia de las Indias de la Nueva España e Islas de Tierra Firme*; it contains fifty illustrations painted by Indian artists of that same period, albeit on European paper.

According to León-Portilla's *Visión de los vencidos*, the first Spaniard to recognize that the vanquished Indians were anxious to preserve their heritage and record their experiences was Motolinía, that is Fray Toribio de Benavente, one of the first group of twelve Franciscans (the number was, of course, significant) who were sent to Mexico in 1524. At the start of the third *tratado* of his *Historia de los indios de la Nueva España*, Motolinía writes: 'Mucho notaron estos naturales indios, entre las cuentas de sus años, el año que vinieron y entraron en esta tierra los españoles, como cosa muy notable y que al principio les puso muy grande espanto y admiración.' (In their historical accounts, these natives of the Indies made much of the importance of the year of the arrival of the Spaniards in these lands, and how at first it filled them with fear and wonder.) That wonder gave way to sadness: a poem in the anonymous Tlatelolco manuscript runs thus:

> On the paths there lie broken spears,
> Torn out hair is scattered about.
> Houses are without roofs,
> Their walls red with blood.
>
> Worms infest the streets and squares,
> And walls are spattered with brains.
> The waters run red, as if stained,
> And when we drink them,
> It is as if we were drinking salt water.
>
> And we were pounding on the adobe walls,
> For our heritage was in shreds.
> Shields had been its defence,
> But they could not protect its solitude.

And another fragment, from the *Cantares*:

> Cry, my friends,
> Understand that with these events
> We have lost the Mexica nation.

After 1521, colonists flocked into Nueva España. New towns were founded throughout the central valley, usually on the sites of Aztec settlements, while some influential Spaniards went into the countryside to enjoy their *encomiendas*. These were grants of land and native labour made to settlers on the understanding that they looked after the Indians and saw to their conversion to the true faith; the Indians were supposed to pay tribute to the *encomendero*, in labour or goods. In many cases, such land grants amounted to grants of social status, since by no means all the settlers were from Spain's upper social strata. Despite the exploitative nature of the arrangement – it was frequently abused by *encomenderos* – the demarcation lines for the *encomiendas* were almost always drawn to coincide with those of existing communities, so that often a city-state (*altepetl*) would be assigned in its entirety to one *encomendero*. The result was that for more than a hundred years after the conquest the pre-conquest social and administrative structures of those communities survived; they no longer made sacrifices and fought wars, but they did organize other aspects of their community life much as in the past. Some members of the Aztec nobility learned Spanish and became involved in the colonial economy, some collaborated with the friars in the business of recording their native heritage, but most of the Nahua people who survived remained in their communities, speaking Nahuatl.[2]

The effective survival of the *altepetl* as a unit made possible the preservation of a good deal of Nahua culture and customs; the outward signs of their religion were gone, but in rural areas in particular traditional patterns of behaviour continued, with some practices surviving into the eighteenth century. In general, Indian languages were still spoken, most people remained tied to the land, and most produced the goods they had always produced. In rural areas, at least, the conquest did not abruptly and totally transform everyday life as it did in some cities, and so it is that in the former the pre-conquest traditions survived longest. In some such areas it would centuries before the Spanish language and its customs made real inroads. Meanwhile, the Indian cultures and languages were having their own effect on the imported one; there was syncretism, there was a nahuatlization of Christianity.

2 Reference was made earlier to the ravages of smallpox in the context of the fall of Tenochtitlan. This was not the only new disease the Indians had to face, for it was followed by measles, typhus, mumps and others that were not identified but contributed to the horrendous decline in the Indian population by the end of the sixteenth century.

3

The Colonial Period

On the site of Tenochtitlan the Spaniards constructed Mexico City. 'Mexico' became the popular name for it and by extension that name came to refer to all the territory that was officially known as 'Nueva España'. This was to be the power base from which viceroys governed territories that by the late seventeenth century extended from southern Central America well into what is now the United States.[1] After the conquest of Peru, a second *virreinato* was established in Lima, and some time later two more in Bogotá and Buenos Aires, but the viceroyalty of New Spain would always be the most significant, and the model for the others.[2] The *virreyes* and other representatives of Spanish authority were invariably natives of Spain; indeed, all significant positions of authority during the colonial period were restricted to Spanish natives, a fact that generated much resentment among the *criollos*, the people of European blood who had been born in the New World.

Although the conquest occurred during the Renaissance, a time when most of Europe was taking a fresh view of the world and of the place of mankind in it, Spain was in many respects still living in the Middle Ages. It went to America as a champion of orthodox Catholicism, high on the recent expulsion of the Moorish infidels, on a crusade. To borrow Unamumo's words, 'España conquistó América a cristazos' (Spain used Christ to beat America into submission). As it turned out, according to both the Spanish and the Amerindian worldviews religion was crucial to government, if not synonymous with it. In the drive to control and convert the natives, the Spaniards used the Indian élite as intermediaries and exploited similarities between pre-Hispanic and Catholic religious customs. While this strategy was not entirely favoured by higher authority, it proved to be a practical way of reaching the Indian populace; in any case, how could those who wished to exercise strict control from faraway Spain do so? The main concerns were how to control the Indians, how to keep a rein on the activities of the *encomenderos* and how to collect taxes.

The difficulty in keeping control from across the water became very apparent when the crown made attempts to better the lot of the Indians, who were often used and abused by settlers. Yet, for all the violence and destruction committed

1 The Philippines were also administered by the viceroys of 'Mexico'.

2 After independence, Mexico suffered significant losses of territory in the nineteenth century: the Central American Confederation separated from it and by mid-century Mexico had also lost Texas and almost all the west and southwest to the United States.

by the Spaniards, for all the greed of the conquistadors, there were also some notable humane deeds, done especially by the missionary friars; it is also important to recognize that official Spain did acknowledge the Indians' humanity both in principle and in law, even if such provisions were not always very effective.

In this regard the deeds of Vasco de Quiroga (1470?–1565) are exemplary. Having been sent to New Spain in his sixties, to be a judge in the *audiencia*, Quiroga set about undoing some of the wrongs perpetrated by his predecessor in the post, Nuño Beltrán de Guzmán, whose record of maltreating Indians had been capped with the brutal murder of one of their chieftains, an event that provoked a rebellion in Michoacán. Once Guzmán had been sentenced, Quiroga turned his attention elsewhere, using his own money to found hospital-schools near the capital and in Michoacán. When Carlos V pulled back from an earlier ruling that the Indians should not be treated as slaves, Quiroga sent him *Información en derecho* (1535), an energetic defence of the Indians and an attack on the way they were being abused by Spanish settlers. Late in life Quiroga took religious vows, and he rose quickly in the ranks, being appointed bishop of Michoacán in 1537. It was in that same year that Pope Paul III issued a bull declaring that the Indians were capable of reason and deserved to receive the sacraments; seen from our modern point of view such a declaration may seem patronizing and culturally self-centred, but it did much to prevent the displacements and slaughter that might otherwise have occurred (and that did occur north of the border). Quiroga, inspired by the writings of Thomas More, was now in a position to try to make the ideal of a utopian community a reality. He established a number of communities where the Indians were housed and fed, and where they received instruction that was not only religious but also in arts and crafts, together with the basics of self-government along rudimentary socialist principles. It was paternalistic, to be sure, but undeniably well-intentioned. Quiroga thought his experiment successful, and indeed there were some utopian communities that lasted into the early seventeenth century, but the fact that the communities effectively deprived the colonial system of part of the labour force meant that they did not spread widely. Quiroga is remembered affectionately as 'Tata Vasco', and his name is enshrined in public places and institutions.

On two occasions during the first half of the sixteenth century Carlos V tried unsuccessfully to put an end to the system of *encomiendas*, which had granted the control of groups of Indians, and most of the benefits of their labours, to individual settlers. The problem with the *encomenderos* had been brought to the king's attention by the writings of Bartolomé de las Casas; as noted in the previous chapter, in his *Brevísima relación de la destrucción de las Indias* he revealed how the Indians were being mistreated under the *encomienda* system. Las Casas himself had had an *encomienda*, and had renounced it before entering the Dominican Order.

Resistance by the Indians to colonial rule is believed to have been an everyday business, but, as Patch notes (Meyer and Beezley: 193), it was not well documented, for obvious reasons. It is clear that physical force was sometimes used to oblige the Indians to conform to the demands of the *repartimiento* system, which was a way of sharing out spoils, particularly, in this case, the spoils of their labours, on a basis that was very favourable to the Spaniards. Some Indians exploited litigation as a means of resistance, some simply ran away and hid in remote regions, and sometimes the resistance was violent. A more subtle form of resistance is apparent in the manner in which they took on the challenge of Christianity, converting to it in ways that were sometimes more apparent than real. They were quick to become nominal Christians, but did not completely abandon their traditional beliefs: they converted not as a result of a spiritual epiphany but by consciously substituting one system for another, by interpreting Christianity in ways that were compatible with their own beliefs. Some of the early friars, recognizing that this was the case, lamented that instead of a thousand deities, the Indians now had a thousand and one. In art and architecture (of which more below) we see material reflections of this assimilative, syncretic process.

The most significant example of cultural syncretism is the phenomenon of the Virgen de Guadalupe. It is said that in the winter of 1531 the Virgin appeared at Tepeyac, near Mexico City, to a Christian Indian labourer, Juan Diego, speaking to him in Nahuatl. She instructed him to exhort the authorities to build a shrine in her honour, and gave him some roses to carry in his cloak to the bishop. When Juan unwrapped the cloak in front of him, instead of the roses there appeared a beautiful *mestiza* image of the Virgin. Accordingly, in 1533 a small hermitage was put on the Tepeyac hill, near where the Indians had had a temple to the earth goddess Tonantzín.[3] The fact that as far as the Spaniards were concerned the site was one where heretical and idolatrous practises had been carried out perhaps made them reluctant to acknowledge the potential power of this legend in the Mexican psyche, but in 1737 the Virgen de Guadalupe was declared patroness of Mexico City, in 1756 Pope Benedict XIV extended her patronage to the whole of New Spain, in 1910 Pius X declared her 'Celestial Patroness of Latin America', and in 1945 Pius XII elevated her to 'Empress of the Americas'. As a place of pilgrimage, her shrine at Tepeyac now rivals Rome. As is the way with such things, people saw what they wanted in the symbol of the Virgen de Guadalupe. To the Indians she was a version of Tonantzín. To early colonial church officials she was proof that their campaign to indoctrinate the natives was having the desired effect. And of course she was reassurance for many people that the *mestizo* was legitimate and particularly Mexican. Somewhat ironically, she was used to rally support at the start of the movement for independence from Spain in the early nineteenth century.[4]

3 References to pilgrimages and worship at Tepeyac are found not only in the archives of the Church, but also in the sixteenth-century writings of Bernal Díaz del Castillo and Fray Bernardino de Sahagún, among others.

4 For more on the Virgin of Guadalupe, see Brading (2002) and Lafaye.

Race, class and society

The blending process took place at all levels, not least racially. We have already seen how Malinche's son by Cortés came to symbolize the new *mestizo* race that would be thought of as characteristically Mexican. Since Spanish women were in relatively short supply in the colonies, it is not surprising that the *mestizos* grew rapidly in number. Thomas Gage, an English minister of religion who visited Mexico in 1625, remarked on the ostentatious lifestyle of the colonial Spaniards, and then added that, even when they did have Spanish wives with them 'many Spaniards, even of the better sort, [were] too prone to venery'.[5] One wonders whether Englishmen would have been very different in similar circumstances.

The Indian population declined disastrously in the immediate wake of conquest. As indicated previously, apart from deaths by violence there were many caused by the incidental importation of European diseases to which the natives had no immunity. There are also accounts of Indians committing suicide or practising sexual abstinence rather than prolonging life under such adverse conditions. With time, the population figures would recover somewhat, but in 1518, faced with the dramatic decline of the workforce, the Spanish crown began to grant or sell licences (*asientos*) for importing slaves from Africa. In the early years they came to the islands, and some escaped from there to lands fringing the Caribbean Sea, but later some were brought directly to Mexico. During the colonial period we therefore have three basic population ingredients: Amerindian, African and European.[6]

A hierarchy of social classes developed, underpinned by a preoccupation with one's family stock in terms of *limpieza de sangre* (purity of blood), a notion that had been used in the peninsula to distinguish Christians from Jews and Muslims. At the top of the colonial social hierarchy were the Spaniards (the *peninsulares* – those born in Spain) and below them those born in the Americas but of European stock (the *criollos*). We have already seen that the positions of power were accorded by Spain to Spaniards; the resentment thus generated among the *criollos*, who could only occupy minor, local *cabildo* positions, would help motivate the push for independence during the nineteenth century. The *criollos* of Mexico coined a pejorative term for the *peninsulares*: 'gachupines'.[7] Despite their frustrations, however, the *criollos* were often economically more prosperous than the *peninsulares*. Many observers, like Thomas Gage, were struck by the self-indulgence of the inhabitants of 'Mexico', as compared with the primitive conditions to which the Indians in

5 *A New Survey of the West Indies*, ed. A.P. Newton (New York: Robert McBride, 1929), p. 86.

6 In the latter part of the colonial period the variety of European immigrants increased considerably.

7 The same happened in the other major *virreinato*, Peru, where the *peninsulares* were dubbed 'chapetones'.

particular were consigned. Below the two élite classes of the *peninsulares* and the *criollos* came the *castas*, a grouping that takes in a variety of racial and ethnic mixes. There were the *mestizos* (people of mixed Indian and European parentage) who, though numerous, were excluded from many social roles; for example, they could become apprentice artisans, but never masters. Others among the many *castas* were the *zambos* (a mixture of Indian and African) and the *mulatos* (black and white). The black slaves were at the bottom of the social scale. But what of the full-blooded Indians? The nobility were relatively integrated with the Europeans, and indeed were accustomed, like the European nobility, to using intermarriage as a means of consolidating alliances. For the rest, the position was a little ambiguous, since Indians were subject to fewer restrictions than were the members of the *castas*, in fact were protected by law in some respects, but they lived somewhat apart from the rest of society. This relative isolation is apparent even today, and it is reflected in the use of the term 'ladino', which in essence means non-Indian and is used especially by Indians to refer to Spanish speakers in general, or to Indians who have adopted Spanish ways. Even in the eighteenth century, when official censuses were still being based on racial characteristics, it was clear that cultural and economic factors were closely correlated with social status. Wealth, income and a Spanish ancestry were the prime factors. There were, however, some prosperous Indian nobles and even some prosperous members of the *castas*.

Mexico was expected by Spain to pay for itself and also to send surpluses to the mother country, but it also soon had more wealthy people than any other colony. Mexico City itself displayed the full gamut of wealth and social standing, with a hundred wealthy 'Great Families' at the top of the ladder; in other parts of New Spain there were only about a dozen more families of comparable wealth, the millionaires of the times. These largely *criollo* families generally intermarried or married Spaniards, with occasional infusions of Indian or black blood that did little to harm their status. They invested profitably, granted each other favours and titles, and lived lavishly. In colonial New Spain, Spanish ancestry was by no means a guarantee of prosperity, but it did help a great deal with social status, as is suggested by the fact that the overwhelming majority of those who called themselves Spaniards were in fact born in the New World. By the end of the eighteenth century most Indians were still living in their native villages, in the south and in the central valley; many were surviving at subsistence level now that a recovery in their population was adding to the general economic strain in New Spain. Black slavery had almost disappeared; fortunately, the blacks did not have to suffer quite the same degree of indignity in Mexico as in the Caribbean, where they were bought and held as symbols of wealth and influence.

At this time women were clearly in the majority, even in the ecclesiastical ranks, and women of the lower classes were a major constituent of the workforce. Marriage to a well-placed man could, of course, lift a woman to a new social level, but there were social hurdles designed to favour women who could claim *limpieza de sangre*, and such hurdles had the support of church and state. Clerics wrote emphasizing the need to marry according to one's status, and for its part in 1776 the state established rules to prevent marriages of unequal status. All the same, by the end of the eighteenth century racial intermingling was widespread. Men and women, in line with both Spanish and Indian traditions, were expected to fulfil very different roles, and educated accordingly. It was thought that women in general did not need to be literate, and such education as there was for them was given privately, in convents, and primarily to white women.

The printed word and the role of the press

Famously, in 1492 Queen Isabel asked Antonio de Nebrija to explain the purpose of a book he was presenting to her, and she was told that it was 'un instrumento de imperio'; it was, in fact, his *Arte de la lengua castellana*, the first grammar of any modern language. This was a time when the new political unity in Spain was consolidating the position of Castilian as the dominant dialect, and this now national form of expression certainly played a vital role in the colonization of the Americas; but so too did the invention, some fifty years before Columbus' first voyage, of movable type. Nebrija's work not only codified and reinforced the language but it did so by means of a book; now the word could be set, copied and spread. In 1539 Juan Pablos was granted permission to import the first printing press into the New World.[8] Somewhat surprisingly, the rate of expansion of printing facilities in Mexico thereafter was slow, but the reason was probably that Church and State were at pains to keep a tight rein on the flow of information. Approved publications toed the official line, while unauthorized ones became the target of suppressive edicts and ever more draconian penalties. For example, the colonial authorities tried to suppress the anonymous broadsides (*pasquines*) that would appear overnight, pasted onto public walls; these broadsides were the satirical precursors of the personal and partisan attacks that *criollo* intellectuals would publish after independence, or of the graffiti of modern times.

Soon after the arrival of the first printing press it became common to publish occasional newssheets (*hojas volantes*) after the European fashion. By the mid-seventeenth century these had become more regular and were known as 'Gacetas'. The first of these that is known to have been produced in a numbered series started in Puebla in 1667. From the *gacetas* there grew what is generally held to be the first true newspaper in the New World, the *Gaceta de México y Noticias de la Nueva España*, which had six consecutive monthly issues, each of some eight pages, based upon which its editor, Juan Ignacio de Castorena y Ursúa, is sometimes referred to as the father of Mexican journalism. Operating under viceregal licence, a later *Gaceta de México* was edited by Father Juan

8 A publishing house bearing his name is still in existence.

Francisco Sahagún de Arévalo; that one appeared monthly from 1728 to 1739. There was then a hiatus resulting from a shortage of newsprint, after which Sahagún resumed publication for a short period under a new title, *Mercurio de México*. A third and final version of the *Gaceta de México* was launched in 1784, with Manuel Antonio Valdés as editor.

Although the various *gacetas* progressed in terms of their efficiency in gathering and disseminating news, the basic formula remained unchanged, as did the underlying philosophy regarding the purpose of the enterprise, which was to document the achievements of the times and not to rock the boat. The editors mentioned were all *criollos*, but they relied heavily on news first published in Spain; indeed, their papers aped those of the old country, trying to show sophistication while at once demonstrating pride in the newsworthiness of the New World. The result was that much of the news was old by the time it reached the Mexican reader. Major Mexican topics of coverage were civic, military and especially religious events, such as ceremonies celebrating the arrival of dignitaries from Spain, official proclamations and inaugurations, together with news of the campaign to indoctrinate the indigenous population, of baptisms, miracles, martyrdoms and canonizations. Functioning essentially as bureaucrats, the journalists of colonial times served the establishment by providing approved information, eschewing comment and avoiding controversy. The subordination of the press to state authority would become even more pronounced as the end of colonial rule approached, as can be deduced from the fact that during the early nineteenth century Valdés' *Gaceta de México* turned into the *Gaceta del Gobierno*.[9]

The first semblance of a modern-style newspaper was Bustamante and Villaurrutia's *Diario de México*, which began in 1805 and survived for twelve years thereafter, thanks to the editors' willingness to acquiesce to the constraints of authority. They avoided alienating the powerful and did not deal with political matters, but they did address a broadly based readership, not just the *criollo* élite, providing information and entertainment and offering an outlet for poets, journalists and historians who previously had had none.[10] There was no lack of material, though it was often penned by writers who felt it prudent to remain anonymous, particularly when commenting on social or economic issues. The *Diario* could also be said to be Mexico's first significant literary publication. What is more, inasmuch as it was neither simply a mouthpiece for the establishment nor rampantly partisan, the *Diario* . . . was objective to a degree that was not seen again until late in the century.

9 In modern times the term 'gacetilla' has been used pejoratively to refer to journalism that is driven by government bribes.

10 It should be borne in mind that literacy levels were low.

Dance, music and theatre

The early chroniclers tell us that Aztec rituals were theatrical, incorporating dance and music, and that their poetry was written to be performed before an audience. Ravicz speaks of a 'culture . . . in which men sang and danced their religious and esthetic devotion' (40). Not that the Aztec performances were solely religious; some, in places such as markets, involved buffoonery and farce and seem to have been simply for entertainment.

As it happened, a similar admixture of performance elements was not uncommon in Medieval and Renaissance Spain. The forms brought to Mexico, primarily from Extremadura and Andalusia, drew on three cultural traditions, the Islamic, the Jewish and the Christian. In Mexico they were used for Catholic ends, with the early missionaries exploiting parallels between Christian and 'pagan' practices as they set about the task of converting the natives. In Father Acosta's *Historia natural y moral de las Indias* we find some suggestions as to how the indigenous proclivity for ceremonial dance might be exploited for the purpose of acculturation and evangelization; given such possibilities, Acosta advocated a permissive attitude to the native dances. The early missionaries noticed that dramatic rituals represented a large part of Aztec life, and that religiosity was a guiding principle; they saw that colour and pageantry were needed in order to substitute one religion for another, and that existing practices were best adapted rather than destroyed. Sometimes, the ceremonies and dances of the Mesoamerican Indians accommodated quite easily to Spanish religious rituals. Indian ritual dance seems to have been the form of artistic expression that Spanish colonial authorities found least alien and most compatible with Spanish ways.

Bernal Díaz del Castillo writes of Cortés' love of music and of how he was accompanied by expert musicians; he describes the lavish musical fare at a banquet for the first viceroy. On colonial music the viceregal court and above all the Catholic Church exerted a pervasive influence, recruiting singers and musicians of all kinds to their service. Carlos de Sigüenza y Góngora (see pages 55–5), in his *Glorias de Querétaro* (1680), describes Indians dancing their dances and playing their instruments in an elaborate outdoor masquerade in honour of the Virgin, while the Spaniards had their own more discreet orchestra that played inside, during intervals in a poetry contest.

Instruments were brought over from Spain, natives were trained in Spanish musical ways; it was soon observed that they were quick learners, and a number of them became quite distinguished musicians. Manuscripts fare less well over time than buildings, and sadly, colonial printing presses were not given to making the copies of musical scores that might have aided their survival.[11] That, together with ignorance and neglect, has led to the loss of much music from colonial times. Robert Stevenson (1952: 100) quotes the experience of a priest

11 An exception was the printer Didacus López Davalos.

who in modern times came across a 280-page manuscript (it became known as the *Valdés Codex*) containing four Palestrina masses, which he found in an Indian community. The community, which had thought the paper worthless, also told him of another such book that it had had – and lost. The archives of Latin American cathedrals confirm that the standard in the seventeenth century was high and the styles imitative of Europe; they reveal that, in addition to the works of local composers, those of distinguished European composers (Lobo, Morales and Guerrero, for example) were also performed in the New World. The main places for ecclesiastical music, in addition to Mexico City, were Puebla, Morelia, Guadalajara and Oaxaca. Puebla Cathedral, the first in New Spain to be consecrated, took on a special role and came to boast a double choir of *diestros* (skilled performers), thanks to royal patronage and the patrician tastes and financial profligacy of Bishop Juan de Palafox y Mendoza. He it was who presided over the consecration of the cathedral in 1649, and for that cathedral Pedro Bermúdez wrote rhythmically lively church music, while its double choir made possible the performance of dramatic antiphonal music in the style of Gabrieli and encouraged compositions by other composers such as Bernardo de Peralta. Juan de Padilla, a Puebla Cathedral chapelmaster, is known for his *Matthew Passion*, which is somewhat on the pattern of Schutz's, but less reliant on rhythm and more chromatic. Some other major composers of colonial church music are Hernando Franco, Juan de Lienas, Antonio de Salazar and the aptly named Francisco López y Capilla. Franco, active in the late sixteenth and early seventeenth centuries, left a number of magnificats and miscellaneous other church pieces. The magnificats, which Stevenson calls Franco's 'most artful compositions' (111), were written in typical sixteenth-century counterpoint, alternating plainsong with polyphony, as was the European custom; he further asserts that 'Franco's technical competence is beyond dispute' (116). There are some hymns with Nahuatl text that some scholars have also attributed to Franco. Manuel de Zumaya and Ignacio de Jerúsalem were the leading figures of the eighteenth century. Zumaya (sometimes given as Sumaya; c. 1678–1755) was an original, Mexican-born composer whose works display great variety and who represents the culmination of the baroque style in Mexico; he was also the first person in the New World to compose an opera (*Parténope*, 1711). Having served as chapel master at Mexico City Cathedral from 1715 to 1738, Zumaya moved to Oaxaca, where he remained until his death. Among Zumaya's works, his *Sol-fa de Pedro*, which is full of word-painting, was an examination piece written in support of his candidacy for the Mexico City post; his *a capella* work, the *Lamentations of Jeremiah* (1717), sometimes seems to echo that of Tallis, and *Celebren, publiquen* is an ambitious composition for double choir. Jerúsalem (1707–69) came to Mexico from Italy, his reputation as a gifted musician having led to his being engaged as a violinist for the Mexico City Coliseo. He was soon writing works for the cathedral and he served as its chapel master for the last twenty years of his life, also becoming known elsewhere in Spanish America. Though his *Responsorio Segundo de S.S. José* is in the high baroque style, Jerúsalem's music is on the whole more emphatically contemporary, his choral music full of blocked chords, sometimes alleviated by the instrumental line; one example is his *Matines para Nuestra Señora de Guadalupe* (1764).

Among the most significant of religious festivals was Corpus Christi, an annual event involving everyone and cutting across the usual social and cultural divides. There were costumes, dances, musical and theatrical events, in which even the dignitaries of Mexico City participated on a similar footing to those of other classes, although in the main procession each social group had its separate place. At some of these feasts of Corpus Christi, for example in 1692, celebrations got out of hand, which led to the Bourbons trying to regulate behaviour, and eventually to the prohibition of dancing, drinking and inappropriat e dress.

After 1700 music in Spanish America gradually moved toward the secular. Popular music and dance are by nature somewhat ephemeral, and inevitably the information we have about them is less than complete. However, it is clear that Andalusian forms dominated early Mexican popular music. Almost all the court and popular songs and dances of sixteenth century Spain, many of them hybrids deriving from the Gypsy and Moorish traditions, had arrived in Mexico. For example, the 'Moros y Cristianos' spectacle that had arisen in Spain with the process of reconquest was brought to New Spain in early colonial days, and there it proved to be very popular and gave rise to a colonial variant known as the 'Danza de la Conquista', in which the Indians played the infidels, as if celebrating the destruction of their own civilization.[12]

Whether we now have reliable evidence as to the true nature of indigenous performances is in some doubt since, as in the case of literature, the heritage has suffered transformation through time and under foreign influences. Generally, it is now held that the imposition of Spanish ways so modified the indigenous ones that their survival in anything like a pure form was impossible. Regarding music, for example, Mayer-Serra (120–1) bluntly claims that nothing authentic has survived. Seeing 'Indian' dances being performed in the Zócalo, Mexico City's main square, one might be tempted to think otherwise, but these are suspect recreations performed for the benefit of tourists, and of course there is no reliable means whereby one can test their authenticity. There are a few descriptions dating from the time, but not many. Ironically, one source of information about performance practices is the official edicts that were aimed at suppressing them on moral grounds.

Yet in some ways the early colonial authorities were tolerant both of songs and dances and of the inevitable confusion of different cultural habits in this new society. Dance could be defended as a way of allowing Indians to express themselves, and as entertainment for the Spaniards; this is demonstrated by the fact that an area beside the viceroy's palace was specially arranged for the

12 'Moros y cristianos' developed a lasting tradition in parts of central Mexico. Anachronistically, the peninsular expression 'Hay moros en la costa' ('There are Moors on the coast', i.e. 'There's trouble brewing') also made its way into Mexican usage.

performance of the pre-Hispanic flying dance; hence its name, Plaza del Volador.[13] But tolerance diminished as the Church became less of a guardian of the Indians and more of an ally of the social élite of *peninsulares* and *criollos*. In 1569 the viceroy tried to contain African exuberance, decreeing that blacks could only dance at certain times and only in the Zócalo, and in subsequent years attempts to control lascivious cavorting in the ranks of the *castas* became increasingly frequent. The colonial authorities, particularly during the Countereformation and while the Inquisition was rampant, kept a tight rein on what was to be performed: Bishop Zumárraga introduced formal censorship in 1574. But in the late colonial period popular song lyrics became more and more critical of the establishment, and in the longer run they played an important part in fomenting resentment against Spain.

Missionary theatre was performed outside, in Spanish, Nahuatl and other indigenous languages, starting in the 1530s. Many of the plays of this era are believed to have been collaborative compositions, and most have been lost. An example of an evangelizing work is *El sacrificio de Isaac*, believed to date from the late sixteenth century; it is a play that emphasizes unquestioning obedience to God and one's elders, Abraham being a noble warrior who is wise and also subservient to God, while God, in turn, is loving and demands no bloody sacrifice. The provenance of *Destrucción de Jerusalén* is less clear, but it may be from the seventeenth century; it emphasizes respect for authority in general and Christianity in particular, taking a few liberties with historical facts along the way.

A work dating from late in the sixteenth or early in the seventeenth century is the *Coloquio de Nueua conberción Y bautismo delos quatro Vltimos Reyes de Tlaxcala en la Nueua España*, an anonymous play whose manuscript only came to light in 1920. It was commissioned by the *cabildo* of Tlaxcala to mark the conversion of the Indians and their alliance with Cortés, which proved highly significant for the Spanish campaign to overthrow the Aztec empire. Indigenous accounts of that alliance suggest that the people of Tlaxcala entered into it because they were keen to avenge Aztec oppression, but in this Spanish play they join the Spaniards because they are visited by an angel of the Lord who persuades them to turn to Christianity forthwith and be baptized.

In his *Historia de los indios de la Nueva España*, Motolinía has left a vivid description of such a performance, which took place at Tlaxcala on the feast of San Juan Bautista (24 June 24) in 1538:

> Lo más principal he dejado para la postre, que fue la fiesta que los cofrades de Nuestra Señora de la Encarnación celebraron [. . .] Tenían cerca de la puerta del hospital para representar aparejado un auto, que fue la caída de nuestros primeros padres, y al parecer de todos los que lo vieron fue una de las cosas

[13] In 1527 Cortés returned to Spain with a troupe of Indians whose acrobatics delighted Carlos V and who then went to the Vatican to entertain the Pope.

notables que se han hecho en esta Nueva España. Estaba tan adornada la morada de Adán y Eva, que bien parecía paraíso de la tierra, con diversos árboles con frutas y flores, de ellas naturales y de ellas contrahechas de pluma y oro; en los árboles mucha diversidad de aves, desde buho y otras aves de rapiña hasta pajaritos pequenos [. . .] y también aves contrahechas de oro y pluma, que eran cosa muy de mirar. Los conejos y las liebres eran tantos, que todo estaba lleno de ellos, y otros muchos animalejos que yo nunca hasta allí los había visto.

Llegada la procesión, comenzóse luego el auto; tardóse en él gran rato, porque antes que Eva comiese y Adán consintiese, fué y vino Eva, de la serpiente a su marido y de su marido a la serpiente, tres o cuatro veces, siempre Adán resistiendo, y como indignado alanzaba de sí a Eva; ella rogándole y molestándole decía que bien parecía el poco amor que le tenía, y que más le amaba ella a ál que no él a ella, y echándose en su regazo tanto le importunó, que fué con ella al árbol vedado, y Eva en presencia de Adán comió y dióle a él también que comiese; y en comiendo, luego conocieron el mal que habían hecho; y aunque ellos se escondían cuanto podían, no pudieron hacer tanto que Dios no los viese; y vino con gran majestad acompañado de muchos ángeles; y después que hubo llamado a Adán, el se excusó con su mujer, y ella echó la culpa a la serpiente, maldiciéndolos Dios y dando a cada uno su penitencia. Trajeron los ángeles dos vestiduras bien contrahechas, como de pieles de animales, y vistieron a Adán y a Eva. Lo que más fué de notar fue el verlos salir desterrados y llorando: llevaban a Adán tres ángeles y a Eva otros tres, e iban cantando en canto de órgano *Circumdederunt Me.* Esto fue tan bien representado, que nadie lo vió que no llorase muy recio; quedó un querubín guardando la puerta del paraíso con su espada en la mano. Luego allí estaba el mundo, otra tierra cierto bien diferente de la que dejaban, porque estaba llena de cardos y de espinas y muchas culebras; también había conejos y liebres. Llegados allí los recién moradores del mundo, los ángeles mostraron a Adán cómo había de labrar y cultivar la tierra, y a Eva diéronle husos para hilar y hacer ropa para su marido e hijos; y consolando a los que quedaban muy desconsolados, se fueron cantando [. . .] en canto de órgano . . .

Este auto fué representado por los indios, en su propia lengua, y así muchos de ellos tuvieron lágrimas y mucho sentimiento, en especial cuando Adán fué desterrado y puesto en el mundo.

(I have left the best part till last: it was the celebration put on by the Guild of Our Lady of the Incarnation. [. . .] Near the door to the hospital they had prepared a place to perform an *auto*, about the fall from grace of our earliest forefathers, and in the opinion of everyone who saw it, it was one of the most memorable events to have occurred in this New Spain of ours. The dwelling place of Adam and Eve was so adorned that it did indeed look like paradise on earth, with trees bearing a variety of fruits and flowers, both natural ones and others made from feathers and gold; in the trees there were many different birds, from owls and other birds of prey to small birds [. . .] and also imitation birds made of gold and feathers, all most impressive. The rabbits and hares were so numerous that the place seemed full of them, together with other little animals that I had never seen before.

> Once the procession had arrived, the *auto* began; it was very long, because before Eve ate the apple and before Adam gave in she came and went between the serpent and her husband and between her husband and the serpent, three or tour times, and always Adam stood firm, and rejected Eve in indignation; she kept begging and bothering him, saying that he really did not seem to love her and that she loved him more than he did her, and by throwing herself upon him she wore him down so much that he went with her to the forbidden tree, and in his presence Eve ate some then gave him some to eat; and when they had eaten they realized the sin that they had committed; and although they hid as best they could, they could not stop God from seeing them, and He came in great majesty, accompanied by a host of angels; and after he had summoned Adam, Adam excused himself and his wife, and she blamed the serpent, and God made a curse upon them and gave them penitence. The angels brought finely worked raiments, which seemed to be of animal hide, and they clothed Adam and Eve. The most impressive thing was seeing them being banished and in tears: three angels led Adam and another three Eve, and they went away singing *Circumdederunt Me*, accompanied by the organ. It was so well done that everyone who saw it was moved to tears; a cherubim was left guarding the gates of paradise, sword in hand. Then they came to our world, to another land that was truly different from the one they had left, for it was full of thistles and thorns and snakes; there were rabbits and hares too. And once the new arrivals in this world had come, the angels showed Adam how to work and till the land, and they gave Eve spindles to weave and make clothes for her husband and children; and with songs of consolation for those who remained unconsoled, they left, to the accompaniment of the organ . . .)

Not all theatre was religious. For example, Hernán González de Eslava (1534–1601?) was a Mexicanized Spaniard who wrote both religious and worldly plays, the latter including some crude, farcical scenes. There are records of satirical farces having been performed in early colonial times, and of their authors facing censure. In Mexico City itself the viceregal court soon became the hub of artistic activity. For instance, in 1578, on the occasion of the delivery of some relics sent by the Pope, an elaborate social event was organzsed, lasting a week, during which there was a procession of all the top dignitaries, followed by the performance of a play telling of the Roman emperors Diocletian and Constantine, and stressing the Christian virtues of the latter. This play is believed to have been written by two Jesuits, and was published in Mexico City, but for the most part, home-grown drama could not compete with the sophistication of Spanish works, and once theatre became an interest of the aristocracy, peninsular dramatists occupied centrestage.

The country's first *corral de comedias* was built by Francisco de León in Mexico City in 1597. Theatrical works chosen followed the fashions of the Siglo de Oro, and the most popular plays were those of Lope and Calderón. A play by Pérez de Montalbán, *La monja-alférez*, about a girl who escapes from a Spanish convent and flees to the New World disguised as a man, was a great popular success. Among successful local, Mexican plays was *Comedia de San Francisco de Borja* (1641) by Mathias de Bocanegra, written to mark the arrival of a new viceroy. Generally, however, the local dramatists had to be content with playing second fiddle, their works serving as *entremeses*, as appetizers before the main peninsular course. *Entremeses*, together with *fandangos* and *mojigangas* or *fines de fiesta* filled out the programme, with songs and dances coming before, during and after plays. The more sensual and suggestive of these, even if of peninsular provenance, were conveniently attributed to the corrupting influence of the New World natives, if not censored. With time, however, there came more freedom of expression, and in 1785 the viceroy acceded to the public performances of airs and dances. All along, the dances and songs brought over from Europe were changing as part of the process of acculturation.

Juan Ruiz de Alarcón and Sor Juana Inés de la Cruz are the two most distinguished playwrights of colonial Mexico. Alarcón (1580–1639) was from a prosperous family, and having studied at the University of Salamanca had been given an important post in the Consejo de Indias, the advisory body to the crown on matters relating to the New World. Not everything was in Alarcón's favour, however. He was physically deformed, and he suffered the derision of some of his contemporaries, a matter that he turns into the theme of one of his plays, *Las paredes oyen*. An *indiano* (a man from the New World who had come to his roots in Spain) whose works were written and performed for the *peninsulares*, Ruiz de Alarcón was fully vindicated by his twenty-five plays, which made him one of the great dramatists of the Golden Age. Characterization is strong in Alarcón's plays, which often deal with moral or ethical issues, but also seem to anticipate a lighter, satirical style of writing. The most famous, *La verdad sospechosa*, is about an plausible liar who becomes involved with two sisters, and it served as inspiration for Corneille's *Le Menteur*.

Although somewhat better known for her poetry, Sor Juana Inés de la Cruz (1651?–95), probably the greatest colonial writer of all Latin America, should also be acknowledged for her contribution to theatre and music. Clearly, she was musically literate, as is demonstrated by a number of her *villancicos* and by her deployment of musical puns. Furthermore, she provided words for music to be performed in Mexico City Cathedral.[14] Her plays include three *autos sacramentales* whose prologues (*loas*) are especially interesting, even explosive: instead of the usual panegyrics in favour of the establishment, this nun attacks outdated dogma, takes a sideswipe at men and argues that the basis of knowledge is doubt! *Divino Narciso* is the best known of the *autos*; it recasts the classical myth in such a way as to make it a Christian allegory, but also highlights the plight of the principal female character, Echo. *Los empeños de una casa* is one of Sor Juana's secular plays, a parodic piece with autobiographical touches; it has a strong leading female figure, and it makes fun of patriarchal society.

14 See her *Poemas de la Unica Poetisa Americana, Musa Dezima* (Madrid: Juan Garcia Infançon, 1690), p. 266.

Great as they were, both Alarcón and Sor Juana demonstrate how Spain dominated the colonial drama scene; both published their plays in Spain, both exemplify the typical aping of Golden Age dramatic styles. The influence of Golden Age drama would be long-lasting, and later peninsular fashions, such as *costumbrista* plays, would be slow to take hold in Mexico.

As time went by the theatrical models ceased to be solely Spanish, but they continued to come from Europe, and there seems to be little evidence of notable home-grown Mexican drama in the eighteenth century. There were melodramas involving spectacular stage effects that were designed to make an immediate impression, rather than aspiring to any lasting dramatic value: thus a dramatic impasse might be resolved by a sudden natural disaster, such as an earthquake. There were farces relying on coarse humour, plays on language, and local colour, forerunners of the nationalistic theatre of the nineteenth century.

Art and architecture

Works of visual art from colonial Latin America are sometimes dismissed as second-rate, as too derivative of European models. Like other countries, colonial Mexico was indeed imitative in many ways, but its art does have distinctive characteristics resulting from its amalgam of traditions and influences. The visual arts developed primarily as a by-product of evangelization, and that development was driven by cultural and economic factors. As with music, the Church was a most important patron of the visual arts; it needed buildings throughout the country and it needed appropriate images with which to fill them. And again as with music, Indians were trained in Spanish styles and techniques; the *Códice florentino* has illustrations and descriptions of Indian performers and artists at work, whether practising newly learned techniques or traditional Indian ones, for example assembling pictures made of feathers.[15] Feathers were stuck in place using natural glues, such as the sap from certain orchids. A fine example of a feather painting, still in remarkable condition, is at the Musée des Jacobins, in Auch, near Toulouse, possibly because it was stolen by pirates. Its subject is the Mass of Saint Gregory the Great (see colour plate 4). This work was made at the workshop of San José de los Naturales in Mexico City, under the supervision of Pedro de Gante, and intended as a gift to Pope Paul III, perhaps in recognition of his edict stating that the Indians were human. Another fine example of feather art is the Christ in Majesty at the Tepotzotlán Convent. Rather as 'mudéjar' is an Arabic word that refers to the art of the Moors under Spanish rule, there is a Nahuatl word that refers to survival of pre-conquest styles into the colonial period: 'tequitqui'.

15 In general, many Indian artifacts made their way to Europe and into the hands of the prosperous and powerful. They also drew the attention and admiration of European artists, though did not particularly influence them. They were seen as exotic and primitive.

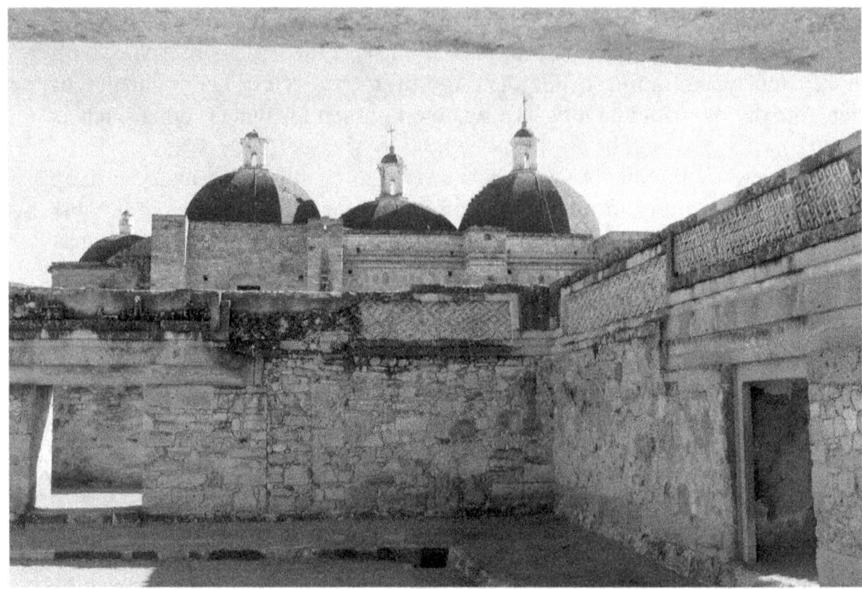

1. A Christian church set upon Mixtec-Zapotec ruins, at Mitla

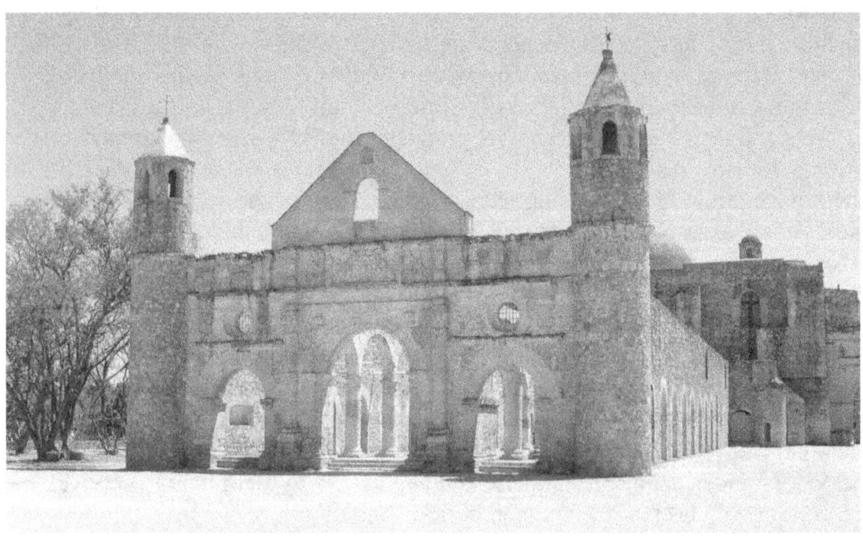

2. The *capilla abierta* at Cuilapán; over the entrance there are Zapotec hieroglyphs. Behind this structure stands a conventional church, attached to a fortress-like monastery.

Imported medieval, Renaissance, *mudéjar* and plateresque styles can easily be found in the early colonial architecture of Mexico, both civic and religious; much of that architecture closely echoes Spain's. City walls in Campeche look like those of a medieval fortress, as do some of the houses of the conquistadors and not a few monasteries, including the one at Cuilapan (Oaxaca); the patio of the Hospital de Jesús in the capital has a calm Renaissance simplicity about it; the town fountain at Chiapa de Corzo, in Chiapas, is a circular brick construction in the *mudéjar* style; the open chapel of the Franciscan monastery at Tlalmanalco, near Mexico City, has a clear plateresque influence. These are only examples. Generally speaking it is in the regions that the best examples of colonial architecture are now to be found, Mexico City itself having suffered the ravages of successive waves of reconstruction and the sad effects of pollution. Unfortunately, much of the country's architectural heritage has suffered from neglect, and many buildings are in a state of decay or have been ruined by insensitive additions, transformations or juxtapositions.

Among distinctively Mexican architectural features of the colonial era we find the *capilla abierta*, otherwise known as the *capilla de Indias* (and in fact uniquely Mexican); this was the friars' solution to the problem of accommodating the masses of Indian converts, a solution that sat well with Indian traditions, in which only the priests would stand in a covered enclosure, while the congregation would be in an open but sacred area (see illustration 2). These open chapels tend to have a small central nave with broad arches to the sides, so that the overall effect is of an open-air theatre. A fine example of a *capilla abierta* is to be found at the Dominican monastery in Teposcolula, about a hundred kilometres north of Oaxaca. Another distinctive architectural feature is the *posa*, or chapel proper, placed at corners of churchyards or cloisters; a good example of this is at the Franciscan monastery at Huejotzingo, in Puebla.

The style for which the architecture of New Spain became famous, and particularly its church architecture, was neither simple nor measured, as is that of the Renaissance, but instead exuberantly baroque, a style that is sometimes called *churrigueresco*, after the name of the Spanish architect (see illustration 3). Some of the most important examples of baroque architecture in the whole of Latin American are to be found in Mexico: the sacristy of the cathedral in Mexico City, the Jesuit seminary at Tepotzotlán, the Convento de Santa Rosa in Querétaro and the Iglesia de Santa Prisca in Taxco.

Highly decorated entrances (the *fachada-retablo*, a transposition of the ornate style of altarpieces to the façade of the church) and interiors congested with details became the norm. Perhaps no façade can hold a candle to the one of the cathedral at Zacatecas. The fabric of buildings sometimes involves the use, to original effect, of local materials such as *tezontle*, a soft volcanic stone that has a sombre, often red hue. *Chiluca* is a whitish stone and the 'piedra cantera' of the Oaxaca region a greenish one. A marked structural feature, found in many places, is the *estípite*, a column that is usually wider at the top than at the bottom and sometimes interrupted by secondary capitals, geometric panels and scrolls; examples can be seen at the convent church of Santa Clara in Querétaro.

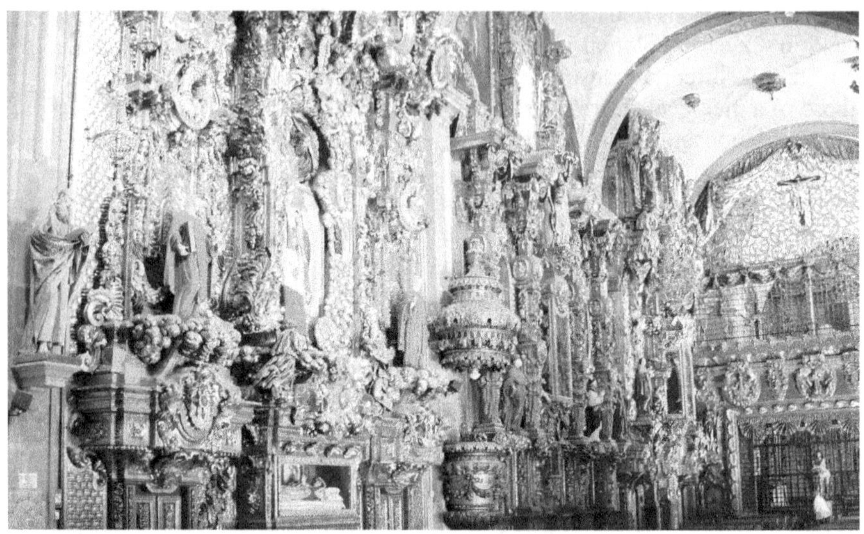

3. Part of the baroque interior of the Templo del Sagrado Corazón, at Querétaro.

Mosaics and tiles adorn some exteriors, such as that of the church of San Francisco Acatepec, in Puebla (see illustration 4), or the so-called Casa de Los Azulejos (once the house of the Conde del Valle de Orizaba) in the heart of Mexico City.

Representations, often quite naïve ones, of animals and plants, together with artifacts from local traditions, found their way into church décor; saints acquired Indian features and plumed head-dresses, and, of course, there are images of conquistadors. It is not only the busy indigestibility of the decoration that one notices, but also the hybridization, the evidence of Indian influence. For example, in the monastery of Acolman there is a Virgin who looks like the Aztec goddess Coatlicue. Also worth mentioning is the church at Ixmiquilpan, in Hidalgo, which has an impressive 1550 fresco that mixes European realism with native colours and abstract shapes. At the extraordinary little church of Santa María Tonantzintla, close to Puebla, there is a plethora of examples of how Indian artisans would mould the Catholic icons into reformulations of their own deities, and give saints Indian features and garb; packed with colourful and gilded images, this church proclaims its otherness (see jacket illustrations). In nearby Cholula there is a frieze that was done after the conquest but seems Aztec. Cholula is a place that impressed Cortés with its number of temples; after conquest it was renamed San Pedro de Cholula and acquired many Christian churches to replace them, including a huge monastery that boasts a seven-naved church, in addition to another large but conventional one. The most symbolic of the Christian structures at Cholula, however, is the church that sits on top of what was once a pyramid. Cholula is still a major religious centre, a

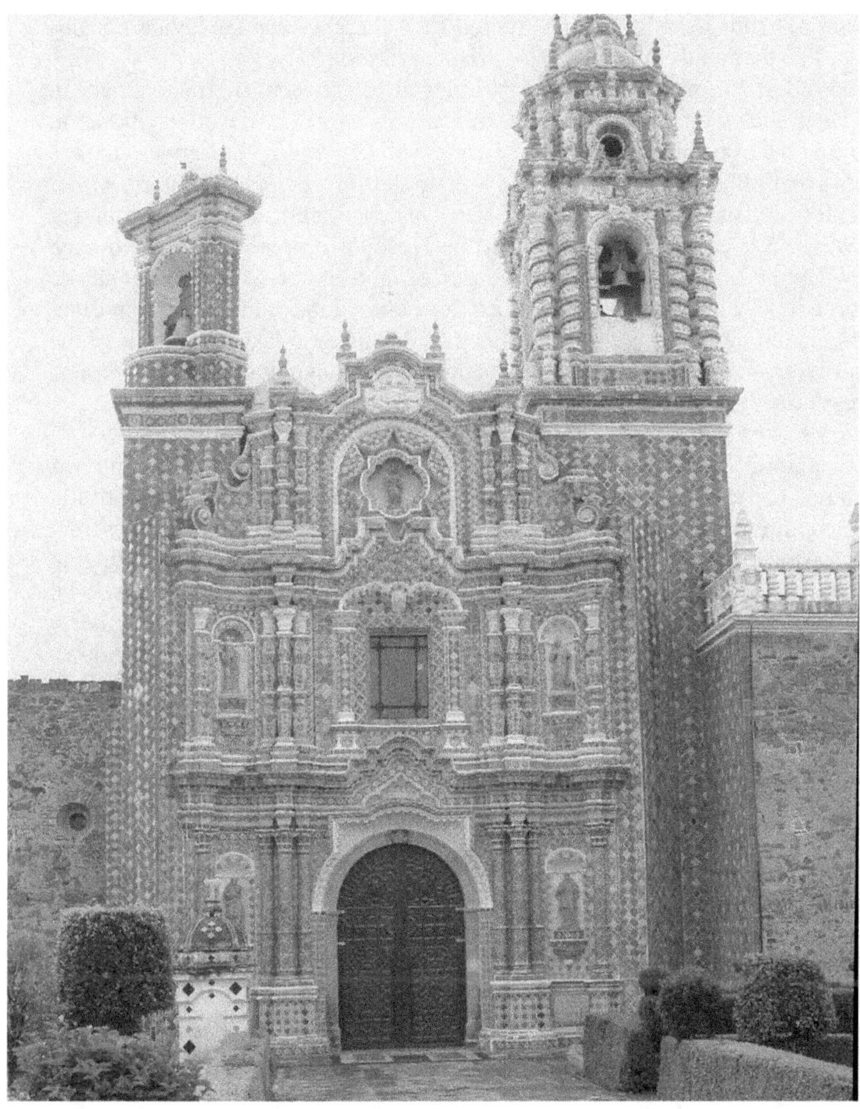

4. The tiled façade of the Iglesia de San Francisco Acatepec; *estípites* are visible on the second and third tiers.

place of pilgrimage and fireworks, dotted with churches that are lovingly maintained, like diamonds in the rough of urban nastiness.

The oldest European mural in Mexico is at the convent of Huejotzingo, in Puebla; it shows the twelve Franciscan friars in an act of devotion. It was in 1523 that the Pope charged the Franciscans with converting the natives, and his order to that effect can be seen at the Instituto de Antropología e Historia. Other examples of visual documentation of Mexico's colonial history can be found at the Museo Virreinal in Tepozotlán, at the Hospital de Jesús, in Mexico City, which has an anonymous portrait of Cortés, and at the Museo Nacional de Historia in Chapultepec Castle, which houses a good number of important works, including a sixteenth-century map of the city and lake, portrayals of the various *castas* and a rather naïve but appealing anonymous oil of a viceregal procession.

'In painting', writes Leopoldo Castedo (113), 'the Old World's triumph was absolute'. Cortés had been accompanied by a Spanish painter who dutifully depicted him in prayer. Other painters from Europe followed, and not only from Spain: Alonso Vázquez and Andrés de la Concha began easel painting in Mexico, but more influential was the Flemish painter Simon Peyrens, who arrived in 1566. An important disciple of his was a man who had come to Mexico from the Basque country, Baltazar de Echave Orio (1548–1620), known too as Echave the Elder, since two of his descendants also painted. Echave Orio was a skilled painter in the Italian style; by contrast the paintings by his *criollo* son, Baltasar Echave Ibía, which are more impressive, sometimes recall those of another Fleming, Joachim Patenier, and hence his nickname 'el Echave de los azules'. A *criollo* protégé of Echave Orio was Luis Juárez (1585?–1636?), whose work Justino Fernández (1969: 104–5) regards as more subtle and delicate than that of his mentor. José Juárez, the son of Luis (1620?–67), was also a painter of some importance; he and Sebastián López de Arteaga (1610–56?) are associated with the arrival of the *tenebrista*, Caravaggio-like style in Mexico.

The Viceroy don Matías de Gálvez, who promoted the training of Indians in the fine arts, is depicted in an eighteenth-century oil that hangs in the convent in Tepotzotlán. It was during that century that José de Ibarra became known as 'el Murillo de Nueva España' in view of his ability to copy the Spanish master, as well as a certain physical resemblance to him. A 1754 painting by Carlos de Villalpando, a prolific artist in the baroque style, captures the splendour of the church of the Betlemitas, and again is in Tepotzotlán, a place that moreover boasts a sixteenth-century Christ in Majesty made of feathers in the Aztec tradition, as well as a 1756 fresco by Miguel Cabrera depicting the apparition of the Virgen de Guadalupe, at the church of San Francisco Javier. Cabrera was acclaimed during his lifetime, but is now remembered primarily for a portrait of Sor Juana, done years after her death. Toussaint observes that Villalpando (1650–1714) and Juan Correa (1645?–1716) initiated the use of lighter colours and painted in an elegant, less sombre style. The latter painter, a black man, used European imagery but has no obvious parallel in the Old World; one of his works, a folding screen measuring over 2 x 6 metres, now in the collection of the Banco Nacional, shows Cortés meeting Montezuma but portrays the latter as a Renaissance-style Roman emperor with a feathered head-dress. (This makes for an interesting comparison with a famous nineteenth-century canvas entitled *Descubrimiento del pulque*, by José María Obregón.) Correa and Villalpando are the painters responsible for the huge works that cover the walls of the *sacristía* in the Mexico City Cathedral.

Colonial Mexico produced no painters of the stature of Velázquez, Zurbarán or Goya, but in a fine 1744 portrait by Rafael Jimeno y Planes, now in the Museo Nacional de Arte, one can at least see signs of Goya's style. The subject of this portrait is the Spanish-born artist Manuel Tolsá, who became known for his equestrian statue of Carlos IV and for his work as an architect in the neoclassical style; among many other projects, he was involved in the design of the Mexico City Cathedral, but his *magnum opus* as an architect was the nearby Escuela de Minas. For that building, Jimeno y Planes did a neoclassical mural, the first painting in that style to have a Mexican theme. Both men were products of the Real Academia de Bellas Artes de San Fernando, in Madrid, and both now found themselves in Mexico City in top positions at the Real Academia de Bellas Artes de San Carlos, which was established by Carlos III in 1783. In the sacristy of the cathedral one can see an altarpiece that is the work of an Indian trained by Tolsá, Pedro Patiño Ixtolinque, and which demonstrates the current tension between the baroque and the neoclassical.

Another painter of note in the late colonial period is José de Ibarra (1688–1756) who is himself subject of a fine portrait by Miguel Contreras, while another Contreras, Juan Rodríguez Juárez Contreras, painted the *Retrato del Virrey Duque de Linares*. More prolific as a portraitist was José María Vázquez (1765–c. 1826). José María de Labástida was one of the most distinguished sculptors, doing work in the neoclassical style.

Elizabeth Wilder Weisman (195–6) provides an interesting angle on the perception of popular art during the colonial era. She argues that it was possible for people to reconcile the intrusion (profusion, one might add, if referring to the baroque period) of popular elements in art – in architecture in particular – with a sense of good taste and moderation because they could be ascribed to Indian or *mestizo* influences (whereas the only reasonable description of the phenomenon is 'Mexican'). Things changed, however, for 'as time passed, the focus seemed to move toward the popular end of the spectrum – or perhaps one should say that folk art became dominant at one end, while strict Neoclassical tenets took over at the other. It is, in a sense, at that moment – when Neoclassicism denounces the rich, irresponsible expressions of the baroque tradition – that popular art, as such, is differentiated.' Popular art is characterized by nothing if not by genuine personal sentiment. Its products may be inept and vulgar and spontaneous, but they come from the heart.

One of popular art's most distinctive manifestations in Mexico is the *exvoto*, the devotional object that invokes or recognizes the intercession of Christ, the

Virgin or the saints at some time of crisis. *Exvotos* are highly personal forms of expression, yet they are also highly public ones, since they are placed in churches, graveyards and shrines for all to see. The experiences that motivate the production of them can vary from minor to momentous: the thanksgiver, or someone close to him, might have successfully overcome one of life's obstacles or an illness, or might feel grateful for the arrival of rain. *Exvotos* can occasionally be quite cynically self-serving, as is illustrated by the case of a husband who, having contracted a venereal disease when visiting a whorehouse, thanks the Virgin for aiding his recovery from it and also for helping him to keep the whole affair from his wife!

The tradition of *exvotos* is a long one. It is recorded that Cortés had one made of gold and emeralds to show his gratitude at having survived a scorpion's sting. If the *exvotos* displayed by some privileged people may be read as ostentatious reflections of their own prosperity and importance, most *exvotos* are humble folk art expressions of religiosity on the part of ordinary people. Miracles are portrayed, written explanations, narratives or poems often incorporated. One characteristic form, widely practised since the late colonial period, is painting on tin. In modern times, *exvotos* may include photographs or photocopies. Some are commissioned from anonymous artisans who make them for a living, but many are designed and made by the thanksgivers themselves. On entering almost any church one can find shrines, side chapels or simply effigies of saints that have strips of coloured ribbon, photographs and handwritten messages pinned or stuck about them. There is a major collection of painted *exvotos* at the Museum of the Basílica de Guadalupe, and another at the Frida Kahlo Museum in Coyoacán, on the outskirts of Mexico City.

Poetry

While theatre was both popular and strategically important in early colonial times, the genre that soon held sway among the privileged classes was poetry. Like theatre, poetry was put to official use, to laud the arrival of new dignitaries, for example. Students of the Real Universidad Pontificia, founded in 1553, were trained to write poems celebrating such things as religious icons and civic occasions. There were poetry contests (*certámenes*). The poetic forms employed were, inevitably, those in favour in Spain, but the audience for them was often local. Indeed, sometimes poetry served the poets' personal agendas; they would jockey for social position, promoting themselves and judiciously flattering the influential. On the popular front there were improvised ballads, based on the conventions of the Spanish *romance*; these were often satirical, and they were to provide the basis for the *corrido*, a sung form that became popular in the nineteenth century and widespread after the Revolution.

Poetry flourished in the hands of writers from Spain who had come to the New World, and increasingly in those of *criollos*. The latter, if pretending to the learned style, published their work in Spain – because of the prestige, because that was where there were more readers, and also because Mexican presses were largely occupied producing official documents. Although much colonial poetry has been lost, *Flores de varia poesía*, an important collection dating from 1577, was published in 1980; it brings together some well-known peninsular poets and the *criollos* Francisco de Terrazas, Carlos de Sámano, Miguel de Cuevas and Martín Cortés (son of Hernán Cortés). Terrazas (1525?–1600?), who was also the son of a conquistador, is considered the first Mexican-born poet of significance.

Bernardo de Balbuena (1568–1627) is remembered for *Grandeza mexicana*, an epic and overblown description of Mexico City and the customs of its aristocracy. This work, dating from early in the sixteenth century (1604), provides a sanguine, hyperbolic view of Mexico as the happy hub of a successful empire. Conforming to the convention of kowtowing to the influential, Balbuena goes out of his way to praise the head of the Consejo de Indias. The poem is interesting, however, for its structure: a programmatic eight-line *argumento* heralds eight developmental sections cast in a form more commonly used in sonnets. The poem is not only descriptive but also 'a playful exploration of the notion of perspective and, in particular, miniaturism' (Hart 1999: 34).

The late seventeenth century saw the emergence of the towering figure of Latin American colonial poetry, Sor Juana Inés de la Cruz. Sor Juana, whose plays were mentioned previously, was illegitimate but had found her way into the viceregal court, serving as a lady-in-waiting and impressing people with her wit and intelligence; quite why she retired from it to become a nun is not entirely clear. By entering the convent she secured control of her inheritance, and in any case it was probably one of few places where a woman of her times could devote herself to study and writing, but it has been suggested that she may also have been retreating from an unhappy love affair. The anti-male invective in her much-quoted poem 'Hombres necios . . .' might suggest as much. Certainly modern feminist critics have found her appealing because of her poems at the expense of men.[16] At any event, once in the convent her life was not a cloistered one; on the contrary, her cell became a place for *tertulias*. Her curiosity and her writings extended well beyond matters religious, as a result of which she incurred the displeasure of the bishop, who admonished her in a document that he published under the pseudonym of Sor Filotea de la Cruz. Her response to that was laced with irony and satire; in *Respuesta a Sor Filotea*, she states that she will not deal in public with theological issues and argues that her passion for secular knowledge is God-given. She even seems arrogant at times, feigning humility in order to be seen to toe the line of acceptability.

Her many sonnets, published, like her plays, in Spain, deal with a wide range of philosophical, historical, religious, social and even erotic subjects. Her

[16] The full text of the first stanza of 'Hombres necios . . .' is 'Hombres necios, que acusáis\ a la mujer sin razón\ sin ver que sois la ocasión\de lo mismo que culpáis' (You foolish men, who accuse\ women unreasonably\ unaware that you are the reason\ for the very things you condemn).

formal skill is considerable, her tone sometimes serious, sometimes satirical. The long poem 'Primero sueño', often said to be her masterpiece, is an ontological speculation but also a literary display, for Sor Juana revelled in plays on words and erudite allusions; her baroque, intellectual style of writing makes one think of Góngora, though, according to Octavio Paz, 'por genio natural, Sor Juana tiende más al concepto agudo que a la metáfora brillante' (*Sor Juana*: 470). Another famous poem, 'Este que ves, engaño colorido', is a clever contemplation of the purpose of portraiture, the value of art and its techniques:

> Este, que ves, engaño colorido,
> Que del arte ostentando los primores,
> Con falsos silogismos de colores
> Es cauteloso engaño del sentido:
>
> Este, en quien la lisonja ha pretendido
> Excusar de los años los horrores
> Y venciendo del tiempo los rigores
> Triunfar de la vejez y del olvido,
>
> Es un vano artificio del cuidado,
> Es una flor al viento delicada,
> Es un resguardo inútil para el hado:
>
> Es una necia diligencia errada,
> Es un afán caduco, y, bien mirado,
> Es cadáver, es polvo, es sombra, es nada.[17]
>
> (This coloured deception that you see\ displaying the delicacy of art\ with false syllogisms of colour\ is a careful deception of the senses.\ This, which flattery has sought\ to excuse from the horrors of aging\ and overcoming the rigours of time\ to triumph over death and oblivion\ is a vain artifice of carefulness\ a delicate flower in the wind\ a futile shield against fate:\ it is a foolish, mistaken diligence\ a fruitless wish, and, seeing clearly\ it is a corpse, it is dust, it is shadow, it is nothingness.)

In 'Detente, sombra de mi bien esquivo', a love poem, Sor Juana deals with the tension between reason and passion; she writes: 'En dos partes dividida\ tengo el alma en confusión:\ una, esclava a la pasión,\ otra, a la razón medida.' (My soul is divided in confusion, torn in two: one part is slave to passion, the other measured by reason.) Sor Juana stands out among all Latin American colonial writers and she was a legend in her time, yet she fell almost into oblivion after it, until a group of writers known as the *Contemporáneos* resurrected her in the early twentieth century.

17 One wonders what Sor Juana might have thought of the fame achieved by Cabrera's portrait of her, had she lived to see it.

Most of the writers of this colonial period were well-connected aristocrats who, as we have seen, tended to dedicate their works to influential people. Indeed, to be published one needed to have connections and be on the right side of the viceregal and ecclesiastical authorities. As the years passed that need became less pressing, yet late colonial poetry, like the other arts, became less interesting. Its writers, many of them artistocrats and clerics, were largely unadventurous as to content and backward-looking as to style, often imitating classical models and writing in Latin, a fashion that perhaps compensated for a sense of cultural inferiority. Surveying the field, Dowling writes that the work of the best-known of neoclassical poets, José Martínez de Navarrete (1768–1809), is highly derivative and 'strikes the reader as *déjà lu*' (*sic*): (Foster, 1994: 73); but he thinks more highly of José Villerías y Roel (1695–1728), famous in his day but now largely ignored.

Prose

It was noted earlier that much prose writing during the early colonial period was in the form of chronicles. Thanks to the Inquisition (established in 1487), imaginative writing was regarded as suspect and many books, including *Don Quijote*, were officially banned. Official edicts sought to suppress works that might encourage people (especially women, the young and the natives) along the paths of nonconformity, even incite rebellion; high on the list of banned books during the late colonial era were those associated with Enlightenment thinking. But, naturally, some of the banned books still slipped through.

Though the novel as a genre rose during the sixteenth and seventeenth centuries in Europe, it was generally slow to develop in Latin America. One of the first imaginative prose works to come from Mexico itself is Carlos de Sigüenza y Góngora's *Infortunios de Alonso Ramírez* (1690). Being expelled from the Jesuit order on grounds of misconduct did not prevent its author from going on to become a university professor and the royal cosmographer, perhaps because he was from a well-known family.[18] He was a controversial figure and also a friend of Sor Juana. *Infortunios . . .* is a short work that is part chronicle, part travelogue and part novel. It tells of Alonso's journey from humble beginnings in Puerto Rico to Mexico in search of fortune, and then on to the Philippines, where he is captured by English pirates. His is a journey of trials and tribulations, but one that ends well, for on returning to Mexico he makes the acquaintance of the viceroy, who puts him in contact with the author. Thus there are clearly picaresque characteristics to this story, but it is also self-referential. The tale is not told in the first person, nor does the author ostensibly keep out of it; on the contrary, Sigüenza makes his protagonist improbably knowledgeable, a character whose behaviour and views reveal that Sigüenza is hiding behind him.

18 He was a nephew of the famous Spanish poet.

Alonso praises the virtues of the viceroy, for example, which was no doubt a prudent gesture on the part of the author.

A man who was influenced by the Enlightenment, and a rather eccentric and controversial one at that, was Fray Servando Teresa de Mier (1763–1827), born in Monterrey and a key figure of Mexican independence.[19] From 1779 to 1803 Mier was a member of the Dominican order, from which he received a doctorate in theology. Among his eccentricities was claiming to be related to Montezuma. In 1794, a month after having given one sermon in honour of Cortés, he gave another, at the Colegiata de Nuestra Señora de Guadalupe, in which he supported the idea of an independent Mexico and for good measure cast doubt on accounts of the Virgin's apparition. This incurred the wrath of the Inquisition: almost immediately he was detained and then sentenced to ten years in a Spanish monastery. However, he escaped, beginning an extraordinary sequence of detentions and escapes that lasted for years, punctuated by periods of relative prosperity and influence. At a low point, finding himself penniless in London, he wrote one of his most important works, *Historia de la revolución de Nueva España* (1813), which he published under a pseudonym. This was only one of many varied works, the most fascinating of which is *Apología y relaciones de su vida*. Mier wrote about the Europe of Napoleonic times, seeing it from the point of view of an educated Mexican, and turning the tables, as it were, making Europe the object of curiosity, the 'other'. After many ups and downs Mier returned to Mexico, only to be arrested once again, but that was in 1822: in May of that year Iturbide was proclaimed emperor of a newly independent Mexico, and Mier was freed from prison and personally received by him. Mier was later elected to the national congress. An extraordinary and resourceful person, he was unorthodox to the end, organizing a public event during which people witnessed him being given his last rites, a few days before his death. His mummified remains are said to have been sold to a circus owner, for exhibition.[20] He was, in Blanco's view (1932: 246), 'el más universal, diverso, audaz e inteligente prosista de las últimas décadas del virreinato y primeras del México independiente' (the most universal, varied, audacious and intelligent prose-writer of the closing decades of the Viceroyalty and the first few of the independent Mexico).

Mier's and Sigüenza's stories, which have picaresque elements and show signs of making an imaginative break from the quasi-documentary chronicles of the past, could be regarded as forerunners of the picaresque novel *El Periquillo Sarniento* (1816) that was to give its author, José Joaquín Fernández de Lizardi (born in 1776), the reputation of being the first true Latin American novelist. Driven by poverty to find his way in the world, the protagonist of Lizardi's novel recounts his own story from his deathbed. He runs through a series of apprenticeships, some for more respectable trades than others but all in some

19 Among Mier's many writings there is a translation of Rousseau's *Le Contrat social*.

20 Mier would later provide inspiration for one of the major novels of the Boom period, Reinaldo Arenas' *El mundo alucinante*.

way devious, until he finally mends his ways. He marries, encounters a Chinese lord, and finds himself having to describe and justify the customs of his native land. Much of this is in the vein of *Lazarillo de Tormes* but Lizardi, unlike the anonymous author of that work, burdens his with pages of tedious moralizing. Nevertheless, *El Periquillo Sarniento* paints a vivid picture of a society in transition, with a burgeoning class of professionals who sometimes abuse power. The main butt of its satire seems to be the Spanish tradition, for instance the belief that anyone of standing cannot stoop to manual work. The satire is often heavy-handed, but is sometimes effective. In the novel's prologue, Lizardi complains about the cost of books; he was fully aware that the printed word could reach a wide public, and indeed dedicated his work to his readers, his true patrons, rather than to a member of the establishment of the day. Though remembered primarily for this novel, Lizardi was in fact an active and revolutionary journalist (and was imprisoned for it more than once). He acquired a nickname taken from the title of one of his newspapers: 'El Pensador Mexicano'. Lizardi and Mier both died in 1827, which means they were alive to witness the publication of Mexico's first republican constitution (1824).

4

From Independence to the Early Twentieth Century

After the defeat of the Armada Invencible in 1588, Spain's military power declined. It lost some of its territories in the Americas to other European countries. Its control of trade with the New World had gradually broken down, and the profits from its discoveries were going in large part to its European rivals, not least because Spain lacked the manufacturing infrastructure needed to exploit the raw materials it brought back from its colonies.[1] Haring (294–5) notes that as early as in 1608 the Consejo de Indias (the king's chief advisory body) reported to him that two thirds of the gold and silver being brought back to Spain was being lost to foreign interests. There were attempts by the Bourbon monarchs to remedy this, to reform the system and increase efficiency, but these were too few and came too late.

Although Spain kept its American empire going for over three hundred years, by the eighteenth century *criollo* dissatisfactions had reached a significant level. Spain had done its best to censor the flow of information into the colonies, yet the new, Enlightenment-led thinking about matters such as human rights and representative government was affecting attitudes in the New World. The American and French Revolutions were seen as inspiring examples by Spanish Americans who were tired of being governed by a Spanish monarchy. However, the spark that set fire to the real drive for Spanish-American independence is often said to have come from Napoleon's invasion of Spain in 1808, when he installed his brother on the throne. The resulting Spanish resistance, initially in the form of *juntas*, or action committees, in some ways served as a model for the *criollos* of Spanish America, who convened *cabildos abiertos* (town meetings) in which their own *juntas* were elected. Ostensibly, the purpose of the *cabildos abiertos* was to support the legitimate Spanish monarch, whom Napoleon had forced to abdicate, but many of the *criollos* clearly saw an opportunity to take advantage of Spain's instability. When Napoleon was finally driven out of Spain in 1814, Fernando VII was restored to the throne, but he rejected a liberal constitution that had been developed during his absence, one that would have allowed him to continue as a constitutional monarch, and in doing so he provoked an armed rebellion in Spain that lasted three years.

1 Ironically, something similar would afflict the Spanish-American countries after independence: they would find themselves (and still do find themselves) exporting raw materials to manufacturing countries and then buying back goods made with those materials.

It was against this unsettled and confusing background that the Mexican movement towards independence sputtered into life. Father Miguel Hidalgo, a priest whose Enlightenment-influenced ideas had already caused him to have brushes with the Church, resulting in his banishment to a small town in the state of Querétaro, began with some friends to plan for Mexico's independence. These self-styled 'men of reason' met under cover of the Club Literario y Social de Querétaro. In the early hours of 16 September 1810 Hidalgo rang the bells of the church in his little town of Dolores, gave a revolutionary address to the assembled throng of humble folk and uttered the now famous 'Grito de Dolores': '¡Viva la Virgen de Guadalupe! ¡Muera el mal gobierno! ¡Mueran los gachupines!' (Long live the Virgin of Guadalupe! Death to bad government! Death to the Spaniards!). A passionate, unruly and poorly armed mob of some 80,000 people then engaged in acts of violence and destruction, of which the most notorious was their attack on the town of Guanajuato, which led to mass killings. This rebel army came close to Mexico City yet pulled back, later to be defeated by Spanish troops. Hidalgo was defrocked and then executed, but before his death he wrote a document expressing his regret at the loss of life to which his actions had contributed. His precise aims were never fully clear, but it seems that his main purpose had been to improve the lot of the poor, and he remains a hero in Mexican eyes.

His banner was taken up by another priest, José María Morelos, who met a similar fate. Other leaders followed, with little progress being made until the time of the aforementioned rebellion in Spain against the king, which brought with it the possibility that Mexico might be governed from Spain by a liberal and anticlerical regime. At that point, onto the Mexican stage stepped an opportunistic military man from an aristocratic *criollo* family: Agustín de Iturbide managed to insinuate himself into the position of Emperor of Mexico, and in 1822 was crowned Agustín I, with full Napoleonic pomp. Iturbide proved to be an unpopular, arbitrary and authoritarian ruler, and in 1823 Mexico was proclaimed a republic and taken over by another military egotist, Antonio López de Santa Anna. Iturbide was driven into exile, tried to return in 1824, but was taken prisoner and – it was rapidly becoming a tradition – executed. Mexico was now destined to have a long series of short-term leaders, with Santa Anna returning to power several times, emptying the public purse and creating havoc on each occasion. It happened that Spain's first ambassador to the newly independent Mexico was married to a Scottish woman; Fanny Calderón de la Barca left a lively account of her experiences in Mexico, and she was clearly not impressed by the political changes. 'One government is abandoned,' she wrote, 'and there is none to take its place, one revolution follows another, yet the remedy is not found.'[2] She was not overstating the problem: during the nineteenth century Mexico had more than fifty rulers. As in other former Spanish colonies, Mexico was ill-prepared to govern itself in an orderly way once inde-

2 Fanny Calderón de la Barca, *Life in Mexico*, p. 433.

pendent; Spain had withdrawn its administrative expertise, leaving a vacuum, and the country's riches had been plundered. The nineteenth century was a turbulent one, with struggles between liberals and conservatives, between one region and another, between federalists and centralists; relations between church and state were often strained, there was mismanagement and corruption, foreign intervention and war.

In 1821, the Mexican government representative in what is now the state of Texas made an attempt to ensure that the territory would be more widely settled, and settled by Catholics; he agreed with a pioneer called Moses Austin that land could be sold off for a song, and so people flocked in, soon outnumbering the Mexicans. Concerned that this might herald the loss of the territory, Santa Anna then tried to impose immigration restrictions and reassert the authority of Mexico City, but that only provoked secession by Texas.[3] In response, Santa Anna marched north; though he was victorious at the Alamo he was soon defeated and obliged to withdraw and concede by treaty that Texas had broken away. When in 1845 the US Congress resolved to admit Texas to the Union, Mexico broke off relations with the United States. Hostilities between the two countries began a year later. Eventually, with the government in Mexico City in chaos, the final encounter of the war took place, the Battle of Chapultepec; it became legendary because the young cadets at the military academy there jumped to their deaths rather than surrender, securing themselves a hallowed place in the national mythology as the 'Niños Héroes', the child heroes. The Treaty of Guadalupe Hidalgo (1848) set the national boundaries we now know, and with that treaty Mexico lost New Mexico, California, Nevada, Utah and parts of Arizona, Wyoming and Colorado, in all about a half of its territory. Its troubles were not yet over, however. Ironically, it had lost out to one of the countries that had served as example to the advocates of independence, and now it was to engage with the other, France.

Mexico finally found a leader of real stature in Benito Juárez, the first president to have Indian blood. His 'Era de la Reforma' brought new laws designed to break up lands held by the Church and reduce its privileges and those of the armed forces; furthermore a new and lasting constitution was drafted. All this amounted to a major attack on the established order, and it naturally met with fierce opposition from those whose interests were at stake. Many Mexico City inhabitants, for example, had large *haciendas* elsewhere that were being managed and worked for them. Sadly, Juárez's reform laws did not create a class of small landowners, as had been hoped; rather, still more lands fell into the hands of the rich and of foreigners. A military takeover then forced Juárez to escape to Panama, but he later returned to Veracruz, and there he set up as alternative president, to announce further reforms separating church and state, encouraging religious tolerance and providing for a public education system that would be secular.

3 Interestingly, the Mexican government outlawed slavery in 1829, as a means of discouraging the ambitions of US southerners.

After much violence, Juárez was formally elected president in 1861, but by that time Mexico was facing huge foreign debts. The French were the main creditors. Napoleon III, who in this situation saw an opportunity to bolster his reputation at home, decided to take control of Mexico and sent French troops to overcome the Juárez government. Although the French were defeated at Puebla in 1862 (the famous 'Cinco de Mayo'), more French forces were sent, and Mexican conservatives were in any case won over by Napoleon's idea that the country should be a Catholic monarchy. He then offered its throne to Maximilian of Habsburg, an Austrian prince. Maximilian and his wife Carlota established a lavish court in Mexico City, but made real efforts to 'go Mexican'. There seems to be no doubt that they were well-intentioned and wished to continue to introduce reforms, but they were out of their depth. The economic problems continued, and the French pulled out. Maximilian tried to hunt down Juárez, who was still in the wings (in what we now know as Ciudad Juárez, to be precise), but popular support rallied round Juárez. By 1867 Maximilian himself had been captured and shot, and Juárez had returned to the capital, to be re-elected for two further terms as president.

The last part of the nineteenth century and the first decade of the twentieth – in all, some thirty-five years – were dominated by Porfirio Díaz. Both he and Juárez were from humble backgrounds, but whereas Juárez had come up through the legal system, Díaz had done so through the army, also becoming a rich landowner. Ousting Juárez's successor, Díaz declared himself provisional President, saw to it that he was then elected, and thereafter managed things in such a way as to stay in power until 1910. Porfirio's rule (the *Porfiriato*) did bring stability and considerable change – the hackneyed slogan of his regime was 'Order and Progress' – but these things came at the price of strong-armed rule and compromised ideals. The progress, paradoxically, was built by preserving old privileges, on the old social order as much as on order in the sense of discipline. Díaz ingratiated himself with conservative landowners by forgetting about land redistribution, allowed the clergy to reassert much of their power, and kept liberals quiet by giving them sinecures. Failing these strategies, to maintain control he also had his 'Rurales', a special militia that wore *charro* outfits and was used to keep people generally in line. Mexico was reputed to be one of the safest places to be in, unless one happened to be a Mexican at odds with the government. Porfirio encouraged foreign investment, and money flowed into cattle-ranching, mines, oilfields and railways, while land was sold off to foreign interests, sometimes having been appropriated from the Indians. Employment levels were high, but the profits generally went abroad and generated little investment in the country's infrastructure. Rather ironically, while Maximilian, the monarch imposed by France, had tried to respect things Mexican, under Porfirio there was an enthusiastic cultivation of things French.

The Press after independence

Let us return for a moment to the time just after independence. Once the lid was off, and colonial censorship removed, newspapers run by *criollos* sprang up all over Mexico, although the readership for them continued to be limited by low levels of literacy. Many of the new publications did not last for long. In the new free-for-all journalists became polemicists or ideological hacks, and they sometimes indulged in wild personal vituperation; the standards of journalism were not high. As a result, there came new waves of censorship, fines and incarcerations, and some papers were washed away by the endlessly shifting political tides. But since governments changed so often the controls were never lasting or pervasive, and information flowed – in fact there was probably more freedom then than before or since. It was newspapers that provided the main locus for public debate about national identity, and moreover it was in newspapers that most literary works first appeared, in instalments. In Mexico City the number of journalists was relatively small, with people often writing for competing publications, thinly disguising themselves under pseudonyms. In the tumultuous, post-independence years of the nineteenth century, newspapers and magazines were the way to spread ideas.

In the early stages of the movement for independence there were several notable publications. One of Father Hidalgo's first acts after taking the city of Guadalajara in 1810 was to found a paper called *El Despertador Americano*, which survived for only a few issues but managed to reach unprecedented circulation figures. Hidalgo's torchbearer, Morelos, was backed by the *Ilustrador Nacional*, a paper founded by José María Cos in 1812, and much to the chagrin of the viceroy. It was soon shut down, but Cos had helped launch another rebel publication, a bi-weekly called the *Ilustrador Americano*, which lasted a year. The loyalists had a publication to counter this last, one pointedly called the *Verdadero Ilustrador Americano*. Andrés Quintana Roo, a colleague of Cos, started the weekly *Semanario Patriótico Americano*, one of whose distinctions was that it published the writings of the rebel priest Fray Servando Teresa de Mier. In fact, in 1812 Spain granted press freedom throughout the colonies, inspiring more brave souls to undertake new ventures, not only in Mexico City but also in the provinces; it was one of these, Puebla's *La Abeja Poblana*, that published a manifesto by Agustín de Iturbide outlining the path that would finally lead to independence. José Fernández de Lizardi, the author of *El Periquillo Sarniento*, was the most important of the liberal reformers, and he was much involved in journalism, writing under the pseudonym of *El Pensador Mexicano*. He began a paper with this as its title in 1812 and earned himself several months in prison for criticizing the colonial authorities. Lizardi argued in favour of such goals as religious freedom and greater social and economic equality.

Early illustrated magazines are exemplified by the *Calendario de las Señoritas Mexicanas* (1838–41) and the *Semanario de las Señoritas Mexicanas* (1841–42). As their titles indicate, these were written (by men) with young ladies in mind; they were miscellanies offering instruction in matters moral and social, together with *costumbrista* accounts of Mexican customs and traditions, and they were sold by subscription. They would evolve into more heavyweight publications that included literary and scientific texts, and that addressed a more eclectic readership, publications such as the *Revista Científica y Literaria* (1845–46) and *La Ilustración Mexicana* (1851–55).

The two outstanding newspapers of the mid-nineteenth century, in terms of popularity, longevity and dependability, were *El Siglo XIX* and *El Monitor Republicano*; both were largely vehicles for committed liberals, although a number of important conservatives also wrote for them at one time or another. The editor most closely associated with the capital's *El Siglo XIX*, Francisco Zarco, became one of the most famous professional journalists of nineteenth-century Mexico. *El Siglo XIX* first appeared in 1841 – during the second period of rule by Santa Anna, of whom it was openly critical – and was published until 1896. In the provinces it was generally the liberal, federalist papers that survived, but so too did some centralist, conservative papers, such as *El Tiempo*, edited by a powerful conservative ideologue, Lucas Alamán. Another, *El Universal*, was to survive into the twentieth century. It seems that Alamán was an influence behind the introduction in 1853 of the Ley Lares, a law that imposed the most oppressive restrictions on press freedom ever seen in Mexico. A few years later, the Leyes de Reforma led to fierce press debates. *El Siglo XIX*, like many others, defended freedom of expression and the separation of church and state, while a weekly called *La Cruz* espoused the conservative case. *El Monitor Republicano*, which had been launched in 1844 by Vicente García Torres, shifted rather surprisingly from one side to another, but did allow space for people of all persuasions to express their views.

In the wake of the North American invasion (1847–48) there appeared the first newspaper in English, called *The American Star*. In the volatile post-war climate newspapers proliferated, generally being highly partisan in style and not long to survive. Following the French invasion, the exiled Juárez government produced its *Diario del Gobierno de la República Mexicana*, while Zarco, in hiding in Mexico City, supported Juárez with his *Boletín Clandestino*. As for the occupiers, they were backed by *La Crónica del Ejército Expedicionario*, and the *Periódico Oficial del Imperio*, which was published both in Spanish and French, and which later simplified its title to *Diario del Imperio*. In 1861 the conservatives brought out *La Prensa*, dedicated mostly to defending the interests of the Church, while liberals founded the satirical *El Monarca*.

Once the French were gone the press entered a period of relative refinement and modernization. The most important arrival on the scene was Ignacio Manuel Altamirano's *El Renacimiento* (started in 1869), the first paper to be devoted exclusively to intellectual and literary issues; it promoted a culture of mature and sophisticated writing, which was something that Altamirano saw as an essential to the process of modernization. In this endeavour he enjoyed the collaboration of all of the leading intellectuals of the day, whatever their political persuasion. Were it not for *El Renacimiento*, it is difficult to see how so many major literary magazines could have followed; the *Revista Azul* (1894) and the *Revista Moderna* (1898), to take two examples, could hold a candle to their European counterparts. The *Revista Moderna* was by no means a magazine of mass appeal, but artists and intellectuals throughout the Spanish-speaking world regarded it highly. Besides the work of leading *modernista* poets, including Darío, the *Revista Moderna* published translations of foreign works and essays on new trends in art and architecture, and topics such as the occult.

The period also saw a gradual but radical change in the relationship between Porfirio Díaz and the press, one that revealed that alliances were changing and exploitation was on the increase. Díaz had come to power thanks partly to enthusiastic backing from a number of liberals, but his style became paternalistic during his second term of office (1884–88) and he began to exercise strict control of the press, buying its allegiance with subsidies, and thereby establishing a precedent for the press in the following century. By 1888, there were thirty 'official' newspapers subsidized by the government, and many more in the provinces. Some journalists found themselves in prison or exile, some were assassinated, and things reached the point where few papers dared oppose Díaz's re-election. Among the most significant opposition newspapers were *Regeneración*, and *El Demócrata*, the latter being memorable because it published an account of the Díaz army's violent repression of an Indian rebellion. The government closed that newspaper, and imprisoned most of its staff. The Flores Magón brothers associated with *Regeneración* were among the most determined advocates of the overthrow the Díaz regime; they had to flee into exile in 1903 and they restarted *Regeneración* in the United States.

Writers

As in other Latin American countries, in Mexico a number of nineteenth-century writers doubled as statesmen, but some came from more humble social origins, and several were partly Indian, Altamirano being a case in point. During this century, prose writing grew in importance, as it did elsewhere, and the reading public grew larger. Newspapers were often the prime outlets for creative writers. They published satirical *costumbrista* sketches by writers such as Francisco Zarco (1829–69), Guillermo Prieto (1818–97) and José de Tomás Cuéllar (1830–94), in the sudden plethora of literary magazines produced by the newly liberated printing presses, while novels – often rather poor quality ones – also tended to come out first as serials in the press.

One of the more adept exponents of the novel was Juan Díaz Covarrubias. The best known of his five works is an historical novel called *Gil Gómez el insurgente o la hija del médico* (1859). Despite declaring that he is abandoning the subjective frivolity of poetry, Díaz Covarrubias writes in a Romantic and poetic style and reserves a prominent place for himself as narrator; there are two story threads, one historical and the other personal, which come together in an improbable conclusion. Luis G. Inclán's *Astucia* (1865) is a refreshingly unpretentious *costumbrista* work, set in rural Michoacán, a didactic story about good and evil, but one that also raises some issues and manages to avoid becoming ponderous in the process. Rather unusually, given the times, Inclán suggests that civilization might be a cause of corruption, not a panacea.

In poetry, representatives of a conservative, neoclassical style of writing, one that upheld the status quo, included Manuel Carpio and José Joaquín Pesado. Guillermo Prieto (also known by the pseudonym 'Fidel') and Ignacio Ramírez are writers who devoted as much energy to polemics as to literature. In his *Romancero* (1885) Prieto chronicles the events of the independence movement, while *Musa callejera* (1883) is in a *costumbrista* vein, all of which helps explain his enduring image as a champion of nationhood. Ramírez was conservative as a writer and more interesting as an energetic advocate of reform and education. He collaborated with Prieto in the latter's Academia de Letrán and in the Instituto Literario de Toluca, which was committed to the education of people from the Indian community. The most popular of nineteenth-century poets, however, was Juan de Dios Peza (1852–1910), who managed to espouse traditional values and patriotism while writing in ordinary language and avoiding the excesses of unbridled Romantics like Manuel Flores and Manuel Acuña.

Ignacio Altamirano (1834–93) had been taught by Ramírez at the Instituto Literario de Toluca. Altamirano's *El Renacimiento*, as already mentioned during the discussion of the nineteenth-century press, was highly influential in promoting a national literature, for he saw how it could help lay the foundations of a modern nation. Altamirano himself tried several genres, notably fiction. His self-conscious *Clemencia* (1869) is skilfully put together and marks a real step forward in the genre in Mexico, but it is marred by a simplistic and didactic portrayal of good and evil. Altamirano's most popular works of fiction were once again *costumbrista* sketches: *La navidad en las montañas* (1870) and *El Zarco* (1901). *Costumbrismo* was still in evidence as the century closed; one finds it in the works of Manuel Payno, who compiled perhaps the most complete inventory of social customs and types, for example in *Los bandidos de Río Frío* (1889–91).

Emilio Rabasa (1856–1930) produced four 'Mexican Novels', each with the same protagonist, who also serves as narrator. In these, the unthinking nationalism associated with Romanticism gives way to a more discerning view: the narrator, while showing signs of having faith in the goodness of things provincial, is clearly aware of the corruption and brutality of the metropolis, whose more affluent inhabitants come in for criticism. Two accomplished realist writers are José López Portillo y Rojas (1850–1923) and Rafael Delgado (1853–1914). Both were traditionalists in terms of social values, but they wrote with some objectivity, López sympathetically (but condescendingly) about the popular classes, and Delgado about members of the upper crust (pretentious and immoral) and the middle class (humble and devout). Sample novels are, respectively, *La parcela* (1898) and *Los parientes ricos* (1903). There was great popular success for Federico Gamboa's Zolaesque novel *Santa* (1903), a fact that is reflected in its several film adaptations. Probably Gamboa's popularity also owes something to the fact that he chose to deal with issues like sex and morality. One of his novels, *Suprema ley* (1896), goes so far as to suggest that passion and sexual desire trump moral values. That said, Gamboa did manage to bring a psychological dimension to his somewhat lurid tales. *Tomóchic* is the most famous novel by Heriberto Frías (1870–1925), a novel that in some respects anticipates those of the Revolution. It is written in a mixture of styles and was first published anonymously in an opposition newspaper in 1893. Frías based it on his experience in Porfirio Díaz's army, which had crushed an Indian revolt in the village that gives the book its title. Although Frías' account is quite balanced, he pulls no punches and consequently this novel caused Díaz some embarrassment.

The influence of *modernismo* in Mexico is evident even in Romantic poets like Manuel José Othon (1858–1906) and Luis González Urbina (1869–1934), and it lasted through key figures such as Salvador Díaz Mirón (1853–1928), José Juan Tablada (1871–1945) and Amado Nervo (1870–1919), and on to Enrique González Martínez (1871–1952) and Ramón López Velarde (1888–1921). The first genuinely *modernista* poet, however, was Manuel Gutiérrez Nájera, who produced refined, though sometimes playful poetry, emphasizing form, colour and sound, and epitomizing the European cultural preferences of the élite of those times. A fine example is his poem 'La Duquesa de Job', published in *Alas y abismo* (1884–87). 'El Duque de Job' was one of several pseudonyms he used when writing pieces for newspapers. Gutiérrez Nájera was rather a dandy, a man for whom poetry provided an escape from the mundane world. He began writing at thirteen, and he dedicated his life to it. He was a prolific critic and also wrote sketches and short stories, but he was distinguished by the genre that the Mexicans call the *crónica*, and by his accounts of the ways of the socially privileged. He was the first of Mexico's full-time creative writers, and he helped found the *Revista Azul* (its title fittingly in imitation of the French *Revue Bleue*), the most important literary magazine in Mexico since Altamirano's *El Renacimiento*. Salvador Díaz Mirón, who perhaps had some influence on Darío, was an individualist, a large-than-life figure in the Romantic tradition, and a writer of passionate poetry, at least in the early stages of his poetic career. Later he evolved towards more refinement, thus being a transitional figure between movements. His poems point up the frustration of writers under Porfirio, professionals who felt marginalized and undervalued by comparison with the poets of Mexico's past.

These were not the only flamboyant figures of Mexican *modernismo*. Amado Nervo left preparing for the priesthood to become a journalist, but the influence of the mystics who had originally interested him is evident in his works. His early poetry, for example *Perlas negras* (1898), *Poemas* (1901) and *Los jardines interiores* (1900), is Parnassian, emphasizing formal perfection and exotic imagery, but with mystical overtones. In later collections such as *En voz baja* (1909), *Serenidad* (1914) and *Plenitud* (1918), one finds an exploration of religious themes and the influence of oriental philosophies, especially Buddhism. The final phase is one of poems of greater simplicity that contemplate life and death. Nervo's poetry is personal, sincere, pure, and expresses both anguish and resignation. He, too, was a prolific writer, like so many of his time; he tried several genres and narrative styles, winning great recognition in his lifetime, though nowadays he meets with a mixed critical reaction.

José Juan Tablada is another major (and eccentric) figure of Mexican *modernismo*, one of Mexico's first cosmopolitans and orientalists. His work spans the range from late Romanticism to the avant-garde, though even in his earliest poems one can see him delighting in being provocative, irreverent and decadent. He was also celebrated in his day, and not only in Mexico, but his originality has only recently been acknowledged. Tablada's taste for avant-garde experiments is very much in evidence in his later works, where for example he exploits the suggestive powers of the haiku, or uses graphic forms influenced by the Orient (and by certain intoxicating substances).

By 1911 another Mexican, Enrique González Martínez, was making himself famous by calling for the *modernista* swan's neck to be wrung, for while the fanciful products of the modernists had their appeal, reality was beckoning. The fact was that *modernismo* in Mexico had never been quite the phenomenon that it was in some Spanish-American countries. González Martínez and López Velarde turned from the exotic and the exquisite to more traditional topics such as family and provincial life. In this return to humbler values they are sometimes held to be poetic counterparts of the novelists of the Revolution, and thought to be reacting against the decadence of Mexico City and seeking refuge in nostalgia, while rejecting the Revolution's chaos and violence. There are indeed poems by López Velarde ('Retorno maléfico', or the famous 'Suave patria') that would support this view, but he was also an innovator. López Velarde's life was not long. Born in Zacatecas, like most writers he moved to Mexico City, where he worked as a journalist, teacher and public servant. Somewhat like Tablada, López Velarde bridges *modernismo* and the avant-garde, and together they laid the foundations for modern Mexican poetry. In López Velarde's case there is a happy marriage of Mexican realities with literary sophistication; his striking use of language appeals to the senses and he treats human emotions in original, subtle and complex ways.

Theatre and music

It would be difficult to claim that the theatre of nineteenth-century Mexico was highly original. In colonial times, as we saw, theatre had been dominated by the needs of the evangelization process, or by the fashions of the peninsula; now, after independence, it continued to be dominated by outside fashions, but not only the contemporary neoclassical and *costumbrista* styles found in Spain. In a process of widening European influences France played the leading role: the *Intervención Francesa* and the brief rule of Maximilian heralded an almost lemming-like frenchification of some aspects of the culture, one that would be further pursued during the *Porfiriato*.

There is an instructive and appealing *costumbrista* play by Fernando Calderón (1809–45), entitled *Marcela o ¿Cuál de las tres?*, a comedy that makes fun of the education of women, overblown Romanticism, and not least the conscious pursuit of things French (despite which this very play is thought to have drawn on Molière). This Calderón nonetheless wrote more plays that were passionately Romantic, as did his contemporary Ignacio Rodríguez Galván (1816–42). Manuel Eduardo de Gorostiza (1789–1851) was basically a neoclassicist, though he wrote a series of *costumbrista* plays satirizing national customs and manners. One important dramatist of the second half of the century was a doctor called José Peón y Contreras (1843–1907), who wrote in a more realistic manner, bringing his interest in mental illness into his plays; yet he gave no great depth to his characters.

There was some official support for works by Mexican dramatists in the form of government subsidies, beginning in 1875, but these subsidies came with strings attached, so that plays became frequent enough yet were often cautious or superficial. There was a lesson learned from the imprisonment of Alberto Bianchi, for a play that critically addressed the practice of pressganging. As a consequence of such pressures, theatre may have been plentiful but it tended to be unadventurous, and dominated by heavy romanticism and slight comedies. Late in the century, when the theatre was going through one of its thin patches, tours by foreign companies were much in evidence, and Mexican actors were having to adopt a peninsular accent. Theatrical activity of this sort, like so much else, would come to a halt in the turmoil of revolution. In general the nineteenth-century theatre, at least insofar as by 'theatre' one understands spoken drama, was neither very distinguished in its works nor very securely established. The fortunes of theatre rose and fell by turns. Drama there certainly was, but in its artistic form it often consisted of imported opera.

Church influence on serious music waned during the nineteenth century and so music came to depend increasingly on the tastes of the bourgeoisie, who represented only a small portion of the population. In many ways the musicians and composers of the new century were leaving behind the colonial musical heritage, which in any case had been declining to the point where even the most serious composers were dealing with trivia and the quality of performances was low. There were problems with inadequate performance spaces, inept musicians, and the promotion of mediocre works and performances done by people who happened to have the right social contacts. 'Mexico has but one place of dramatic exhibition', wrote an English traveller in the 1820s. 'It is a building of considerable size [but] the orchestra is indifferent, and the performers in general below mediocrity.'[4] The first place to grant music status as an academic subject was the Escuela de Minas, designed by Manuel Tolsà, which did offer a good performance area.

4 W. Bullock, *Six Months' Residence and Travels in Mexico* (London: John Murray, 1824).

On the educational front the most significant contribution came from José Mariano Elízaga, 'Citizen' Elízaga, as he preferred to be called, who evinced musical talent while still a toddler and who benefited from having as enterprising a promoter in his father as had Mozart in his. After a period in Mexico City, Elízaga returned to his native Morelia, became a cathedral organist and piano tutor to the future wife of Iturbide, and under the latter's aegis was able to publish the first of several important didactic works, *Elementos de la música*. Elízaga also composed and he established a printing press for music; he was associated with a conservatory of music that had a grand opening in 1825, but it did not survive for long, owing to uncertain financial support.

Following the brief appearance of a Sociedad Filarmónica in mid-century, the Conservatorio Nacional de México was established (1866); for years its curriculum was based on the Italian model. Soon there was a national piano competition, and anyone who had any social pretensions had to have a piano. Fanny Calderón, a competent pianist herself, wrote: 'In every part of Mexico, town or country, there is a piano . . . there is evidently a great deal of musical taste.' She felt, however, that there was a stifling of Mexican talent and that this was attributable to the instabilities of government. She was less than enthusiastic about some performances that she attended during her years in Mexico. Of a *Miserere* sung at Mexico City Cathedral one Good Friday she wrote: 'The very spheres seemed out of tune and rolling and crashing over one another. I could have cried "*Miserere*!" with the loudest; and in the midst of all the undrilled band was a music master with a violin stick, rushing desperately from one side to another, in vain trying to keep time. . . . The calm face of the Virgin seemed to look reproachfully down.' On another occasion, having been subjected to some Strauss waltzes during a church ceremony to which only the cream of society had been admitted, she remarked on their inappropriateness (*Life in Mexico*: 338, 139 and 156 respectively.)

Throughout the nineteenth century there was a cross-fertilization between popular songs and refined, European forms, and when all is said and done the Mexican popular tradition provided a good deal of inspiration for classical composers. Large numbers of foreign virtuosi visited Mexico in the middle of the century, and many performed arrangements of Mexican popular songs to pander to the sensibilities of local audiences. Foreign performers were being favoured over local ones, regardless of talent. After José Aldana, a talented Mexican violinist, had been poorly received by a concert audience, an anonymous letter in the *Diario de México* (3 October 1805) suggested that he might be well advised to change his name to Mr. Aldam or Signor Aldani.

There were many productions of Italian operas but also some home-grown products, such as Cenobio Paniagua's *Catalina di Guisa* (1845) and his pupil, Melesio Morales' *Ildegonda* (1866). The star Mexican soprano Angela Peralta sang in first performances of both the latter work and Aniceto Ortega's one-act 'musical episode', *Guatimotzin* (1871), an opera that conveniently cosseted patriotic instincts at a time when the nation was resisting the French. It was a huge success, a national opera that exploited the apparatus of Italian opera while romanticizing the Aztecs. This reception compares revealingly with the case of an opera that dates from thirty years later, Gustavo Campa's *Le Roi Poète*. As this title suggests, the use of French was in vogue by this time, during the *Porfiriato*; Campa himself loved the language and, besides, no singer would have wanted to sing in such a vulgar language as Spanish. And yet his opera gives a sentimental and romantic view of the poet-king Nezahualcóyotl and of the Aztecs.

Angela Peralta, the 'Mexican Nightingale', was a native of Puebla, a person endowed with a spectacular voice and natural musical instincts. She made her début in Mexico in *Il trovatore* at fifteen years of age, was sent to Spain and from there graduated to performing in Italy. Thereafter she made a number of international tours, and in Mexico City in 1867 she founded her own opera company, specializing in the standard repertoire of nineteenth-century Italian grand opera. Her final performance, before dying (not of tuberculosis but) of yellow fever, was again of *Il trovatore* (1883). One of the accompanying violinists at that performance was called Juventino Rosas.

Rosas' *Sobre las olas*, composed in the style of a Viennese waltz, was the most conspicuously successful salon piece of the nineteenth century, and it is a work that exemplifies the tendency to give imported forms a Mexican flavour.[5] Julio Ituarte, a pianist and the composer of a lyric drama called *El último pensamiento de Weber*, is sometimes credited with writing the first truly accomplished stylization of popular Mexican songs, in *Ecos de México* (1880), a work that included arrangements of such popular numbers as 'Las mañanitas' and 'El palomo'; this was 'romanticismo a la mexicana', as Moreno Rivas puts it (1989: 23). Another man who deserves recognition is Ricardo Castro, composer of the opera *La Légende de Rudel*, which is similar to Campa's *Le Roi Poète* in that it too has a libretto in French, though it was first performed in Italian, in Mexico City in 1906; Castro has been called 'the most *europeizante* of the nineteenth-century Mexican composers'.[6] But the key figure at the end of the nineteenth century, about whom more anon, was Manuel Ponce, the 'father' of Mexican classical music.

It was perhaps in the field of music, and musical theatre, that the most vibrant developments took place. All sectors of the public were in some way passionate about music and on the whole governments took it as a given that musical activities should be subsidized. The growing popularity of light opera during the nineteenth century was to encourage the production of local works in the style of the *zarzuela*. José Elizondo's *Chin-Chun-Chan* (1904) was the first Mexican *zarzuela* to run to a thousand performances, and he was also a composer of reviews, another form, replete with stock characters, that rose in

[5] In 1951, for the MGM film *The Great Caruso*, Rosas' song was Americanized into 'The Loveliest Night of the Year'.

[6] William Berrien, *Concerning Latin American Culture* (New York: Columbia University Press, 1940), p. 157.

prominence during the second decade of the century. Mexican *zarzuela* spawned the lyrical *canción mexicana*, but it was a song type that really came into its own only after the Revolution, in its variant form, the *canción ranchera*. In the more sophisticated dance salons, the waltz and the polka caught on with an urban élite that also appreciated Italian operatic music, and the *bel canto* style of singing. The preferences of people in rural environments were less refined; songs were commonly reduced to two rhymed verses of four lines plus a repetitive refrain, the melodies and harmonies also being simplified – two or three chords, unadventurous harmonies – but the rhythms, even if based on European traditions, assumed a characteristically Mexican pattern (a mixture of 3/4 and 6/8).

The *corrido* is one of the most popular and best-known genres of popular Mexican music, and it has its roots in the Spanish romance, brought over at the time of conquest. *Corridos* and other song forms of the early nineteenth century told stories of the turbulent lives of settlers in northern Mexico. When the Republic of Texas was established in 1836, there was an influx into the border area of people such as Germans and Czechs who brought their own musical traditions, and a certain amount of socio-cultural tension, with them. As the century progressed, the *corrido* came to focus on racial and class oppression, sporting pistol-wielding heroes who were out to defend their rights; by then it had travelled a long way from its Spanish roots. Finally, with the Revolution the *corrido* moved deeper into Mexico, to recount the adventures of people like Pancho Villa.

Visual arts

For the most part, nineteenth-century painting followed classical and Romantic figurative styles, concentrating on religious and historical subjects. Academic painting took on a special character, consciously dealing with Mexican subjects, especially historical ones, and many portraits were painted. Popular art acquired new interest, while architecture on the whole declined.

Although attempts were made during the nineteenth century to deal with things Mexican, the choice to do so happened to coincide with a certain European taste for the exotic, and since the way in which such subjects were treated was often stylized and laden with the trappings of neoclassicism, a general sense of artificiality and of dependence on Europe persists. Juan Cordero's *Retrato de los escultores Pérez y Valero* (1847) portrays clearly *mestizo* faces but is otherwise in the classical style; he, Pelegrin Clavé (1810–80), José Salomé Piña (1830–1909) and Santiago Rebull (1829–1902) were the principal practitioners of academic painting and the dominant forces in art education during the nineteenth century.

When concluding the discussion of colonial art above, reference was made to a work by José Obregón, *El descubrimiento del pulque* (1869), which is a painting that also exemplifies the influence of neoclassicism in that the Indians are portrayed rather as if they were Greek gods. Another example is an 1887 sculpture of Cuauhtémoc being tortured by Cortés, done by an artist who had trained in Italy, Manuel Vilar, and now on the Paseo de la Reforma in the centre of Mexico City. Vilar (1812–60), tackled a number of national and especially indigenous subjects, including Iturbide and Malinche; one of his best pieces is his 1851 evocation of Tlahuicole, a leader from Tlaxcala. Other nationalistic and indigenist paintings that are worth mentioning are Leandro Izaguirre's *El suplicio de Moctezuma* (1893) and his naturalistic *Tortura de Cuauhtémoc* (1892), Manuel del Valle's *Moctezuma en Chapultepec* (1895) and José María Jara's *Fundación de la Ciudad de México* (1889).

Luis Coto (1830–91) is one of few painters of the time to do landscapes, but his work in that area pales by comparison with that of the century's star painter, José María Velasco, who for some forty years painted the flora and fauna and above all the dramatic geography of his country, developing a style of his own. If Velasco has a precedent, it is in the works of foreign visitors to Mexico during the previous century who applied a scientific eye to the study of nature and topography. One thinks of people like Alexander von Humboldt, of Claudio Linati, who introduced lithography to Mexico, and of Daniel Thomas Egerton, an Englishman who left a large number of paintings of Mexican country scenes. And if looking for later artists who worked in a similar vein, then one thinks of Dr Atl who, albeit in a less delicate and subtle manner, used art much as Velasco did, as a means of exploring the physical and scientific realities of the nation.

Velasco was the first notable Mexican landscape artist. At the Academia de San Carlos he came under the influence of an Italian master, Eugenio Landesio, who taught perspective and composition and asked his students to practise by painting rock formations and foliage. Early paintings by Velasco showing Landesio's influence include the splendid *Patio del Ex-convento de San Agustín* (1871), *Peñascos del Cerro de Atzacoalco* (1873) and *La Alameda de México/ Un paseo en los alrededores de México* (1866). Velasco is best known for a painting of Oaxaca Cathedral and for his varied and expansive landscapes of the central valley, which he began to paint in the 1870s and continued to produce for the next thirty years. He emphasizes the grandeur of the landscape by using diminutive human figures and downplaying the city, and he pays a great deal of precise attention to detail. A number of examples of his work can be seen at Bellas Artes and at the Museo Nacional de Arte, both of which are in the capital. In the small Oaxaca canvas, which was the product of a trip Velasco made in 1887, he uses a subtle control of perspective and light to capture the quality of the building; this painting was presented to Pope Leon XIII. Velasco also produced some fine seascapes, such as *Bahía de la Habana* (1889). His direct contributions to Mexican natural history have been less widely recognized, but he did a series of lithographs on the flora of the central valley and also provided illustrations for the journal of the Mexican Society of Natural History; he painted canvases for the Museum of Geology; he made pictorial records of archaeological excavations at Teotihuacan, and of its pyramids; and for some thirty years at the end of the century he was chief illustrator for the

National Museum. It was only late in his career that Velasco ventured outside Mexico: in 1889 he was sent to Paris to represent the government at an international exhibition, then in 1893 he went to Chicago to show a number of his paintings. His work was well-received internationally and thought as good as that of the leading European landscape painters of his time. According to Burke (1998: 72), Velasco's genius lay in his ability to combine the influence of Claude Lorraine (a painter much appreciated by Landesio) with touches of baroque, scientific detail, and a sense of compositional discipline.

Izaguirre and González Pinedas left us, respectively, interesting evocations of Shakespearean characters in *Yago* (1898) and *Otelo Dando Muerte a Desdémona* (1879), while Felipe Gutiérrez (1824–1904) gave us, *inter alia*, portraits of Saints Jerome and Bartholomew, and, curiously, the only nude of the period in *La Amazonas de los Andes*. Like Gutiérrez, Gonzalo Carrasco (1859–1936) painted in a naturalistic manner, but as the century progressed other painters evinced signs of sentimentalism. The culmination of Mexican Romanticism was the work of Julio Ruelas. Ruelas served as the principal illustrator for the *Revista Moderna*, which as we have seen was one of Mexico's first significant literary reviews, one that served the interests of the *modernistas*. Ruelas worked with figurative forms, but he used them symbolically and allegorically, to represent dark forces, archetypes and the spiritual side of life. His two most famous works are firstly an etching entitled *Crítica*, which is a self-portrait in which a devil with a top hat and a rolled-up newspaper sits astride the artist's head, as if threatening him with its long beak, and secondly a painting entitled *Revista Moderna* (1904), which portrays the main collaborators of that magazine as birds, devils, satyrs or centaurs, and shows them greeting their patron, who is on a white horse. Ruelas was clearly heralding a new era; according to Justino Fernández (1969: 127), everything in his work is symbolic. Ruelas also exemplifies a healthy collaborative tendency among Mexican artists, not simply of one visual artist with another, but across the range of artistic activity.

Occupying a place of his own is Hermenegildo Bustos (1834–1907), a painter who spent his whole life in a small town near Guanajuato, studied locally and always thought of himself as an amateur. In addition to his portraits, which combine skill with a dose of naïveté, he is known for a pair of still life compositions of fruit, painted with an almost surreal quality and perhaps intended as part of the tradition of documenting flora and fauna; he includes a scorpion, no doubt as a *memento mori*. Bustos' portrait subjects sometimes appear to be staring directly out as if into the lens of a camera; during the nineteenth-century photography was all the rage, and there is no doubt that it was a major influence on painting. The daguerreotype arrived in Mexico in around 1840, and many professional photographers came to the country from abroad, either to serve the vanity of the upper-middle class, or to help with scientific cataloguing, or to aid the engravers who made book illustrations. The world's first accurate war photos were the work of an anonymous Mexican photographer during the war with the United States. Also of major interest are the splendid photographs by Agustín Casasola that record the epoch of Porfirio Díaz and the process of industrial modernization that went with it. As the technology advanced and photography was put within the economic reach of more people, clubs and exhibitions proliferated, but far later than similar developments took place in Europe and the United States.

Two skilled engravers were Jerónimo Antonio Gil and José Joaquín Fabregat, who based his fine plate of the *Plaza Mayor* (1796) on a drawing done by Ximeno. Fabregat also produced an engraving of a plan of Mexico City whose accuracy and detail make it of both artistic and historical significance. Engraving grew immensely in importance during the nineteenth century, and not only in the official, academic sphere; it was also used to illustrate popular celebrations, stories and songs, such as the *corridos*. Manuel Manilla (1830–90?), though far less well-known than José Guadalupe Posada (1852–1913), worked with him for Vanegas Arroyo, a publishing house; they made cuts in wood, copper or zinc that became images on poor-quality paper, aimed at feeding popular sentiments of piety and humour. The papers in which such illustrations appeared had titles like *El Centavo Perdido*, *El Jicote* and *La Gaceta Callejera*; others, such as *El Argos*, *Fray Gerundio* and *El Fandango*, had a more political slant. The marriage of art and socio-political criticism was, of course, nothing new: there were plenty of English precedents; there was, not least, the precedent of Goya's *Caprichos* in Spain; and then there was Daumier in France. In fact, Claudio Linati, the man who had introduced lithography to Mexico, had used it himself for political criticism, in a magazine called *El Iris*.

Posada's early illustrations and cartoons are delicately drawn and in half-tones, a little like French political cartoons of the 1860s. However, he moved the tradition forward towards expressionism: he was quite capable of skilled work in the traditional style, but chose to progress to other things. Much of Posada's work is the product of his imagination; it is the work of an artist who feels free to let go of traditional ideals of proportion and perspective and adapt the medium to his personal ends, rather than making any attempt to represent reality in an objective or detached way. Posada's habit of transforming public figures into skeletons can be seen in many works: for example, *Calaveras de Periodistas* (1889–94) shows a press group on bicycles trampling a fallen skeleton, and *Calavera Catrina* (1913), one of his most famous, portrays a lady-like skeleton wearing a large hat, a feathered boa and a fancy gown, the message being that vanity is empty, that flesh turns to dust. Diego Rivera later incorporated a representation of this work into his mural at the Hotel del Prado. *Calavera de Don Quijote* shows a skeleton figure galloping along and scattering skeletons in its wake. Posada's fantastic world allowed him to criticize the real one, somewhat as had Goya with his *caprichos*; in the manner of Daumier, with his invented character Robert Macaire, Posada invented Don Chepito, a free and rather absurd character who appears in all sorts of situations, getting beaten up, falling in love with the wrong person, fighting bulls and making political pronouncements. In what seems to be an attack on mindless progress, *Calavera de las Bicicletas* shows Time, accompanied by other representative cyclists, running over Tradition, and watched by a saintly figure and two others who seem to represent the *charro* and the *china poblana*.[7] We shall return to Posada in the next chapter.

There were a number of major initiatives in architecture and town planning during the nineteenth century under Maximilian and Porfirio. Architectural interest shifted from imitation of Spain, all but forgot the Indian tradition and turned to France. In the capital, the Napoleonic pomp of Iturbide's coronation at the beginning of the century had somehow set the tone for things to come. However, in other cities – Puebla, for example – this tendency to lean on France was less pervasive, and in rural areas it was far less noticeable. In the capital, Maximilian planned a major avenue to link the Chapultpec Castle to the National Palace, a project that was further developed under the restored liberal government and under Porfirio. To mark the liberal triumph the avenue was named the Paseo de la Reforma and it acquired some statues of historical significance. By the late nineteenth century the Paseo was losing its rural character; in 1899 avenues were created to cut across it, and more statues were placed at the junction roundabouts. The whole business was modelled on France, on the Champs-Elysées and the boulevards. In the twentieth century the Paseo's leafy retreats for prosperous families gradually disappeared, giving way to skyscrapers, luxury hotels and financial institutions; it is now a tree-lined artery punctuated by statues of national heroes that cuts across the city, close to its historical centre, and it exudes an air of prosperous modernity that contrasts with the run-down and disorderly state of other parts of the city.[8]

7 The *charro* and his female counterpart, the *charra* or *china poblana*, became the very embodiment of national identity and patriotic honour. These stereotypes still find their way into many Mexican tourist promotions and are used commercially in advertising. For more details, see Standish and Bell, 62–3 and 68–70.

8 The Palacio de Bellas Artes and the Palacio de Correos, both impressive but derivative buildings, date from the time of Porfirio Díaz.

5
The Revolution and Since

The *Porfiriato* and its violations of civil liberties did not go unchallenged by Mexican liberals. At San Luis Potosí they held congresses reaffirming the principles of the 1857 constitution, but persecution drove many of them to seek asylum in the United States. It was from there, in St Louis, in 1906, that the Flores Magón brothers and others issued a proclamation calling for the overthrow of Porfirio Díaz, and it was there that they resumed the publication of *Regeneración*, copies of which were smuggled across the border. Francisco Madero was nominated as their candidate for the 1910 elections, but he was jailed and Porfirio unscrupulously held on to power.

In that same year, on the centenary of Hidalgo's call for independence, Porfirio arranged for a large-scale self-congratulatory celebration at which, even though eighty years old, he declared his intention of seeking a further term in office. To mark the occasion, Mexico City was refurbished and purged of undesirables, buildings were inaugurated, monuments unveiled and lavish banquets attended by the cream of society and the diplomatic corps. All this drove the opposition into action. Madero, having been released and gone into exile in the US, drafted the Plan de San Luis Potosí, calling for restoration of the democratic priciples of 1857 and declaring himself provisional president of the country. Rebel groups were already becoming active against their regional governments. Eventually, with mobs in the streets screaming for his demise, Porfirio stepped down and slipped away to France. In 1911 Madero duly became president.

It was not surprising that Mexico turned to Revolution, given the inequalities, the political dissatisfactions and the sense of repression shared by so many people, but it should not be thought that its Revolution was very coherent or driven by a shared ideological vision; if there is a single word to describe it, perhaps that word is 'chaotic'. Another period of short-lived and unsuccessful leadership ensued, with the country falling prey to warring regional *caudillos*. Principal among them were Venustiano Carranza, Alvaro Obregón, Emiliano Zapata and Pancho Villa. Carranza seized power, with the help of Obregón, but then the latter betrayed him, took over, and subsequently had him put to death. Villa was little more than a thug who raped, murdered and pillaged his way around Mexico, but he acquired a mythical reputation, largely because he launched a raid into New Mexico and managed to elude US troops. Carranza was probably behind the death of Villa and certainly his troops shot Zapata. Zapata, who operated primarily in the south, was not so driven by personal interests; he was an idealist who tried to improve the lot of landless peasants and he remains a popular hero to this day. As for Madero, his position was threatened also by a revolt organized by Porfirio's nephew, Félix Díaz, and when Victoriano Huerta, the unscrupulous leader of the federal forces, saw his opportunity to seize power, he abandoned loyalty to the president and staged a coup. Madero was arrested and later assassinated, along with his deputy. Huerta himself was forced to resign in 1914. Carranza, the leader of the northern coalition, called a conference of revolutionary leaders, but it proved too divisive to come to an agreed course of action. Carranza, however, had the ear of the United States (as had Huerta) and emerged victorious; at a meeting in Querétaro he presented his draft of what would become the landmark constitution of 1917.

Though 1920 is often said to be the end of the Revolution, the violence continued for years beyond that date. Everyone had been caught up in the Revolution but many had seen no real improvements stemming from it. Nonetheless, military and Church powers were reined in, and some post-revolutionary leaders did bring about improvements for humble people. Obregón, who was president from 1920 to 1924, began to implement some of the provisions of the 1917 constitution. One of the most important ministerial appointments he made was to the post of secretary of education, for which he chose José Vasconcelos, a lawyer and teacher who had opposed the ideas of the *científicos* (the positivist advisers to Porfirio). Vasconcelos set about reforming schools, sending teachers out into remote regions, building libraries and calling on artists to help promote his agenda. The constitution provided for land redistribution and limits on foreign ownership; in implementing these things the Obregón government was cautious, and yet US oil companies, fearful that he might appropriate their assets, led a campaign against Obregón, which eventully led to a compromise. Nevertheless, Obregón's chosen successor, Plutarco Elías Calles, was a more radical politician who did launch into serious agrarian reform while continuing to support improvements in education. In 1926 there arose a major confrontation with the Church when Mexico City's bishop declared that the religious provisions of the constitution could not be upheld, despite which Calles pushed ahead with changes that outlawed processions, led to the deportation of foreign clerics and closed Catholic educational establishments. The Church responded by refusing to administer the sacraments, and then violent revolts broke out in the provinces, under the cry '¡Viva Cristo Rey!' So began the Cristero Rebellion (1926–29), a revolt that brought attacks on government officials and led to the destruction of public schools; but by 1929 it had largely been contained and the government was back in control. By then, despite a rule forbidding re-election, Obregón had returned to the presidency, only to be assassinated by a religious extremist before taking office. This ushered in a period that became known as the 'Maximato', during which Calles continued to pull the political strings from behind the scenes while others were ostensibly in power. Vasconcelos fell out of favour because of his opposition to the authoritarianism of the 'jefe máximo', that is Calles, the *de facto* president. During the last two years of the *Maximato* the government moved appreciably to the right, persecuting communists, dissolving organized labour and allowing the rise of fascist organizations. All the same, under pressure from his party Calles nominated as the next presidential candidate a man who would go down in history as a significant reformer, a man who had already acquired a reputation for his support, while governor of Michoacán, of public education and workers' rights. This was Lázaro Cárdenas. He nationalized foreign assets, including the oil industry, and made radical changes in land distribution; about 70 percent of Mexicans at that time were working in agriculture, many of them under the old colonial *hacienda* system. Cárdenas was popular, at least in most of Mexico; foreign powers were rather less keen on him.

On the cultural front, the 1920s and 1930s were rather a special period for Mexico, because the European avant-garde movements coincided with the country's early post-revolutionary years, a time when change was in the air and Mexico was viewed as a place to try out new ideas. The political and cultural agenda held a number of disparate artistic tendencies together for a while: most strikingly there was on the one hand a preoccupation with technological change and the effects of capitalism, and on the other an impulse to return to the simplicity of the primitive, to magic, myth and intuition. Whatever their personal preferences, a host of significant radical intellectuals, writers and artists came to Mexico at this ebullient time: D.H. Lawrence, Eisenstein, Trotsky, Copland and Breton, to name only some. Later, there would be a second influx of ideas and talent, in the form of refugees who fled to Mexico from Franco's Spain; Luis Buñuel, the film director, was among the most important of these. In the second half of the century, in particular, Mexico served as a place of refuge for beleaguered Latin Americans from other countries and that, too, led to an influx of artistic talent.

Like most Latin American countries during the second half of the twentieth century, Mexico suffered severe economic crises, but in the political arena it was unique and, in its own way, stable. During the presidency of Miguel Alemán (1946–52) the ruling party adopted a new, self-contradictory name: it became the Partido Revolucionario Institucional (PRI), the rationale being that by then the aims of the Revolution had been broadly achieved and it was time for a period of stability. The fact is that Mexican politics were by then doomed to one-party domination for a period of seventy years; thanks to a combination of clever organization, the avoidance of political dogma and the tolerance of corruption, the PRI remained in the driving seat. In such circumstances it became difficult to see what was still revolutionary.

A major hiccough in the system occurred in 1968, against a background of political unrest in other parts of the world. Just as the country was on the verge of hosting the Olympic Games, there was a demonstration at Tlatelolco. The Plaza de las Tres Culturas, at Tlatelolco, has pre-Hispanic ruins, a colonial church and some soul-less modern high-rise buildings, all juxtaposed; it was and is a symbolic place. The 1968 demonstration there had been timed in such a way as to focus international attention on the country's problems and put pressure on the government for change, but it was an event that ended in tragedy when armed forces fired on the demonstrators, causing several hundred deaths. Official Mexico was very slow to acknowledge the cost of the incident, which to many people seemed to be comparable to acts of repression that had recently been seen in Prague and Paris. Moreover, Tlatelolco uncomfortably echoed the Mexican tradition of authoritarian regimes, such as the *Porfiriato* of pre-revolutionary days.[1]

Curiously, it was Luis Echeverría, a senior official in the outgoing government, and one who had been closely associated with the massacre to boot, who then became became President (1970–76) and introduced popular left-wing policies. Echeverría lost no opportunity in presenting himself as a man in the Cárdenas mould. He increased the number of state enterprises and used subsidies to keep down the prices of essential goods at a time when most countries were suffering high inflation. Echeverría was no communist but he showed that he was not in the pocket of the US, for example by being the second Latin American head of state to visit Castro's Cuba and by welcoming Salvador Allende's widow to Mexico. His policies were aimed at stimulating the economy and redistributing wealth. Unfortunately, the delicate relationship between the government and the business community took a turn for the worse, investors lost confidence and government debt increased.

Economically, the next president, López Portillo, was saved by the oil boom, able to continue to stand up to the United States but unable to prevent his now-rich nation from being one of haves and have-nots. While the country was awash with money, and the value of its currency was high, his promise to invest in projects that would support long-term growth was never fulfilled; the money was spent, but not productively, and graft increased, inflation rose. In the public mind he was now 'López Porpillo' the crook who had done very nicely himself while the country went to ruin.[2] When Miguel de la Madrid came to power in 1982 the situation was dire and there were increasing signs of public dissatisfaction with PRI rule, a dissatisfaction that was only exacerbated by a new austerity package that he announced, apparently under pressure from the International Monetary Fund. The wealthy were able to shield themselves from its effects; the gap between rich and poor grew ever greater. However, steps were taken to crack down on corruption and profiteering. There were also tensions with the United States during those years. Mexico had adopted a conciliatory attitude towards rebel political forces in Central America, in contrast to the US drive to support regimes that it found politically acceptable even though they were unpopular and oppressive in dealing with the people they were supposed to represent. Mexico had supported Castro and also the Sandinistas, almost defining its foreign policy in stubborn contradiction of the United States. There

[1] Octavio Paz, who was his country's ambassador to India at the time, resigned in protest.

[2] 'Pillo' is 'crook'.

were also increasing problems related to drug trafficking and migration. But the US and others recognized that Mexico could not pay off all its debts.

Then, in 1985, the country was hit by two major earthquakes that left thousands dead or homeless and brought a new economic burden.[3] Aid money poured in, but a lot of that disappeared, presumably into the pockets of the powerful. With the government unable to deal adequately with the aftermath of the disaster, the people took the situation into their own hands in an outpouring of civic solidarity. They organized volunteer groups to help and there emerged a popular hero, 'Superbarrio', who, dressed like the famous wrestler known as 'El Santo', acted as an intermediary between the people and the authorities. There was no violence, no subversion, simply a grass-roots effort to help make things better. Carlos Monsiváis, the cultural and social critic, was instrumental in giving this popular activism publicity, later gathering his articles about it in his book *Entrada libre: crónicas de una sociedad que se organiza* (1987).

Dissatisfaction with the PRI continued, and in 1986 some of its members, led by Cuauhtémoc Cárdenas, formed a subgroup called the Corriente Democrático, whose main concern was to democratize the workings of the party, in particular the practice whereby the outgoing president would choose his successor (a process known as the *dedazo*). Ostracized by the party establishment, Cárdenas then stood as an independent candidate for the presidency in 1988, advocating a return to the principles of the Revolution; he was backed by a coalition of left-wing interests that eventually acquired the name Frente Democrático Nacional. Cárdenas, a *mestizo* and a son of the former president, had a lot of popular support in a country now sick of the PRI's machinations. The official PRI candidate at the 1988 elections was Carlos Salinas de Gortari, who won by a slim margin, far less than his predecessors; there is a good deal of evidence to suggest that the election process was tampered with and absolutely no doubt about the fact that two of Cárdenas' aides were assassinated. Once in power, Salinas, a friend of the United States (he had been to Harvard), brought about a new wave of privatization, reversing some of the popular measures introduced by Echeverría; but he also increased confidence among foreign investors.

In 1994, just as the North American Free Trade Agreement was being sealed, Indians in Chiapas, calling themselves Zapatistas in homage to the hero of revolutionary days, staged an armed rebellion. Their masked leader, Comandante Marcos, was backed by huge spontaneous public support in the capital; at a demonstration in the Zócalo, about a hundred thousand people cried 'Todos somos Marcos' (We are all Marcos), emphasizing their solidarity with the rebels and effectively protecting Marcos himself. There was little violence; instead the Zapatistas soon became a pressure group advocating Indian rights. But foreign investors did not like it, and money fled the country. As for NAFTA itself, it had the effect of putting many Mexicans out of business. It also provided a cheap

[3] The government estimate of the number of deaths was 10,000, but others thought the number three times as high.

labour pool that allowed multinational corporations to grow richer; a major factor affecting the economy was the development near the US border of *maquiladoras*, massive assembly plants for putting together consumer products destined for the US (and, later, for other industralized countries), using materials and components generally made outside Mexico.[4]

Salinas also amended the constitution, abandoning the *ejido* system of communally owned land and restoring powers to the Church. Foreign policy changed too, because of the wish to stay on the right side of investors in general and the United States in particular. In all, Salinas' policies were extremely unpopular, even with sections of his own party; rivalry between Salinas and his fellow technocrats on the one hand, and between the technocrats and the 'dinosaurs' of the PRI on the other culminated in several assassinations, and it is possible that Salinas himself was instrumental in these. At any event, as far as public opinion was concerned he became the most hated man in Mexico. Another of the technocrats, Ernesto Zedillo, inherited the presidency; he deflated the peso, but that deflation did not produce the desired results. Crime rates rose dramatically, there was high inflation, many job losses and bankruptcies, and another international aid package became necessary before Mexico regained a degree of economic stability. Zedillo did take steps to strengthen democracy. But the seventy-year pre-eminence of the PRI was nearing its end; there were continuing tensions in the party, corruption was again rife and there were more political assassinations. Finally, in 2000, Mexico elected President Vicente Fox, the PAN (conservative) candidate, an entrepreneur and former head of Coca-Cola in Mexico. The Prague-like euphoria that followed his election was shortlived, for while Fox had ambitious plans he was unable to get them through Congress, where the PRI still had a majority. There is little doubt that Fox had ideas, and constructive ones, too; he tried to make peace with the Zapatistas, to build on NAFTA by opening up the border for people to travel freely, hoping to raise the standard of living of ordinary Mexicans by a process of regional integration similar to that of the European Community, which raised the standard of living in countries like Portugal and Greece. However, Fox's *sexenio*, ending in 2006, brought less progress than expected.

The visual arts

After the Revolution, several architects, including some who had studied in Europe, began to adopt modern European styles, particularly the functional style for which Le Corbusier became famous. Governments recognized the

[4] One effect of NAFTA has been to weaken some traditional Mexican sources of income, such as the cultivation of maize. Corn is now being imported from the US Midwest, from farms that receive subsidies from the US government. In the process, it is suspected that genetically modified strains are contaminating centuries-old strains that have hitherto been cultivated in Mexico.

cost-effectiveness of such architecture in an era of expansion of services and when faced with a growing population to house. O'Gorman was a pioneer of functional architecture. Félix Candela (1910–97), a Spanish immigrant, was one of the first to use concrete shell construction, facing a good deal of scepticism among architects who doubted that such designs could withstand Mexico's difficult environment, where soil conditions were not the best and earthquakes a constant menace. Candela attacked prevailing architectural practices, claiming that reinforced concrete had strengths that had yet to be recognized. During the 1950s he had commissions from the business and government sectors; for example his simple vaulted concrete structures were used in some rural communities, such as at Ciudad Victoria (Tamaulipas), for which he designed a school. But Candela needed more freedom to express himself. In Mexico City's Iglesia de la Virgen Milagrosa (1954–55) he used concrete to ape the Gothic style. For a restaurant called Los Manantiales, at Xochimilco (1957), he chose a vaulted octagonal structure, giving the concrete shell free-form edges. Candela believed that in that kind of construction it was form, not mass, that gave support, and in this particular instance of it one has the impression that the tiled exterior supports itself.

Much of the mid-century architecture in Mexico City can be attributed to Mario Pani, whose work was influential in other parts of Latin America. Pani (1911–93) was from a family of diplomats, and educated in Europe; he took more fully to the international style than did most Mexican architects. After redesigning the Hotel La Reforma in the 1930s (a building that became the flagship of modern architecture), he worked on a large number of buildings for the main streets of the capital. His work is not always beautiful, but is usually on a grand scale. Pani was instrumental in bringing the skyscraper to the capital; tradition and a steel shortage had combined to hold back the construction of tall buildings prior to the Second World War. In common with many of his contemporaries, Pani saw architecture and urban planning as things that went hand in hand. During the 1950s he collaborated with Enrique del Moral in designing the campus of the Universidad Nacional Autónoma de México, marrying the visual arts with functional architecture. Several of the buildings there were covered with mosaics, the most famous being O'Gorman's for the library. The university's stadium, one of the largest in the world, is fronted by a mosaic done by Rivera. The campus project as a whole covered 600 hectares and over a hundred architects were involved in it. Pani also undertook huge housing projects, of which the biggest was at Tlatelolco, begun in 1964. There, in marked contrast to adjacent historical sites, he put a 101-building complex to accommodate 70,000 people in 11,916 flats, with thirteen schools, three clinics, a cinema, shops and social spaces.

Naturally there were reactions against functionalism. Juan O'Gorman and Luis Barragán, who had also worked with functional architecture, turned to organic architecture, as defined by Frank Lloyd Wright. Barragán (1902–88) became known primarily for his single-family structures built for the upper end of the market. He came into his own in domestic architecture and residential urban planning, and this was because they gave him greater freedom than large-scale functional projects. His first real success was the development known as Los Jardines del Pedregal, begun in 1945, and in that he followed Lloyd Wright's precept of harmonizing architecture with the (in this case volcanic) landscape. In the late 1920s Barragán and some other architects, known as the 'Guadalajara Four', were associated with the Partido de Acción Nacional and its condemnation of the changes brought about by the Revolution. In particular Barragán rejected the institutionalized Indigenism that was overcoming art. Yet his mind was not closed to other cultural influences: study in Europe had given him an interest in Islamic architecture, African art and Art Deco, all of which influenced his neocolonial designs of the late 1920s and early 1930s. Residential architecture could only succeed, he thought, if it provided tranquillity and privacy. Instead of glass looking on to the outside world, he chose a central garden or patio with surrounding rooms opening on to it; this, of course, was a common characteristic of Mediterranean dwellings, but so too was it of those of Mesoamerica. One of Barragán's finest houses is the Casa Gilardi (1976, in Mexico City). Younger architects who were influenced by Barragán include Ricardo Legorreta and Mathias Goeritz, the latter collaborating with Barragán on La Plaza de las Cinco Torres (1957–58), where they placed concrete towers of different colours to mark the entrance to a part of Mexico City known as the Ciudad Satélite.

We saw in the previous chapter how Ruelas was a transitional figure in painting; so too was Saturnino Herrán (1887–1931), who tackled the portrayal of the native heritage during the touchy time of the *Porfiriato*. Herrán was somewhat influenced by the contemporary fashion of Europeanizing the culture of Mexico; his paintings of indigenous subjects and scenes from popular life bring together a stylized realism and disciplined, classical composition. *Labor* (1908) is an early composition that typifies Herrán's portrayals of the Indian plight: it shows a couple feeding their child in the shadow of a building, with labourers in the background struggling to move a huge construction stone under the blazing sun. Herrán was probably the first painter to use his art as a way of voicing social concerns. Best known during his lifetime as an illustrator for magazines such as *El Universal Ilustrado*, Herrán also spent some time working for the government agency responsible for keeping track of archaeological sites, and he was commissioned to copy the Teotihuacan frescoes for the Anthropological Museum. Among his most memorable canvases are three that depict the legend of Iztaccihuatl, while his most famous work, *Nuestros dioses* (Our Gods 1918), was done for the new Teatro Nacional building and represents an Aztec sacrificial rite. Although he and Diego Rivera were so different in personality – Herrán preferred to stay at home, Rivera travelled widely – there are several characteristics of the latter's work that are heralded in the former's, particularly the reverence for the strength, dignity and stoicism of the Mexican people. Herrán was a close friend of the poet Ramón López Velarde, and some of his art, *Nuestros dioses* for example, has parallels in the poet's writings. Another of his friends was the musicologist Manuel M. Ponce, about whom more in a moment. All three were conservative nationalists who felt as uncomfortable with the foreign pretensions of Porfirian high society as they did with the cosmopolitanism and frivolity of the *modernistas*.

Other painters who deserve comment are Joaquín Clausell (1866–1935), Abraham Angel (1905–24), and Francisco Goitia (1882–1960). Clausell was a painter of late impressionist landscapes that are very different in style from the more academic approach of Velasco. In fact Clausell is strikingly his own man, and he painted with more contrastive lines and colours than did the European impressionists; his works are generally more appealing than the equally personal and no less striking landscapes done by the prolific and influential Dr Atl. In all, these three landscape artists – Velasco, Clausell and Atl – make for an interesting comparison. As for Angel, one wonders what he might have done had he lived more than nineteen years: as it is, the works of his that can be seen at the Museo Nacional de Arte and the Museo de Arte Moderno, such as *La mulita*, are impressive and inventive. Goitia is a painter with a very subjective, surreal vision; he did landscapes and human figures, often with dark tones that emphasize suffering and the weight of oppressive forces, for example in *Campo mortuorio revolucionario del Charquito Colorado* (1922) and *Tata Jesucristo* (1927). However, Goitia is known above all for his bleak images of the Mexican Revolution. Following some success with exhibitions in Spain he returned to Mexico at the beginning of the Revolution and accompanied the forces of Pancho Villa, recording the desolation of the war in some of its most sober images, such as *El ahorcado* (1917). Goitia became a close friend of Tamayo. He also became increasingly eccentric over the years. After the Revolution, he travelled around Mexico taking part in archaeological and ethnological projects, painting scenes of indigenous peoples and traditions (such as *Las danzas indígenas* [1921]) as well as of psychological states. In his final years he once again used his revolutionary experience, for paintings like *Paisaje con ahorcados* (1959). He died in Xochimilco, living a life of extreme poverty in an Indian community.

We come now to the movement that dominated Mexican art for three decades after the Revolution. Like ancient Mesoamerican art, Muralism focused the artistic world's attention on Mexico. It not only became the dominant artistic mode, it became *de rigueur*, official, so much so that painters who preferred alternatives felt excluded by the prevailing dogma. Posada was a formative influence upon the muralists, who resurrected him from the oblivion to which he had been consigned since his death in 1913. One can see Posada's influence, for example, in Diego Rivera's skeleton and skull motifs, in the cartoon-like quality of much of his work and in his festive popular scenes; but Posada had also been a social critic, and that was perhaps more significant.[5] Among the

5 Many of the key figures in the muralist movement took part in the open-air painting classes led by Dr Atl, whose aim had been to distance art from the conservative academy and give it back to the people.

students at the Academia de San Carlos who also worked with Posada was José Clemente Orozco, whose cartoons of the 1920s reflect his admiration for Posada's work. At Posada's worshop simplified, expressionistic cuts were subsequently hand-coloured in lurid tones, the intention being to make them readily accessible and appealing, to send obvious messages to poor people, whether urban or rural. In this, Posada was highly successful, reaching all corners of the country with topics ranging from horrific to comic, from edifying to outrageous. Posada was later to give us some memorable images based on the Revolution. *Calavera zapatista* shows a horseman-skeleton dressed as a traditional cowboy *charro*, clutching a banner emblazoned with the symbol of death, while the horse's feet are surrounded by bones, as if to say that Zapata is at once the harbinger and trampler of Death. In later life Posada adopted a freer technique, illustrating ballads, battle scenes and the life of the soldiers, for instance in *Despedida de un maderista y su triste amada* (1910?). Clearly enough, his works influenced future graphic art, for example the work of José Chávez (1909–2002); they also fostered an interest in Mexican popular culture among other artists.[6]

The muralists seemed to empower ordinary people, to elevate their status by covering the walls of official buildings with their images. These artists gave expression to the ideals of a Revolution that had captured the world's imagination. Muralism seemed novel (though in fact there was a long national tradition of it), it was provocative, and it was in tune with the radical thinking of avant-garde intellectuals, not least foreign intellectuals. Muralism thus became a source of national pride.

It came into its own under the wing of the post-revolutionary minister of education and writer, José Vasconcelos. Vasconcelos' agenda, which drew partly on the Soviet experience, aimed to eradicate illiteracy, promote the fine arts for pedagogical purposes and bring Indian minorities into the mainstream of society. There were to be more rural schools and the popular arts and crafts were to be revived; those aspects of the culture that had been played down during the pre-war years were now to receive due recognition. There were also more grandiose pretensions: in *La raza cósmica* (The Cosmic Race, 1925) Vasconcelos speaks of a utopian Latin America in which the races have harmoniously fused, and he sees Mexico as the torchbearer.

The muralist movement lasted a good deal longer than Vasconcelos did as minister, and it lasted notwithstanding real differences between the artists involved. Rivera and the other two leading figures, José Clemente Orozco and David Alfaro Siqueiros, all went along in some way with the Vasconcelos vision, according to which artists were expected to go to work regularly in the service of society, just like other workers. In 1923 the three of them signed a manifesto along these lines, drawn up by the union of technical workers, painters and sculptors. But in fact the three artists were remarkably different

6 Posada's printmaking tradition has also been continued by Chicano artists.

people, and the nature of their political involvement reflects some of their differences. Orozco, the most sceptical of the three, saw the course of the Revolution first hand since he stayed in Mexico, while Rivera, who had left for Europe in 1907, stayed there assimilating contemporary trends in art and dreaming up Muralism with Siqueiros.[7] Not that Siqueiros, the younger man, lacked direct involvement in the political process: on the contrary, he was clearly the most ideological and dogmatic of the three; imprisoned at an early age for political reasons, he then took up with revolutionary groups, and he fought on the Republican side in the Spanish Civil War. One might say that Rivera, the most successful of the three, was also the most opportunistic, the best at self-promotion.

In its most vehement forms, Muralism was aggressively anti-capitalist . . . and yet its financial patrons were often capitalists. Bearing this in mind, the story of a painting commissioned from Rivera (at a time when his international reputation was well established) by the Rockefeller Center in New York is particularly instructive. With the work well under way, Rivera's patrons realized that the composition included a thinly disguised portrait of Lenin; Rivera was asked to remove it, refused to do so and therefore was paid off, after which his unfinished work was destroyed. But two years later he took revenge by painting another version of that same mural for the Palacio de Bellas Artes in Mexico City, under the title of *Man, Controller of the Universe*, and by including Rockefeller in it. Mexican post-revolutionary governments have been less troubled by such images; rather they have found ways to cynically exploit them. All the same, Muralism did establish a commitment to two revolutionary principles: that art was for the masses and that it should enjoy government sponsorship. The movement not only dominated Mexican art for some thirty years, but also influenced painters elsewhere, in the US (the Chicago movement of the 1960s, not to mention modern Mexican-American art) and in the Andean countries (the work of Kingman and Guayasamín).

Rivera's first mural was done in the early 1920s for the Anfiteatro Bolívar, at the Escuela Nacional Preparatoria, near Mexico City's main square; this is a place frequented by the political élite and sometimes used for presidential functions. The work in question, *La creación*, includes figures with Indian and *mestizo* features but its overall design and conception draw on the Renaissance tradition; it is an allegory done by the Rivera who had recently returned from Italy, yet its message is clearly in tune with Vasconcelos' vision. In following years Rivera moved on to decorate the nearby Secretaría de Educación, and there began to develop his dramatic and distinctive treatment of Mexican themes. On the lower floors, around the first courtyard, he put scenes of daily life, of labour on the land or in the mines, and of rural education, while around the second he painted scenes of popular fiestas, including his famous depiction of the Day of the Dead celebration. Rivera put both himself and his then wife,

[7] There are some paintings by Rivera that are clearly Cubist in style.

an actress called Lupe Marín, in among the festive crowd of *pulque* drinkers in this mural. Unfortunately, especially in the context of a building that stands for education, the paintings he did for the top floor are no more than tedious and simplistic propaganda: the peasants and combatants of the Revolution are idealized, the rich, the clergy and the powerful are lambasted. Lest the message be lost, this series is linked by a frieze across the top whose words come from revolutionary *corridos*. However, at about the same time Rivera produced what some critics consider to be his masterpiece, for the National Agricultural School at Chapingo, where in a much freer vein he created voluptuous human figures, integrating them into an overall design that admirably fits with the baroque architecture of a former chapel. On one side he portrays natural evolution, on the other social transformation, and the two are brought together by an allegory on the back wall that represents Mother Earth and mankind's technical mastery of Nature, both in harmonious co-existence. The murals that Rivera painted at the Palacio Nacional in Mexico City give a powerful view of Mexican history: one wall offers an idyllic vision of pre-Hispanic times, another emphasizes the violence and turbulence of subsequent history, with the lower sections dedicated to the conquest, and the upper arches depicting the protagonists of such major events as independence, the war with the United States, the era of reform, the struggle against French intervention, and finally the Revolution. Another wall, whose painting was completed in 1935, is entitled *The Mexico of Today and of the Future*, a sanguine view of the revolutionary future and a critique of reactionary capitalism. Rivera returned later with the intention of painting a chronological series depicting moments from Mexican history, but he died before completing it. A scene that he did complete there, however, was his much- reproduced portrayal of Tenochtitlan.

One of Rivera's last murals was *Dream of a Sunday Afternoon in the Alameda Park* (1947–48), which he did for the Hotel del Prado, bringing together many of his favourite images and historical figures, and significantly placing Posada and a skeleton at the heart of it; for good measure he inserted portraits of himself and Kahlo. By that time Rivera was known worldwide and had been commissioned to work abroad, especially in the United States. Among his first works in the US was one for the San Francisco Arts Institute entitled *The Making of a Fresco*, a self-conscious composition in which the painter himself is shown at work; in New York he painted *Frozen Assets*, which is far more didactic, in fact a bitter attack on capitalist speculations; in Detroit he painted a rather laborious homage to industrial progress; and then there was the abortive Rockefeller Center mural described above.

Critics have spoken of a number of contradictions relating to Rivera's work. He glorified Mesoamerican civilizations, presented the Indian as at the very heart of Mexican cultural identity, but did so under the auspices of a government that called itself revolutionary while only paying lip service to the cause of social justice. Moreover, there is often a contradiction between the ostensible purpose of the murals and their practical effect, in that they were inspired by a utopian Marxist ideology, claimed to reflect the reality of the masses and to speak to them, and yet could be fully read only with education, which was something those masses generally lacked.

Such was Rivera's notoriety that the other muralists suffered in his shadow; Rivera revelled in public attention, was flamboyant and provocative, and managed to secure the plum commissions. But many historians of art would say that Orozco had the greater and more original talent, and that it was he who had the greater influence on subsequent painters. Orozco was less idealistic, less dogmatic, less of a party hack and freer in style, aware of artistic trends but able to develop individually. The sharp, geometric lines of his *The Trench* at the Escuela Nacional Preparatoria make one think of Cubism, while other works have an expressionist feel about them. Perhaps there is some tension between his aims and his practice too; for example, the powerful abstraction of *The Trench* is a long way from accessible art with a clear message. His mature work can seem violent, dramatic, sinister and even chaotic. At times Orozco evokes impassioned grief in the face of human flaws, at others he denounces violence and exploitation, and sometimes he expresses wonder over the strength of the human spirit, and faith in humanity's potential. This last is perhaps best seen in his giant *Prometheus* at Pomona College in California (1930). Fire as a cleansing force is a common motif in Orozco, visible, for example, in his mural at the Hospicio Cabañas, in Guadalajara. He makes frequent references to the crucifixion, especially in his paintings entitled *Christ Destroying His Cross*, and he also paints realistic scenes of the horrors of revolutionary violence. He was anticlerical, and above all a man who resisted vain hopes, hypocrisy and idealism. He was a sceptic and a pragmatist, both of which set him apart from Rivera and Siqueiros. Yet Orozco's work was a target of public criticism and even of vandalism: his first major commission, for the Escuela Nacional Preparatoria, led to protests by both radical students and members of the establishment.

Orozco may have been a sceptic, but Siqueiros, as noted previously, was a card-carrying, orthodox communist. During the 1920s he worked on a series of allegorical murals, *Los elementos*, but soon he turned to more aggressively didactic work: for example, *Entierro de un mártir obrero* (Burial of Martyred Worker, 1923–24), inspired by the execution of a left-wing activist, sports a hammer and sickle. One has the feeling that Siqueiros, had he been born a little later, would have loved using spray cans. In Los Angeles he painted the controversial *Tropical America* (1932), an attack on US imperialism that showed an Indian being crucified under the US eagle; as a result Siqueiros was deported and the work destroyed. One of his last and most complex murals was *Marcha de la Humanidad en Latinoamérica*, which was installed at the Poliforum Cultural during the 1960s. Some of Siqueiros' most impressive work was done on canvas, including *Ethnography* (1939) and *Our Present Image* (1947).

The library building at the Universidad Nacional Autónoma is known for the mosaic façade done by Juan O'Gorman (1905–82), a painter but more famously an architect who was also associated with the muralist movement. His functional designs include houses for a number of members of Mexico City's élite,

Rivera among them, and a host of buildings besides, including housing projects and schools. It was during the 1950s that he turned away from functionalism on the grounds that it took account neither of nature nor of Mexico's Indian tradition, and that is when he did the library façade, covering it with historical scenes and allegories. Other, less well-known artists who were associated with the values and techniques of muralism were Alva de la Canal, Jorge González Camarena, Gabriel Fernández Ledesma, Fernando Leal, Roberto Montenegro, and Fermín Revueltas. Foreigners also took part, the most notable being Jean Charlot, who for example has works at the Secretaría de Educación that are at least as good as those of Rivera, and that seem to be every bit as Mexican.[8] Charlot was one of the artists associated with *Estridentismo*, a movement that began in Mexico City in 1921 under the leadership of the poet Manuel Maples Arce. This group, with its vision of a society that would be improved by technology, sponsored avant-garde activities, including exhibitions, and it issued a series of scandalous manifestos; yet like so many other artistic ventures, it too was overshadowed by Muralism.

One of the effects of increasing technology and the march towards modernization was to hasten the decline of folk traditions, so it is ironic that there should at the same time have been a resurgence of interest in them among the very ranks of the avant-garde. One result of this increase in attention to popular art was that several prominent painters cultivated a naïve style, which they fashionably applied to folkloric subjects. Many of Mexico's leading intellectuals also began to gather collections of Mexican arts and crafts, Kahlo and Rivera included. Dr Atl was partly responsible for this interest, in that he encouraged the scholarly investigation of popular traditions with his massive *Las artes populares en México*, published in 1922. At the time of the hundredth anniversary of Mexico's independence Atl, Roberto Montenegro and Jorge Enciso received government funding for an exhibition of Mexican popular art.

Despite Muralism's sway, other painters had been at work in different ways, one of the most distinguished being Rufino Tamayo (1899–1991). Tamayo, who was from a prosperous Oaxacan family, was impatient with the muralists and their dogma, and he doubted that they really spoke to ordinary people or reflected their lives. Art, he argued, was universal, and the triumvirate's attempt to limit it to nationalistic subjects was stifling. Tamayo's own work hints at the pre-Columbian tradition, with its distinctive palette, its animal and vegetable motifs, and its figurative forms that are often dark-skinned, though cast in his own geometrical and rather flat style. In his *Juárez* (1932) and *Zapata* (1935), there is admiration for the two national figures: the Juárez painting has an Indian woman in the foreground contemplating a bust of the former president; the Zapata one has him in celestial surroundings that would do the Virgin of Guadalupe proud. Neither picture has much of a message; rather they make lyrical use of colour and form. Tamayo's work, however, like that of the

[8] Revueltas had two famous brothers: the classical composer Silvestre and of the novelist José.

muralists, has been criticized as self-consciously primitivistic and oversimplified. During the 1940s Tamayo produced expressionistic works, such as *Muchacha atacada por un extraño pájaro* (Girl Attacked by a Strange Bird, 1941), and then he turned more abstract, as in *Sandías* (Watermelons, 1968); in short, he tried several styles. Tamayo was invited to make his own contribution to the walls of the Palacio de Bellas Artes; this consists of *Birth of our Nationality* and *Mexico Today*, two huge, bold and abstract displays of colour that, their titles notwithstanding, are very different from the works left there by the muralists.[9]

Tamayo's fellow Oaxacan, Francisco Toledo (b. 1940), is sometimes said to have followed in his footsteps, but many other artists whose style does not necessarily derive from Tamayo's found inspiration in his independence of mind. The *Generación de la Ruptura*, dating from the 1950s, gave Mexican art an abstract, experimental and decidedly cosmopolitan look, and it broke quite deliberately with the tenets of Muralism, with the 'nopal curtain', as their leader, José Luis Cuevas, aptly called it. Other artists in the group were Manuel Felguérez, Vicente Rojo, Roger von Gunten, Francisco García Ponce, Lilia Carrillo and Alberto Gironella. Apart from Tamayo's, there was the influence of foreign artists who had come to Mexico; Artaud, Breton, Weston, Eisenstein, Modotti and Toors are among the many foreign intellectuals and artists who, together with anthropologists and folklorists, found themselves attracted by early post-revolutionary Mexico and influenced its forms of cultural artistic expression. Some of the artists among them produced significant, though largely unheralded work during the 1940s and 1950s, for example Leonora Carrington from England and Remedios Varo from Spain. Both, working independently of one another, were influenced by Surrealism, and both later enjoyed a cult following. These two women had had direct contact with the surrealists; not so Rivera's wife, Frida Kahlo (1907–54), whose work nonetheless evinces signs of Surrealism's influence. In fact André Breton, the doyen of surrealists, once said that Mexico was the land of Surrealism *par excellence*.[10] He it was who identified a surreal quality in Frida Kahlo's work, though she herself thought otherwise. Certainly her work has an oneiric quality. It is also somewhat naïve in style. Even in the many paintings in which she is her own subject she includes plenty of Mexican trappings, and there is generally ample evidence of her interest in *exvotos*. Kahlo's life was dogged by misfortune, illness and an unhappy marriage, but she won late recognition and has since become a cult figure.[11] María Izquierdo (1902–55), another painter who is said to have been

9 Tamayo left his collection of Indian art to his native city, and in Mexico City there is a museum dedicated to his own work, an impressive building in Chapultepec Park.

10 There was a major Surrealist exhibition in Mexico City in 1940.

11 She has also been the focus of at least three films: Marcela Fernández Violante made a short called *Frida Kahlo* in 1971, Paul Leduc the full-length feature *Frida: naturaleza viva* in 1984 and more recently Julie Taymoor has made *Frida* (2002). (*Carrington* [1995], directed by Christopher Hampton, is set in England and deals with Leonora's relationship with Lytton Strachey and members of the Bloomsbury Group.)

something of a surrealist, was also interested in the idea of 'Mexicanness'. For a few years in the early 1930s Izquierdo was the partner of Tamayo, that great critic of Muralism; ironically, more than a decade after that relationship had ended she had the distinction of being commissioned by the government to paint a mural, the first Mexican woman to receive such an invitation, but that opportunity was lost when the big three weighed in, questioning her suitability.

Two artists who cultivated an apparently naïve but really rather modern style were Miguel Covarrubias (1904–57) and Antonio Ruiz (1897–1964), both of whom were active during the 1930s and 1940s. In his time, Covarrubias was famed above all as a caricaturist, but later he became known for having amassed collections of pre-Hispanic and folk art. Like his friend Kahlo, Ruiz embraced the traditions of folk art and genre painting, and so his work is in some ways indigenist; his humour and style, however, distinguished his approach from the earnest activities of other artists. A painting that will serve as an example is *The Bicycle Race* (1938), which reminds one of the naïveté of Henri Rousseau and also of the approach of Surrealism. It is set in Ruiz's native town of Texcoco, and has the atmosphere of a country fair, with a host of participants who are painted in a slightly caricatured fashion. By contrast, and more in the indigenist vein, Ruiz's *El sueño de la Malinche* (1939) has free, flowing lines and a dream-like quality, as seems appropriate to its subject; here the dreaming Malinche lies in a bed whose covers are the landscape of Mexico, with Cholula's church-topped pyramid in the centre.

Although he was not Mexican, mention must be made of the role of Carlos Mérida (1891–1984), who was born in neighbouring Guatemala. He went to Paris at quite an early age, then to New York, moving to Mexico in 1919, where he collaborated with Rivera, with whom he had become acquainted in Europe. In 1927, back in Paris, Mérida turned from figurative painting to more abstract and surreal styles. His travels had brought him into contact with most of the leading lights of the art world – Modigliani, Mondrian, Picasso, Klee, Miró, Kandinsky, Léger. Mérida was highly influential upon the Mexican art scene, and his example inspired a number of abstract artists, such as Gunther Gerzso (1915–2000) and Vicente Rojo (b. 1932).

Nueva Presencia (confusingly, also known as *Los Interioristas*) was an offshoot of *Ruptura*, and was active during the early 1960s. *Nueva Presencia* rejected social realism and didacticism, but also abstractionism; instead its proponents favoured neofiguration, a trend that had emerged in Europe, the US and Latin America during the 1950s. While European neofigurative painting sometimes expresses existentialist angst in the context of the post-war world, in Latin America it was industrialization and urban growth that drove artists' concerns. The members of *Nueva Presencia* learned of Existentialism thanks to the writings of Octavio Paz, the 'Beat Poets' and writers like Camus and Kafka, while revealingly, the group's alternative name comes from a book by a US author, Selden Rodman: *The Insiders: Rejection and Rediscovery of Man in the Arts of Our Time* (1960).

One of the most important members of *Nueva Presencia* was Alberto

Gironella (1929–99), a man of Catalan extraction. Gironella studied Spanish at the Universidad Nacional Autónoma de México and became interested in the work of Gómez de la Serna and Valle-Inclán. In the early 1950s he turned to painting, and together with Vlady (Vladimir Kibalchich Rusakov), founded the Galería Prisse, which was to prove an important outlet for artists who were trying to break away from the muralist stranglehold. Characteristic of Gironella's own mature work is his appropriation of masterpieces by people like El Greco, Velázquez and Goya. An example is *Entierro de Zapata* (Burial of Zapata, 1957), for which Gironella's starting point was El Greco's *Entierro del Conde de Orgaz* (Burial of the Count of Orgaz).[12] Nor was Gironella the only painter to lean on the works of the old masters; that same El Greco painting was used by Alejandro Colunga as the basis for his *La pasión de los locos 1* (Passion of the Lunatics 1, 1981), while another Greco, the *Vista y mapa de Toledo* (View and Plan of Toledo) inspired Juan O'Gorman's *Ciudad de México* (Mexico City, 1942).[13] Gironella's key works are those in the *Serie de las reinas* (Queen Series, 1960s–1970s), in which he deconstructs images of Queen Mariana of Austria painted by Velázquez, with sinister results. Gironella was fascinated by the dark side of life. The series begins by using an expressionistic style and making the queen almost abstract, then Gironella introduces *objets trouvés* and finally he is making collages. In the one called *Gran Obrador* (Great Maker, 1964), he portrays the queen as a dog; *La reina de los yugos* (The Queen of the Yokes, 1975–78), becomes a statement about colonial power. The link between Mexico with Spain also appears in *El sueño de doña Marina 2* (The Dream of Doña Marina, 1977), for there she has become Malinche, both a traitor to and a symbol of Mexico.

Now to Cuevas (b. 1934), the leader of the group. Although self-taught, by 1953 he had already had an important exhibition at Gironella's Galería Prisse. He became famous not only because of his talent, but also because he attacked the muralists, demanding artistic freedom. Most of Cuevas' work comprises drawings and prints. Expressionistic and subjective in its representations of the human figure, it can be compared with the work of other neofigurative artists, and not only Mexican ones, of the 1950s and 1960s. Echoes of Goya's dark view of human nature, of a world peopled by grotesque and marginal figures, can be seen in Cuevas' *Loco* (Madman, 1954), *Estudios de Kafka y su padre* (Studies of Kafka and His Father, 1957), and *Autorretrato en la noche* (Self-Portrait at Night, 1978). Cuevas won some international acclaim and was the only painter of this group to approach anything like the renown of the Muralists and Tamayo. At home in Mexico he and the group were very influential, thanks to their cosmopolitanism and openness to new ideas; their importance was acknowledged by the creation of the Museo de Arte Contemporáneo.

12 Zapata had become a national myth, the iconic representation of the traditional values of the *campesino*.

13 One could add to the list the highly successful modern Colombian artist Fernando Botero.

Unlike the muralists, the *Ruptura* artists never claimed to be abandoning high art; but when all is said and done, how far had the muralists really abandoned it?[14]

Occupying his own place is Juan Soriano (b. 1920), a painter who is difficult to characterize, a brilliant and idiosyncratic *enfant terrible* with his own ideas and approaches. Some of his work is defined by sharp, expressionistic lines, some is blurred in the impressionist manner, and his colours and vivid and striking. Some of it is simple and orderly, some complex and chaotic, some of it playful, some gloomy, some cosmopolitan and refined, some primitivistic, some traditional-looking, some very modern. Figurative, sometimes allegorical or symbolic painting in the early years gave way to greater stylization and abstraction. Here is an artist who worked in several media and with artists in other fields, following the national collaborative tradition. Let us take just one sample from this varied panoply: his *La vuelta a Francia* (Tour de France/Back to France, 1954). It is a picture that makes for an interesting juxtaposition with Ruiz's *Bicycle Race*, whose jolly naïveté in dealing with a similar subject is replaced in the Soriano by a far clearer rejection of realism and a loud celebration of colour.

Rocío Maldonado (b. 1951) is one of the most important exponents of neo-Mexicanism, a term applied to the work of a number of artists who came to prominence during the 1980s and whose painting once again turned to ideological matters. Maldonado is interested in historical representations of women and in popular culture. In early works, such as *La Virgen* (The Virgin, 1985), dolls made of painted leather or papier mâché are often accompanied by representations of human genitalia, the idea being to point up the passivity of the roles that have traditionally been accorded to women. In more postmodern works of recent years one finds her expressing her feminism by combining images from the history of art and religion. In *Extasis de Santa Teresa II* (Ecstasy of Saint Teresa, II, 1989) for instance, she uses a Bernini sculpture to explore a number of dichotomies: past/present, sacred/profane, passivity/activity.

Nahum Bernabé Zenil (b. 1947), another neo-Mexicanist and one of the most important artists to have emerged in Mexico in the late twentieth century, makes himself the focus of his art – as did Kahlo and Cuevas before him. Indeed, the art of Frida Kahlo was a source of inspiration to all the so-called neo-Mexicanists. Zenil's works are generally of small dimensions and often involve the use of mixed media. Portraying himself in traditional cultural contexts and subverting established symbols, Zenil questions sexual attitudes, particularly homophobia. In the somewhat narcissistic *Retrato de boda* (Wedding Portrait, 1988) all members of the wedding party have Zenil's facial features. *Bendiciones* (Blessings, 1987), exploits the idea of the *exvoto*; here he and his longtime gay companion appear beneath the image of the Virgen de

14 In essence the *rupturistas* were playing a similar role to that of the composers of classical music who tried to break away from Carlos Chávez's nationalism, or the 'mafia' generation writers who rallied round Octavio Paz.

Guadalupe, who showers blessings of roses over them.[15] A related work of the same year, called, precisely, *Ex voto*, shows Zenil bare-chested in the foreground to the left, the Virgin above and to the right of him, and below her a huge human heart being pierced by a dagger. Beside the heart there is a lengthy inscription that *inter alia* tells of Zenil's personal life and his continuing prayers to the Virgin. At her feet, instead of a cherub, we find another tiny portrait of Zenil's head. This painting seems to have an obvious precedent in Kahlo's *The Two Fridas*. The most intriguing question, however, may be whose is the hand that is thrusting the phallic dagger into the heart?

Two other artists among the many who have achieved some international prominence are Yolanda Gutiérrez (b. 1970) and Gabriel Orozco (b. 1962). Gutiérrez works with open spaces and nature. For example, she has collaborated with Mexico's Ministry of the Interior to produce nesting structures designed to attract birds back to areas devastated by hurricanes. Her famous work entitled *Umbral* is an installation of cattle bones arranged to mimic birds in flight. As for Orozco, he is an example of an artist who divides his time between Mexico City and those meccas of modern art, New York and Paris. He too creates installations, but he is also known for his sculpture and photography. Orozco exploits the possibilities of found objects and industrial products – an inner tube, a tin of cat food or a yoghurt pot – creating unexpected combinations and celebrating the mundane aspects of urban life. *La DS* (read 'La Déesse', 1995) is a Citroën DS that was cut into three and then reconstituted, omitting the middle section: the result is a remodelled icon. *Ping Pond Table* (1998) is a table tennis table with a lily pond in the middle; like *Oval with Pendulum* (1996), inspired by the game of billiards, it illustrates Orozco's interest in the dynamics of play. His photographs record chance events (the coincidence of several identical mopeds at one place, for example) or images at fleeting moments such as that of his own breath on the surface of a piano, or the circles made by his bicycle as he rides through a puddle.

Much of the art of the latter part of the twentieth century was personal and apolitical. The neo-Mexicanists, although apparently dealing with national subjects, had little to say about current social and political realities, living instead in a subjective and almost mythical world. They did well commercially, at home and abroad, possibly because they 'presented a palatable image of Mexico as a colorful, festive country filled with age-old traditions and untouched by the complex troubles of present-day life' (Gallo: 7). By the 1990s a new, socially conscious art movement was in evidence. Artists like Eduardo Abaroa, Pablo Vargas, Abaham Cruzvillegas, Daniela Rossell and Sofía Taboas turned from easel painting to installation and performance art, to global media images rather than national ones, and to pop culture. Abaroa's *Invasión metafísica de los hombres desperdicio* (1995) is a typical installation, consisting of soap sculptures strategically placed on a pornographic magazine, as if to

15 In Mexico there are few cultural icons to match her. It will be recalled that roses were the means whereby she conveyed her message via Juan Diego to the bishop.

suggest the cleansing of sins. The reality is that in modern Mexico such magazines (often imported from the US) can be seen more readily than images of Aztecs and their art. Even so, 'the brash contradictions that mark everyday life are visible only intermittently as decorative detail in most of the art of the post-NAFTA era' (Fusco: 64). After the Salinas presidency this changed; for example, one enterprising man, Vicente Razo, gathered a collection of anti-Salinas ephemera (expressions of public indignation at the Salinas regime, an indignation that was widespread at the time) and these eventually became the basis of his Salinas Museum. Artists such as these, whose work at first seemed uncommercial, have since been exhibiting in major galleries and selling well. *Twenty Million Mexicans Can't be Wrong* was the title of a major exhibition of such work at the South London Gallery in 2002; *Zebra Crossing* was a similar exhibition at the Haus der Kulturen der Welt in Berlin; there have also been several exhibitions in the United States. Mexico was once again in fashion.

Photography, the new art that had begun to acquire such importance in the nineteenth century, naturally saw considerable development during the twentieth. In Mexico the first major contribution was the work of Agustín Casasola, who took official photographs of Porfirio Díaz and of the stars of the Revolution. A large number of photographs related to the Revolution itself have been attributed to Casasola though in fact most were taken by journalists and soldiers who were there in the fray. What Casasola certainly did do was collect and archive them, publishing many in a multi-album set entitled *La historia gráfica de la revolución* (Graphic History of the Revolution). He was not alone in showing an interest in the Revolution; foreign photographers like Edward Weston and Tina Modotti were also active in the Mexico of the 1920s.

The other truly significant photographers of the time were Manuel Alvarez Bravo and his wife Lola, both of whom were at one time teachers at Bellas Artes. During the 1920s they became interested in documenting indigenous life, her approach to the subject being more detached than his. Lola served as a staff photographer for a number of magazines, in addition to which she did portraits of some artists, including Frida Kahlo. Manuel (1902–2002) has the more lasting reputation; he was closely associated with the muralists, though in his photographs he was less blatantly propagandistic than were the painters. His fine images, often of working people, are striking, inventive, interestingly composed and sometimes dream-like in quality.

From the Alvarez Bravo studio there emerged another generation of photographers. One was Flor Garduño (b. 1957), who caught indigenous people engaged in traditional activities, though her first internationally acclaimed photographic series, *Bestiario* (Bestiarium, 1987), portrays them in the zoomorphic costumes related to pre-Columbian rituals that have fused with Catholicism and show signs of modern influence. Like Garduño, Graciela Iturbide (b. 1942) became professionally active in the 1970s, and she too was one of Manuel Alvarez Bravo's assistants. Both women, following the style of their mentor, use black and white. Iturbide's work has been the more widely ranging in subject, often dealing with human dignity and the attempt to keep a sense of individual or group identity. For example, she has photographed gypsies in Spain, unemployed women in Newcastle, street gangs in Los Angeles and *santería* rituals in Cuba. Appropriately, a number of her Mexican photographs look at death. Mariana Yampolsky (1925–2002) was a photographer who often worked in rural areas, documenting the lives of impoverished indigenous people. In addition to Gabriel Orozco, whose work was briefly reviewed above, other photographers to achieve prominence in the second half of the century were Lázaro Blanco, Ignacio López, Pedro Meyer and Yolanda Andrade; their subjects range from city life and psychological trauma to the effects of poverty and violence. Daniela Rossell published *Ricas y famosas*, a collection of photos, most of them of women from Mexico's most corrupt and influential families; here they are, at home, surrounded by the trappings of wealth. Though the subjects are unnamed, these are the women of the PRI politicians (Salinas, not least), whose houses sport images of Zapata and symbols of the Revolution – essentially images of causes betrayed by such powerful people.[16]

Music and dance

In closing the discussion of musical developments during the nineteenth century, mention was made of Manuel Ponce, who began his career as a composer, conductor, teacher and critic. Ponce showed his nationalistic colours in a number of ways, serving music in much the same way as Velasco and Dr Atl served the visual arts, that is to say by applying his professional expertise to documenting things Mexican. In 1913, Ponce published a musicological work, *La música y la canción mexicana*, together with some arrangements of traditional tunes like 'Cielito lindo' and 'La Valentina'. The most famous of his early songs is 'Estrellita' (1914). His main aim was to preserve the most valuable and authentic of Mexican folksong. For example, he recognized the tempi and rhythms and the irony of the lyrics of the *canción norteña*, viewing them as a reflection of a bold frontier spirit. Unfortunately, he also overlooked some regional forms, and so his work led to the canonization of selective types of Mexican music (and ultimately to their conversion into stereotypes). Ponce spent some time in Paris during the 1920s, under the tutelage of Paul Dukas, and after his return he began to write in a more impressionistic style, in concise, contrapuntal compositions, leaving the romantic, folksy style of his early works behind. Ponce wrote some of the first successful Mexican symphonic works, and a great number of minor works, including many for the guitar of Andrés Segovia, a close friend. Some his best works in this new vein are *Canto y danza*

16 Gallo (66–8) takes her to task for not guiding the reader with captions and for not grouping the photos so as to point up their political or regional significance; the effect, he feels, is of a shallow, voyeuristic coffee-table book, 'a book version of *Hello!* magazine'.

de los antiguos mexicanos (1933), *Tres poemas arcaicos* and the *Concierto del sur* (1941).

As we have already seen, musical culture had undergone some change during the nineteenth century, thanks to the influence of German and East European immigrants, the French intervention, and fashionable trends that favoured the Old World. After the Revolution, the rise of nationalistic awareness brought with it a new appreciation of rural musical traditions, in particular the *corrido* and the *canción mexicana*. A subgenre of this last was the *canción ranchera*, which was made popular by Pedro Infante, Jorge Negrete and others through cinema and the media. Later, musics from other parts of the Americas also made their mark on Mexico. Also worth noting is the increasing clarity of the divide between popular and art music after the turn of the century, so that whereas on the one hand Mexico cultivated its own folkloric traditions, on the other it was promoting its own forms of classical music.

As far as the popular forms were concerned, the one that became most vibrant was the *corrido*, derived from the old Spanish *romance*. During the nineteenth century it had been a northern phenomenon that told of frontier life and later of racial and class struggles, of resistance to injustice and of armed conflict. The *corrido* eventually moved deep into the heartland of the country, becoming indelibly associated with the Revolution and its key figures. In fact it is unlikely that it would have become so popular were it not for the Revolution. In a conveniently anonymous way it told stories of revolutionary exploits to illiterate people, celebrating the 'heroes' and pouring scorn on others, including the gringos.

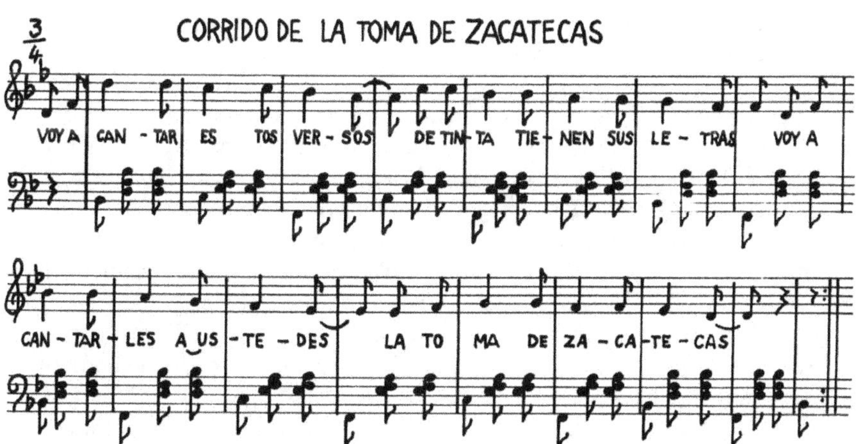

El día veintrés de junio,
hablo con los más presentes,
fue tomada Zacatecas
por las tropas insurgentes.

Al llegar Francisco Villa
sus medidas fue tomando
y a cada uno de sus puestos
bien los fue posesionando.

. . .

Estaban todas las calles
de muertos entapizadas,
lo mismo estaban los cerros
que parecían borregadas.

Andaban los federales
que ya no hallaban que hacer,
pidiendo enaguas prestadas
pa' vestirse de mujer.

Lástima de generales
de presillas y galones,
pues para nada les sirven
si son puros correlones.

(On the twenty-third of June – I say to those around me – the city of Zacatecas was taken by the rebel troops. When Pancho Villa arrived, he did what was necessary and took possession of his posts. [. . .] All the streets were strewn with bodies, and the hills looked like a slaughterhouse. The Federal troops were going around, no longer knowing what to do, asking to borrow petticoats so they could dress like women. Woe betide the generals, with their ribbons and medals that do them no good when all they know how to do is run away.)

Once the Revolution was over, the *corrido* turned to matters of love and life in general. Like so many aspects of the dominant culture, however, it never really reached the south of Mexico. When the *corrido* was in its heyday it was also exploited by printers like Vanegas Arroyo, who happened to have the popular engraver José Guadalupe Posada in his employ: illustrated with a Posada caricature, the *corridos* would sell like hot-cakes. But commercial attempts to exploit the *corrido* after the Revolution were not very successful. Nowadays it is primarily of historical and cultural interest, but is still part of the repertoire of the *orquesta típica*, especially in *norteño* music, and in the borderlands a new subgenre has emerged, the *narcocorrido*, telling of the activities of drug dealers. It is subject matter that is used to distinguish between different types of *corrido* – they can be romantic and sentimental, exemplary, nostalgic, tragic, denunciatory or humorous, and they can tell stories; in all some ten varieties have been identified. Structurally speaking, the *corrido* usually has a preamble sung by a man who introduces himself and his topic, followed by the substance of the song and then a moral or summary conclusion, sometimes capped with an *envoi*. Singers may accompany themselves on the guitar or be accompanied by a *mariachi* ensemble.

For the name 'mariachi' there are two possible explanations; according to one, it is of Indian derivation and comes from a word for a platform used by dancers; according to the other, it is a corruption of the French word *mariage*, the argument being that it came into use at the time of French occupation, when errant musicians would entertain guests at weddings. The latter perhaps seems the most plausible explanation, but the former has in its favour the fact that *mariachi* traditions are particularly strong in Jalisco, and that is where the Indian word in question comes from. The *mariachi* ensemble has grown over the years, having once consisted simply of a harp, a *guitarra de golpe*, a *vihuela* and violins. Then the *guitarrón* became a basic instrument in the ensemble; this is an oversized, six-stringed guitar that evolved because of the need to have a portable instrument to replace the harp. The *guitarrón* provides the bass line. Trumpets first joined the ensemble in the 1920s. Apart from *corridos*, the standard repertoire of *mariachi* groups now includes regional *sones* and *canciones rancheras*. The traditional musicians' garb – dating at least from the occasion in 1907 when Díaz demanded it of a band engaged to perform for a visiting US diginitary – consists of a wide-brimmed sombrero and a silver-embroidered *charro* costume. Stereotypical though it may be, it should not be thought that *mariachi* music has become merely a spectacle for tourists; on the contrary, it is a ubiquitous feature of social life in a country where popular music seems to be everywhere. Bands can be found at private functions, but also in parks and at restaurants, often charging by the song.

Norteño, the popular music associated with the north and the borderlands, has vestiges of musical traditions that developed when the southwestern United States belonged to Mexico. The colonial fare – not only the *romance* but also dances like the *jarabe* and the *jarana* – came into contact with new, predominantly Czech and German imports, such as the waltz and the polka, and there were major changes in instrumentation. Enter the *conjunto*, a new, guitar-based ensemble featuring the *bandoneón*, which is an instrument derived from the accordion and normally played by the lead (male) singer. In songs about the trials of border life, simple chordal accompaniment during the verses gives way to decorative instrumental interludes. The *polca* became one of the favourite *conjunto* forms. Like many aspects of border culture, this *norteño* music spills over into (the undiplomatically termed) Mexican-American culture. There is a big band version of *norteño*, called *banda*, whose origins are in Sinaloa; *banda* grew in popularity at the end of the twentieth century.

The dance known as the *jarabe* in essence dates back to the fifteenth century, though the name first appeared in the eighteenth referring to a dance that at the time was thought rather improper, the *jarabe gitano*.[17] Despite various attempts

17 The 'Mexican Hat Dance' is known in Spanish as the *jarabe tapatío* (i.e. the *jarabe* from Jalisco).

by church and state authorities to suppress this licentious corruption of the *seguidilla manchega*, its popularity grew and regional characteristics were added, such as the dance gestures of the Huichol Indians in the Jalisco area. Another important dance, the *habanera*, came from Cuba during the nineteenth century. An amalgam of elements from opera, *zarzuela*, Mexican song and the *habanera* generated the lyrical Mexican variety of the romantic song known as the *bolero* (not to be confused with the Spanish *bolero*). Agustín Lara (1897–1970) was the most famous of composers of Mexican *boleros*; alter a difficult start in an unhappy family, after playing the piano in brothels and suffering facial disfigurement when attacked with a bottle, Lara ultimately became very successful. Along the way he had written some songs with the names of major Spanish cities as their titles, and towards the end of his life General Franco presented him with a house in Granada, in recognition of their popularity.

Now to classical music. In this, Mexico made little impression on the international scene before the twentieth century, but then Carlos Chávez (1899–1978), Silvestre Revueltas (1899–1940) and others were noticed. Their grand 'native' compositions were the musical counterpart of the works of the muralists, and like the muralists they received official backing to compose them. Nationalistic music involved the conscious evocation of pre-Hispanic music (albeit largely imagined) and yet the musical culture of the composers concerned was undeniably European.

Chávez dominated the musical scene much as Rivera did the pictorial. He was a conductor, a theorist, an administrator and a teacher, and by far the most famous of all Mexican composers. Like Rivera's, Chávez's art was never really for the people, but he did attract attention to his country and win international acclaim. Like Rivera, he drew on the avant-garde, exploited the post-revolutionary cultural climate, helped impose the current dogma; and like Rivera he was criticized for it. His main formal inspiration came from Stravinsky, and he was closely associated with Varèse and Copland.[18] In 1921 he produced a ballet called *El fuego nuevo*, just as Rivera was returning from Europe; it was dubbed his 'Aztec ballet'. Some people found it exhilaratingly new and trendy, while others thought it fed European fantasies about an exotic Mexico. His reputation is based on *indigenista* compositions like this and the famous *Sinfonía india* (1935–36), which nowadays is viewed as an artificially modern and foreign evocation of indigenous music. Since no ancient music had been preserved, Chávez used material that had evolved among isolated, northern, nomadic tribes. Despite the dubious sources, Chávez's originality is undisputed; he used new instrumentation, upset the prevailing harmonic conventions and emphasized melody and rhythm: in general his music is rhyth-

18 Aaron Copland wrote a number of compositions inspired by Mexican popular melodies and musical motifs.

mically complicated and dissonant, consciously breaking with romanticism. In addition to his indigenist works, Chávez wrote many abstract, avante-garde pieces that had little to do with Mexico itself. *Energía* (1925), for example, celebrates technology, as does the 'Danza de los hombres y las máquinas', one of the episodes in *H.P., caballos de vapor* (1925–26). *Exágonos* (1923–24) is a set of six pieces whose geometric abstraction could be thought of as the musical counterpart of Cubism; these are musical evocations of images in the poetry of Carlos Pellicer. Chávez also produced a number of relatively unsuccessful populist works, which he hoped would embody the principles of the Revolution. In later years he wrote some of his most ambitious and accomplished pieces, including several chamber works, four symphonies, an opera called *The Visitors* and a ballet called *Pyramid*. Chávez was also influential in other aspects of musical life, for example as chief conductor of the Orquesta Sinfónica de México for some twenty years following its foundation in 1928, and as the director of the Conservatorio Nacional from 1928 to 1934.

Chávez had such prominence that he came to overshadow his former duo partner Silvestre Revueltas. Like Chávez, Revueltas trained and worked for years in the US; then he became deputy conductor of Chávez's symphony orchestra. That does not mean to say that he is now regarded as playing second fiddle. On the contrary, his compositions are thought by many musicologists to be more original and interesting than those of Chávez. Revueltas' early death, coupled with the fact that he came from a family that was making such a mark on various aspects of the cultural scene – one thinks especially of the notoriety of his brother José, the novelist – helped give him a special aura and a cult following. As for the works themselves, they are less ponderous, more upbeat, apparently more spontaneous and intuitive than those of Chávez, though they are borne of the same nationalistic feeling, and they use similar driving rhythms and dissonances. Revueltas seems to capture the vibrancy of daily life and festivities, drawing on popular music and the folk traditions, such as *mariachi* music, but also managing to be strikingly inventive at the same time. The titles of some of his pieces suggest their inspiration in everyday things, such as *Feria* (Fair), *Esquinas* (Corners), *Caminos* (Roads) and *Alcanías* (Collection Boxes). Revueltas also composed scores for many Mexican movies. *Ocho por radio* (Eight for/on the Radio, 1933), a light medley for chamber orchestra, provides evidence of his interest in bringing the elevated and the popular closer together. His reputation as a composer, however, was built on his works for full orchestra: *Cuauhnahuac* (1930), the first, identified his personal style; *Janitzio* was written for the movie of that title and has a Mexican provenance (an island in a lake in Michoacán). Revueltas also looked beyond Mexico for inspiration. Some of his work was inspired by Lorca, including *Homenaje a García Lorca*, performed in Spain shortly after the poet's death. His most famous composition, the symphonic poem *Sensemayá* (1938), was based on Nicolás Guillén's poem; Revueltas' work recognizes the African influence on popular music and also reveals his high regard for Ravel and Stravinsky. While he assimilated lessons from the work of composers such as these, Revueltas was not a slavish imitator.

His expressive and very personal style as a composer is certainly Mexican, but not clichéd.

Chávez founded and led the National School of Composition, whose activities helped to create a unified front as art music broke away from the old romanticism. This still had proponents among older composers such as José Rolón and Candelario Huízar, but their works also slotted into the nationalistic ethos: Rolón wrote *Cuauhtémoc* (1930), Huízar the symphonies *Oxpaniztli* (1935) and *Sinfonía Cora* (1942). Chávez's protégés at the Conservatory, Daniel Ayala, Salvador Contreras, José Pablo Moncayo and Blas Galindo – also known as the Grupo de los Cuatro (if Russia had 'The Five' and France 'The Six', why not a Mexican 'The Four'?) – made sure that its rule lasted for years, though without quite the flair of Chávez and Revueltas. The modern classics among the works of the 'Grupo de los Cuatro' became Galindo's *Sones de mariachi* (1940) and Moncayo's *Huapango* (1941), both skilful and appealing arrangements of and improvisations on popular themes that are regularly wheeled out at civic ceremonies. After a relatively dry period, new life flowed in musical nationalism, particulary in the ballet of the 1940s; compositions from the National School were revived and newly choreographed, and many new pieces were composed for the ballet, in the school's established tradition.

Luis Sandi (1905–96) became another leading figure in musical nationalism, as composer, conductor and administrator; as a composer he is known for his arrangements of Indian music, such as *El venado* (1936) and *Música yaqui* (1941), compositions that once again played up characteristics that were supposed to be typically Indian (the pentatonic scale, unusual instrumentation and so on). The compositions of Miguel Bernal (1910–56) frequently reflect his assocation with Morelia and the state of Michoacán. *Tata Vasco*, enthusiastically received in 1941, at home in Morelia, had its première in Mexico City held up on fears that it might provoke religious controversy; it is based on the life of Vasco De Quiroga, the friar who had established utopian communities in Michoacán. It is an opera that perhaps makes up for a lack of plot with its juxtaposition of different musical styles: the Indians sing neo-indian music, the clergy Gregorian Chant and the conquistadors *romances*. At the end of the decade a reduced version was taken by Bernal to Spain at Franco's invitation, and there it met with great success.

Rodolfo Halffter (1900–87), somewhat less famous than his brother Ernesto, is one of a number of foreign musicians who contributed to the Mexican musical scene. He had come from Spain and was not encumbered by nationalistic Mexican baggage; he tried using dodecaphony, and even received some support from Chávez for his endeavours. Rafael Elizondo (b. 1930) and Manuel Enríquez (1926–94), together with Mario Kuri-Aldana (b. 1935) are members of a group known as *Nueva Música de México*, many of whose works do have nationalistic features. Chávez conducted workshops on composition in the early 1960s, and many of the prominent figures in contemporary classical music passed through them – Héctor Quintanar (b. 1936), Eduardo Mata (1942–95), and Mario Lavista (b. 1943); Mata became director of UNAM's Orquesta

Filarmónica and also of the Bellas Artes opera company. Under the influence of musicians like John Cage, these people incorporated chance into their compositional technique, and they moved away from the dominance of rhythm, melody and harmony towards pure sound. *Quanta* is the name of an improvisational group that was set up by Lavista, whose output includes an opera based on the Carlos Fuentes novella *Aura* (1988). As elsewhere in the musical world, there was experimentation with synthesisers, with Héctor Quintanar directing the electronic studio at the National Conservatory. Daniel Catán has produced several interesting compositions, including *Mariposa de obsidiana* (1984) and *La hija de Rapaccini* (1988), inspired by works by Octavio Paz.

As far as modern popular music and the recording industry are concerned, Mexico is the largest market in the Spanish-speaking world. In addition to international companies, there is a company called Fonovisa, owned by the TELEVISA group, and it has had a major share of the national market. Spanish-language music has remained strong despite the onslaught of Anglo-American products. The general popularity of Latin music and the increasing international availability of Spanish-language television have reinforced this strength. In 1996, for example, 47 percent of sales were of music by Mexican artists, while Latin American artists accounted for a further 20 percent. The country's popular music ranges from salsa and *cumbia* (a dance form believed to be African in origin but imported from Colombia and especially popular in Mexico in the late twentieth century) through media-promoted pop to songs of protest. Just as cinema and radio in the past made the reputations of people like Jorge Negrete, so today's television, often with the teen market in mind, has made stars of pop singers like José José, Lucía Méndez, Daniela Romo, Mijares and Gloria Trevi. From the youth counterculture of the 1960s and 1970s, especially from Avándar, Mexico's answer to Woodstock, came a tradition of rock music that is much stronger than in most Latin American countries. The most famous exponent of this is a band called El Tri; other popular rock bands have been Café Tacuba, Caifanes, Jaguares, Lost Acapulco and Maldita Vecindad.[19]

A brief comment was made earlier about ballet. At about the turn of the century, under Porfirio Díaz, classical ballet began to gain support as a professional activity and there was also encouragement for the performance of popular dances in theatres. The Teatro Juárez was built in Guanajuato (1903), the Teatro Degollado in Guadalajara (1906), and then there was the Palacio de Bellas Artes in Mexico City. The result was that by the end of the *Porfiriato* theatrical dance was flourishing, with performances by companies both national and foreign; the number of theatregoers had increased and their tastes had diversified. A high

19 Paul Leduc, the film director, made a movie about counterculture: *¿Cómo ves?* (What do you think?, 1986).

point was the visit of the ballerina Ana Pavlova in 1919, during which she pandered to local audiences by including a *jarabe tapatío* and other dances for which traditional *china poblana* and *charro* garb was worn.

The Escuela Nacional de Danza (National School of Dance), directed by Carlos Mérida, was founded in 1932, that is, some ten years after the establishment of the Orquesta Nacional under Chávez. Both were initiatives of the Secretaría de Educación Pública and came under the umbrella of Bellas Artes. Here, in the Escuela de Danza, were the Campobello sisters, dancers who had previously come to Mexico City and set up their own school; Gloria taught Mexican dance, and Nellie (who was also a significant writer) acted as deputy to the director. Guillermina Bravo, who became so influential in later years, was a student there in the 1930s. It was during that same decade that Waldeen and Ana Sokolow, two US dancers, introduced Martha Graham techniques into Mexico, but some felt, rather predictably, that this was compromising national artistic identity.[20] The Ballet Nacional de México dates from 1948, and Bravo was appointed to lead it; she had previously studied with Waldeen and collaborated with her in setting up the company called Ballet Waldeen, which set out to break free of the confines of classical ballet and exploit indigenous dance practices. As leader of the Ballet Nacional Bravo won considerable support from the government even though she choreographed some controversial themes that brought her into conflict with it. She also improved conditions for dancers. Since 1991 the Ballet Nacional has been based in Querétaro; it has maintained a good standard over the years, and gone on several world tours. Other state-supported companies are Ballet Independiente de Mexico and Ballet Teatro del Espacio. Mexico was the first of the Latin American countries to set up a folk dance company, its Ballet Folklórico de México, founded in 1952 under the direction of Amalia Hernández, which was so successful that smaller regional companies of a similar sort arose later. The Ballet Folklórico is based at Bellas Artes in Mexico City, where since the 1960s it has been giving frequent performances, largely for the benefit of tourists; it, too, has toured the world.

The media

If there had been any hope that the press might be free after the Revolution, that hope was quickly dashed as the old pattern of censorship came back into operation, either subtly or overtly. Broadly speaking, it is a pattern that remained in place throughout the twentieth century, with successive governments manipulating the press, and the related newsprint and paper industries, by means of permits and subsidies. As in the time of the colonial *gacetillas*, unofficial disbursements to journalists and newspapers were made in exchange for the publication of press releases, while payments for carrying the right sort of

20 Her full name was Waldeen Feldenkrais (1913–93).

advertising were made available by state and federal bodies. Beneath a false veneer of self-censorship by the press there lies a well-oiled system that serves the interests of those in power.

Within this culture of collusion there were, of course, variations, but the way in which President Obregón operated will serve as an example. He established a relaxed, old boy network among journalists; he would hold off-the-record meetings and favour journalists with inside information, and in interviews he liked to give the appearance of openness while in fact carefully controlling the proceedings. This established a precedent of the government paying attention to the press because it recognizes that journalists can present its policies favourably, but also cultivating the impression that the press is independent. Presidents Calles and Cárdenas were less relaxed and permissive than Obregón. Calles tried to exercise more direct control, while Cárdenas attempted to get the media to commit to his socialist agenda by establishing the state-owned newsprint monopoly, PIPSA, in 1935. Ever since, PIPSA has served to keep newsprint available at subsidized costs, but also as a means of government control. The official organ of Calles' National Revolutionary Party was *El Nacional Revolucionario*; later, under the shortened title *El Nacional*, Cárdenas had this paper more directly under the federal government. Despite the fact that thereafter *El Nacional* became a 'readerless', uncontroversial paper, its Sunday supplement, *La Revista Mexicana de Cultura*, has had quite a distinguished history.

Controls and pressures notwithstanding, during the first half of the century the press was sometimes a lively force, as exemplified by the role of the conservative journalist Martín Luis Guzmán, who returned from the US in 1920 to run the editorial page of *El Heraldo de México* and to found *El Mundo* shortly after. He was an irritation to the government, a thorn in Obregón's side, and by 1925 he found himself once again in exile. Returning to Mexico in the early 1940s, he founded *Tiempo*, a political magazine. Other, younger intellectuals supported Vasconcelos, who had his own mouthpiece, *La Antorcha*, begun in 1924. Led by the charismatic muralists Diego Rivera and David Alfaro Siqueiros, many artists took on the role of the workers' party intellectual. Conservative, Catholic publications that supported the Cristero Rebellion, such as *El País*, were countered by the muralists and other left-wingers in papers such as *El Machete*, the official organ of the Communist Party, and many of those who wrote for that paper also wrote for *El Popular*, which was the newspaper of the Confederación Mexicana de Trabajadores. Intellectuals with less firm political agendas produced the literary review *Contemporáneos*, which appeared monthly between 1928 and 1931 and proved to be extremely influential, in the manner of the *Revista Azul* and the *Revista Moderna* in the previous century. *El Hijo Pródigo* and *Tierra Nueva,* to which Octavio Paz contributed, the *Revista Mexicana de Literatura*, *Cuadernos del Viento*, *Plural*, *Vuelta*, *Nexos* and, more recently, *Letras Libres* have continued in this vein, while universities have produced *Revista de la Universidad* and *Casa del Tiempo*.

El Universal and *Excelsior*, both dating from the second decade of the twentieth century, are dailies that have had a comparable role to that of *El Siglo XIX* and *El Monitor Republicano* in the nineteenth. They were modelled on the then current format of US dailies, and they updated the Mexican industry with changes in typesetting, abundant illustrations and new production methods, including the use of telegraphic news sources. Astute marketing and public relations by the editor of *Excelsior* led to it generally getting the better of its arch-rival *El Universal*. First serving as a mouthpiece for the conservative wing of the Constitutional Assembly of 1917, *Excelsior* later showed sympathy with the Cristero Rebellion and so fell into disfavour with President Calles. In 1932 it eventually came under the control of a workers' cooperative, and in doing so established a precedent that was followed when *Unomásuno* and *La Jornada* were set up years later (in 1977 and 1984, respectively). As we shall see in a moment, *Excelsior* became important once again in the 1960s and 1970s, a crucial time in the history of the press in Mexico. *El Universal* had backing from the US thanks to its support for the allies during the First World War, and it remained financially buoyant well into the 1940s, when it went through a difficult time, facing new competition. *Novedades*, started in 1939 by Ignacio Herreras, soon came to rival *Excelsior* and *El Universal* for prominence among the national dailies, and became most influential in the mid-1940s, when it supported the pro-business policies of President Miguel Alemán Velasco. Its parent company began *The News*, which is still Mexico's major English-language daily, but *Novedades* itself these days is one of few dailies that feature photos of social events involving the political and business élite, and as a newspaper it has lost much of its political significance. After the end of Alemán's presidential term, he became a business partner of Rómulo O'Farrill, the chief editor of *Novedades*, and they devoted their energies both to the media and to tourism; eventually they joined forces with the Azcárraga family as partners in the Televisa media empire. During the 1960s and 1970s Novedades Editores went into regional markets, with offshoots like *Novedades de Acapulco* and *Novedades de Cancún*.[21]

Fernando Benítez, a journalist who for a number of years was associated with the successful *México en la Cultura* (one of several incarnations of the cultural supplement to *Novedades*), is widely credited with having transformed cultural journalism in general, making it more lively and effective in promoting literature and the arts. Benítez and his colleagues enhanced the reputation of a number of cultural publications: the supplement of *El Nacional*, *La Semana en la Cultura*, *La Cultura en México* (initially a supplement to the political weekly *Siempre*), *La Jornada Semanal* and finally the *Unomásuno* supplement entitled *Sábado*.

El Universal Gráfico, an evening paper dating from 1922, became known for its freedom from any particular ideology, and for the standard of its reporting. Many of Mexico's periodicals also started at about that time, including the *Revista de Revistas* (1910) and *Jueves de Excelsior* (1922). *Ovaciones* (1947)

21 Alemán knew how to feather his nest. He acquired large tracts of land around Acapulco, prior to its development for tourism.

addressed itself to a mass readership with its tabloid format and its devotion to sports and entertainment. Extras and supplements to existing papers grew in popularity in the 1930s and 1940s; *Excelsior* produced *Ultimas Noticias*, for example, and that became famous for up-to-date reporting on the Second World War. 1962 saw the appearance a racy and widely circulating afternoon edition of *Ovaciones*, complete with girlie photos in page 3 style. The two significant national dailies that started in the 1960s were *El Día* (anti-imperialist and supportive of the left wing of the PRI) and *El Heraldo de México* (conservative, anti-communist and anti-populist).

In Carlos Fuentes' novel, *La muerte de Artemio Cruz*, there is a character who is said to be based on José García Valseca, a man who became a newspaper tycoon despite having little education. García Valseca's first success was in publishing *historietas* on cheap paper, beginning with *Paquito* (1935) and *Pepín* (1936); these appealed to semi-literate readers and reached daily circulation figures as high as 300,000. In 1941 Valseca invested in publishing Mexico's first sports daily, *Esto*. After that he turned his attention to providing serious news coverage in the provinces, with papers such as *El Fronterizo* (in Ciudad Juárez), *El Heraldo de Chihuahua* and *El Sol de Puebla*, and in following years a 'Sol' rose in several regional capitals. His entrepreneurship was highly successful: *El Sol de Guadalajara*, for example, soon acquired a reputation for quality and was selling at the rate of one copy for every four Guadalajara residents; by the late 1960s, García Valseca's share of the overall national market was roughly 22 percent. Other media moguls rose to richness and power by venturing into several fields; Valseca alone stuck to the press. The government, it seems, became uneasy about his increasing power and so Valseca was obliged to sell his holdings to it, following which they passed once again into private hands.

In another novel, entitled *Los periodistas* (1976), Vicente Leñero documents the story of the trouble with *Excelsior*, which again provides an interesting case history in relations between government and press, in this case involving President Luis Echeverría during the aftermath of the Tlatelolco massacre. Under the editorship of Julio Scherer García, *Excelsior* had been notable for its unflinching support for the protesters and for its criticism of the government. When Echeverría came to the presidency in 1970 he decided to favour *Excelsior* with exclusive news bulletins and interviews, presumably in order to restore Authority's battered image or to persuade the paper to become more of an ally; but *Excelsior* was not prepared to pull punches or refrain from criticizing the president, with the result that a union takeover was orchestrated, Scherer García deposed and many journalists driven to leave. The government's presumed role in bringing about the takeover turned into a *cause célèbre*; journalists came to see it as another nail in the coffin of freedom of the press. However, Scherer García and his supporters rose from the ashes and went on to create two new champions of critical freedom in *Unomásuno* and the political weekly *Proceso*, which ever since has been a visible watchdog, known for its investigative journalism. *Excelsior*'s literary review, *Plural*, was closed down. Its editor, Octavio

Paz, together with some other writers from it, launched a new magazine called *Vuelta*, while others started a rival that was concerned more with politics and popular culture; this was *Nexos*, whose first editor was another of the leading cultural commentators of the century, Carlos Monsiváis. Since the death of Octavio Paz in 1998, *Vuelta* has been replaced by *Letras Libres*, directed by Enrique Krause. *Nexos* and *Letras Libres* now represent the views of the left and right wings, respectively, of the cultural establishment. *Excelsior* almost went out of business in the late 1990s, as the old system of government financing began to fall away and readers turned to independent papers.

The late twentieth century was a period of change; communication between journalists improved and some tried to be free of the old forms of patronage that had so compromised the press, but not everyone was ready for change, if change meant loss of privilege. So when President Salinas attempted to do away with government control of access to newsprint, something that had provoked a great deal of criticism in the past, it was the journalists and editors themselves who stood in the way of that initiative. Journalists who have spoken out against corruption in the modern era have faced threats, violence and murder, and many such crimes have gone unpunished. As the quality of journalism improved, it seemed that the risks to journalists increased; powerful figures, whether public or private, were not used to public scrutiny, and they were lashing out. The system of state control has, however, begun to break down, and if there is control, it has to become more subtle, more a matter of 'spin-doctoring'.

In 1993 the family that owns Monterrey's respected *El Norte* started a new national daily called *Reforma*, which has also challenged the 'culture of collusion'; refusing to be compromised by the system, it has been largely dependent on street corner sales, and nonetheless has had a meteoric rise. *Reforma*, and a few other papers, have made efforts to keep the business and editorial sides of their operations separate. In general, as the PRI monolith began to decline the press ethos changed, journalists came to rely less on personal relationships with the powerful and more on building their reputations for exposing political scandal. The press corps is now on the whole more professional, better paid and better educated than it once was.

In many Spanish-American countries the press is dominated by one or two newspapers; not so Mexico, where there has been a plethora, but the result, bearing in mind literacy levels, has been relatively low circulation figures that have encouraged a reliance on political patronage as a way of staying financially viable. Serious Mexican papers do not do well by comparison with editions in Spanish of foreign (usually US) magazines, even less well by comparison with adult comics (*historietas* and *fotonovelas*) and mass-marketed magazines related to radio and television. Something like a third of the country's population is now concentrated in Mexico City, yet even there, only the sports tabloid *Esto* can boast a circulation of 300,000; circulations for the best dailies – *Reforma*, *La Jornada*, and *El Financiero* – run to about 130,000. Among regional papers only Monterrey's *El Norte* has comparable circulation figures.

A tradition of critical graphic art can be traced back to the lampoons of colonial days, one that reaches a high point in the nineteenth century, particularly in the work of José Guadalupe Posada, whose satirical etchings did so much to bring art to the masses. Others kept up the tradition and in modern times it is flourishing in the work of Rius (b. 1934), a pseudonym for Eduardo García del Río, and El Fisgón (b. 1956; Rafael Barajas Durán) and in the healthy sales of *historietas* and *fotonovelas*. In a country whose literacy levels have generally been low it is understandable that this sector of the market has prospered, but cartoons are also a visible part of sophisticated publications. Exaggerated graphic conventions, influenced by Disney, can be seen in *Siempre*, for example, making fun of superpower politics; Mexico City magazines are great masters at using cartoons to satirize the political establishment.

At the beginning of the twentieth century, short comic strips made their appearance in the US, and Mexico came up with its own in *Don Lupito*, which was the work of Andrés Audifred. For the next three decades, Mexican comics more or less aped outside trends and were often simply translations of US originals. In 1936 Germán Oliver Butze started *Los supersabios* and in the following year Gabriel Vargas brought out *La familia burrón*. Adventure strips became even more popular than humorous ones, leading to the comic book in the mid-1930s. Serious publishers such as Grijalbo have brought out comic books; examples are Rius' *Marx para principiantes* (1972) and El Fisgón's *El sexenio me da risa* (1994). In the 1950s Manuel de Landa created the minicomic, which had the advantage of being cheaper. Minicomics such as the best-selling *Lágrimas, risas y amor* come especially from Editorial Argumentos. Romantic stories (*fotonovelas*) told in pictures with captions are the most popular material after comics; these were first imported from Spain. Since the advent of television there have been co-productions of *fotonovelas* and *telenovelas* (the latter – soap-operas – are sometimes called *culebrones*), and for these, Mexico now controls much of the market in both Central America and the Caribbean. There are several types of *fotonovela*. The *fotonovela rosa* tells of poor, innocent women who face rich, evil women in a struggle for the love of rich, cynical men who are torn between base and noble impulses. The *fotonovela suave*, though based on similar scenarios, is more middle-class. The *fotonovela roja* is essentially down-to-earth in theme, its characters rarely have stable jobs, and they tend to be darker-skinned and less prosperous; female sexuality is often portrayed as an irresistible temptation, and so the *fotonovela roja* manages to emphasize the importance of being virtuous and moral while at the same time approaching soft porn. A fourth, more explicitly sex-based type, is the *fotonovela picaresca*; a couple of titles will give an idea of its tenor: *Sexy risas* and *Fiebre de pasiones*.

Developments in electronic media and cinema all came in the wake of the Revolution. We shall now look at radio and television, both of which came to function and be administered in similar ways. In the post-revolutionary era they served a state that, despite the rhetoric, was authoritarian, paternalistic and at bottom capitalist. Government and private interests weighed in, both Mexican and US, with heavy investments that generated large profits; a handful of entrepreneurs took control. While following the US model of organization and programming, accommodations were made to meet the needs of the local market, and so there was an impression that cultural domination from north of the border was being resisted. As in the US, there was a close relationship with the film industry.

The first radio broadcasts in Mexico were in 1921, not long after the invention of radio, but it was some time before there was an adequate infrastructure to take full advantage of this new medium. In that same year there were about seven hundred radio stations in existence in the US, but eight years later there were still only fifteen in Mexico. Significant change came in the 1930s, after Emilio Azcárraga Milmo had launched Radio XEW; Azcárraga would go on to become the most powerful media magnate in the country, creating the Televisa empire. In addition to their predictable concentration in Mexico City, radio stations cropped up in some other regions, but mostly in the north, and particularly in Monterrey. There, a powerful group of entrepreneurs managed to resist the challenges of foreign capital from the US and also keep a degree of independence from the powers of Mexico City. It was from this environment that the Azcárraga family emerged. The fact that media control has been concentrated in these two parts of the country is merely a symptom of their general dominance in Mexican life; rivalry between them is a given.

In 1923 the government established a Department of Radio, but other government agencies also took a hand. It was partly in opposition to government use of the airwaves that interest groups were formed, the first being the Liga de Radiodifusores and the Liga Central Mexicana de Radio. Under the leadership of Azcárraga, these groups eventually became powerful lobbyists: the Asociación Mexicana de Estaciones Radiodifusoras Comerciales (AMERC) and the Cámara Nacional de la Industria de la Radiodifusión y la Televisión (CIRT). There is evidence of an early US incursion into the Mexican market in the shape of Radio CYJ, which was used by General Electric to promote its products. In 1926 a Ley de Comunicaciones was brought in, to govern radio broadcasting.

Programme formats were largely derivative, following the US style and exploiting the popularity of vaudeville. Music was interlaced with adverts and news, which initially gave considerable coverage to official events and ceremonies. In Mexico, radio has always meant competition between commercial and non-commercial stations. According to the critics, commercial interests have had too free a hand and there has been too little broadcasting of quality or of educational value, but paradoxically some of those same critics have also been quick to denounce government involvement in broadcasting. There is no doubt that successive governments had a major role in shaping the development of the media, and their strategies led to the domination of those media by a few people who were closely allied with the interests of the PRI. The goal seems often to have been to limit US interests in the media (but not to lose the advertising revenues), to encourage Mexican entrepreneurs and to make sure the government kept control of broadcasting.

In 1930, another member of the Azcárraga family, Emilio Azcárraga Vidurreta, started Radio XEW, and this soon became the most powerful radio station in the Western Hemisphere. It would be the start of a network of regional affiliates, and in later years the seed for TELEVISA, which for some time almost monopolized the Mexican television industry. The Azcárraga fortune that made this possible had been amassed through dealings with US industry. Thanks also to a timely marriage into a family that controlled French banking resources, Azcárraga was well placed to use his connexions: he secured rights from RCA-Victor, set up a company to sell sheet music, records and sound equipment, and astutely played off US interests against national ones. He managed to satisfy advertisers by using the right programmes to attract a mass audience, and at the same time to keep the government happy by rallying the nation. Commercial interests became regular sponsors of certain programmes, just as in the US: Vicks VapoRub sponsored a talk show called 'La Doctora Corazón', while the Mexican cigarette manufacturer El Aguila underwrote the variety show 'Mi Album Musical'.

In the US, radio drama and comedy became common, but in Mexico music was the core of programming. At peak hours three-quarters of what could be heard was music, increasingly popular music, and much of the time was given over to Mexican songwriters and performers, most of the rest being Latin American. The fact that stations that were not his were much more open to foreign material speaks of the degree to which Azcárraga was hand in glove with the government. He was not the only media magnate at that time, but he was certainly the most powerful one. Azcárraga's empire became the *de facto* guardian of the national interest in broadcasting. By the mid-1940s, Radio Programas de México, Azcárraga's production company, had agreements with half the radio stations in Mexico, and it was distributing taped programmes to affiliates in at least ten other Latin American countries. Some of these tapes were of serialised melodrama – the *radionovela*. This was the other great popular success in programming, apart from music. There have also been many cases of interaction and cross-promotion between different arms of the media; for example, Gamboa's best-selling novel *Santa* generated a theatrical review, a radio drama and several film versions.

Musicians from across the country flocked to the capital city hoping to make their mark, some of them later finding success abroad. Mexican popular music flourished, helping crystallize a national musical culture that encompassed traditional songs, marimba bands and dances such as the *jarabe*. Once obscure and unknown regional *mariachi* bands migrated to the capital, and eventually, in this heyday of radio and cinema, such bands became the very icon of Mexican popular music. Two musical forms became dominant, the *bolero*, a sentimental, romantic ballad, and the *canción ranchera*, whose popularity was much boosted by its key role in cinema's *comedia ranchera*. The *bolero* is often associated with the name of Agustín Lara. The most famous names associated with the *canción ranchera* are Jorge Negrete, Lucha Reyes, Chucho Monge and Lola Beltrán. Lara's controversial music came under fire from conservatives for not being Mexican enough, not to say improper, and they accused him of hastening the death of what they saw as genuinely popular. The *canción ranchera*, on the other hand, tended to be reassuring and make the urban masses feel that the traditions they had known were lasting.

The 1917 constitution had included safeguards against the intrusion of foreign interests and encouraged Mexican entrepreneurship. Moreover, the government made it clear that it intended to influence the media. By the 1930s commercial broadcasters were required to have 30 minutes of government programmes a day, and they had to ensure that at least 25 percent of the music broadcast was Mexican. Commercial channels tended to attract the largest number of listeners; they were no less nationalistic than more highbrow government ones, which broadcast music by the new nationalistic classical composers, such as Carlos Chávez and Silvestre Revueltas, coupled with poetry recitals and lectures.

As elsewhere, when television arrived in many ways it eclipsed radio, but in Mexico radio remains important and the more wide-reaching medium. The role and the management of radio changed with the advent of television, its talk-shows and news programmes grew in importance, and it came to be trusted more than television. As far as the management and evolution of television are concerned, these closely followed radio's precedent, early experiments quickly giving way to uniformity of style and to commercial pressures from US equipment manufacturers. As with radio, US formulae were copied but infused with a Mexican flavour. The Mexican government showed a much closer interest in television than it had radio. After beginning with broadcasts of public events, television then co-opted radio's established stars and programme types, so that there were news, sports, talk and variety shows, and the usual dramatic forms – comedy and melodrama (the *telenovela*). It was all very successful and the Mexican television industry became powerful throughout the Spanish-speaking world.

In 1947 President Alemán set up a commission under the Instituto Nacional de Bellas Artes, charging it with studying how television was being run in other countries and making recommendations for Mexico. The leading technical member of that commission, Enrique González Camarena, favoured following the advertising-dependent US model, while Salvador Novo, a multi-faceted intellectual best known for his plays and poetry, preferred the example of the BBC. González Camarena, a man of considerable influence who had been experimenting with television since the 1930s, even inventing his own colour system, effectively won the argument and in 1949 was appointed technical adviser to a committee set up by the Secretaría de Comunicaciones y Obras Públicas to regulate national television.[22] Perhaps, in commissioning the INBA

22 He had also worked as a technical adviser for Azcárraga.

study, Alemán was simply trying to make sure that his own family had a piece of the cake, and that Azcárraga did not scoff it all; that view would seem to be supported by the fact that the first licence to broadcast went to Rómulo O'Farril, who became Alemán's business partner. XHTV, the first television channel in the country, began in 1950 with a special musical programme broadcast from the Jockey Club of the Hipódromo de las Américas. Soon after, Alemán took the opportunity to address the nation. Azcárraga, in the corporate person of TELEVIMEX, was granted the third licence, and his XEW-TV started in 1951 by transmitting a baseball game; a year later he had TELEVICENTRO, which he inaugurated with a broadcast of professional wrestling.

According to Mejía Barquera, by 1951 only five thousand television sets had been sold to Mexican homes, compared with some ten million in the United States. In 1952, about 40 percent of advertising revenue was going to radio, 30 percent to the press, and for the rest, television was having to compete with other direct forms of advertising. Competition between the television channels was fierce and their financial situation precarious, and so during the 1950s the three negotiated over possible mergers, a process that culminated in 1955 in their merger into Telesistema Mexicano, S.A. (TSM). Azcárraga, O'Farril and González Camarena were to be joint owners, but Azcárraga the chief executive. All operations moved to his TELEVICENTRO. This rationalization produced the hoped-for economies of scale and shared programme costs; it was agreed that the three stations would continue to run, but that they would offer different fare. Eventually each tried to serve the interests of a particular market sector. It was a cost-effective, competition-free arrangement that led to increased profits and expansion of the industry.

In discussing the illustrated press we saw that *historietas* and *fotonovelas* became very widely read. Television soap-operas, *telenovelas*, have also been immensely popular and, just like their printed counterparts, they have been sold all over Latin America and their well-tried formulae have been followed in the products of other countries. The plots tend to be simple enough and their messages obvious. They often deal with the trials and tribulations of the rich. Sometimes the plot hinges on a pivotal discovery affecting the identity of the protagonist. Sometimes the protagonist is born into one social class, raised in another and returns to his true 'home'. *Rosa salvaje*, from the 1980s, exemplifies one common plotline, the one about the young penniless woman whom chance brings into contact with a man who lifts her into a better class. The messages of *telenovelas* are usually black-and-white, a matter of good and evil (humble folk are decent, rich people corrupt, and so forth) but rarely is there any real rocking of the social boat; rather, these *telenovelas* allow viewers to dream and to see how the other half lives. To give an illustration of how popular soaps can be, *Cuna de lobos*, which was transmitted by Televisa in the late 1980s, was watched by about half the population, and it brought the country to a halt on the day when the final episode was aired. There is even a television channel devoted wholly to *telenovelas*.

Direct government involvement in TV began in 1959 and declined in the

1990s. The first venture was Channel 11, whose programming was put under the control of the Instituto Politécnico Nacional; it was initially troubled by limited financing but survived without advertising to provide a valuable service to the country. In addition to buying cultural programmes from Europe it began its own production service, but until 1989 its signal only covered Mexico City. At that time new financial regulations allowed private and government sponsorships, with the result that the signal was strengthened to reach nearby states, and more programmes were produced. The Channel 11 news programme entitled 'Hoy en la Cultura', in particular, is respected in intellectual and artistic circles, and many of this élite audience protested when, in 1992, there was a plan to sell to Imevisión. In a compromise solution, a part of the operation, as Canal 22, was safeguarded by being put under the control of the Consejo Nacional para la Cultura y las Artes (CONACULTA).

In the wake of the 1968 Tlatelolco tragedy, critical decisions were made that changed the face of television. Just as TELEVISA was being formed, President Luis Echeverría challenged Azcárraga's power by making the decision to enter the television field in a serious way and providing an alternative voice. Echeverría hoped to give the government a better image, to make Mexico a leader among developing nations, and to answer the critics who were arguing that government had abandoned its social, cultural and educational obligations by putting control of the media in private hands. Echeverría created a new division of the Secretaría de Comunicaciones y Transporte to oversee broadcasting; there followed attacks on commercialism and violence in the media, and rumours of possible nationalization. The Echeverría government came up with Televisión de la República Mexicana, designed to bring government television to remote rural areas, particularly in the south. There were indeed major developments: for example, by 1976 TRM had a network of about one hundred local stations scattered across the provinces. But there was too heavy a debt incurred in the process, and that, together with mismanagement, left government television in a parlous financial state. With the arrival of President López Portillo in 1976 there was a major overhaul, in the course of which the president's sister was made director of a new governing body for the media, the Dirección de Radio, Televisión, y Cinematografía. The results were disastrous. Policy-making was erratic and programmes suffered; an attempt to appeal to mass audiences and draw viewers away from TELEVISA failed, but perhaps it did do enough to make TELEVISA aware that it needed to cultivate its public relations and image, and to address its social and cultural responsibilities. Under the administration of López Portillo's successor, Miguel de la Madrid, government television operations were once again reorganized. The administration of radio, television and film was separated, and the government's television enterprises, among which there had frequently been tension, were brought together in 1983 under IMEVISION, the Instituto Mexicano de Televisión.

In 1993 President Salinas sold off state-owned television assets. One of these, surprisingly, came to rival TELEVISA; it was called Televisión Azteca, and the buyer, though unrelated to the president, was Ricardo Salinas. TELEVISA now lost its dominance as the provider of nightly news to most Mexicans; now they could watch something other than kowtowing to politicians. Azteca's coverage still favoured the PRI, but it was less deferential and took more risks, such as interviewing Comandante Marcos, the leader of the Chiapas rebels. It was not long before Azteca was drawing almost half the peak-hour viewers, and the competition led to TELEVISA's improving its coverage and changing its style.[23] Nonetheless, the dominant impression left by modern Mexican television is one of low quality, of a television based on noisy and vulgar gameshows, sensationalised news and melodramatic serials.

Given the long history of collusion with the PRI, and despite an evident bias in that party's favour, especially on radio and television, it is reassuring to note that during its reporting of the 2000 presidential election the media made an important contribution by helping to make the process transparent and keeping an eye out for irregularities. But things deteriorated as the race for power became closer, until the person presiding over the Instituto Electoral Federal issued a statement saying that media coverage of presidential candidates was no longer balanced. Once elected, Vicente Fox was quick to act on his election promise that freedom of the press would be respected. Late in 2000, at a conference on the right to information, a code of ethics was drawn up by a panel representing journalists, employers and consumers; nowadays, professional organizations such as the Academia Mexicana de Derechos Humanos, the Centro Nacional de Comunicación Social and the Sociedad de Periodistas are visibly active.

Literature and theatre

Of the many artistic groups that came into existence during the first half of the twentieth century, some had quite an effect on writing. One such was the Ateneo de la Juventud, a group that was founded in 1909 and whose members, like the *modernistas*, helped make creative writing a professional activity. Some *ateneístas* went on to illustrious literary careers after the life of the group as such had run its brief course. Both *modernista* and *ateneísta* authors had been marginalized during the Porfiriato, and to that marginalization they had reacted in different ways, the *modernistas* by withdrawing and the *ateneístas* by becoming activists. Though this activism coincided with the Revolution and though the *ateneístas* generally sympathized with it, at least at the start, they were not political revolutionaries, but rather high-minded intellectuals,

23 Cable television has been available since 1954, consisting almost exclusively of English-language programmes from the US with subtitles in Spanish. Some people naturally see signs of cultural imperialism in this. However, use of cable is relatively limited and the cost is prohibitive for the majority of the population. Cable channels like CNN do provide programmes in Spanish, though most are not directed specifically at the Mexican market.

philosophers and humanists who stood for universal values and were interested in the spiritual side of life. Where they did prove to be revolutionary was in their effect on higher education. Their protests against the positivism that had informed cultural and educational policy under Porfirio were loud and very public. Alfonso Reyes (1899–1959) and Pedro Henríquez Ureña (an expatriate from the Dominican Republic) were the chief literary critics in the group. Another member, Antonio Caso (1883–1946), was something of a polymath but above all a leading philosopher who did much to establish that discipline in Mexico and usher in a later generation of philosophers, which included Samuel Ramos. Some creative writers among the *ateneístas* exploited the essay in their own ways, often mixing fact and fiction; Vasconcelos, the man who was later Minister of Education, was a case in point. Probably the most important of the writers, however, was Martín Luis Guzmán, one of the leading exponents of the novel of the Revolution.

This genre, the novel of the Revolution, amounted to a Mexican version of the regional novel that could be found in Spanish America generally during the twenties and thirties. By the thirties it seemed that the novel of the Mexican Revolution was almost as obligatory in fiction as was Muralism in art. It provided fodder for the films of the golden age of Mexican cinema, and as a literary genre it lasted well beyond the time of the Revolution itself: around the middle of the century Agustín Yáñez published *Al filo del agua* (1946), Rulfo his *magnum opus Pedro Páramo* (1955) and Carlos Fuentes his Boom novel *La muerte de Artemio Cruz* (1962). Novels that deal with the Revolution, at least indirectly, can still be identified in modern times, for example Angeles Mastretta's popular success *Arráncame la vida*. The novel of the Revolution first drew interest because it was an alternative to news reports, and that interest was shown outside Mexico as much as in it. Mariano Azuela's *Los de abajo* (The Underdogs) and Martín Luis Guzmán's *El águila y la serpiente* (The Eagle and the Serpent) are the classic early examples: both their authors were well-educated (Guzmán, as noted above, was an *ateneísta*, Azuela was a doctor of medicine), both works are fictionalized stories based on personal experience and both imply a visceral reaction to the Revolution. Both men sympathized in principle with it, both were in awe of its leaders and joined the bands operating in the northern part of the country, and both came out of the experience disillusioned. Yet their novels are quite different in form and style. Azuela's *Los de abajo* first appeared in instalments in a Texan newspaper in 1915 (in Spanish), and was published as a book in 1924. Guzmán's *El águila y la serpiente* was first published in Spain, in 1928. *Los de abajo* is short, episodic, passionate and staccato, as if trying with its form to capture the atmosphere of conflict. It deals with the activities of a small rebel group from the north, giving no precise dates but enough information to make it clear that we are in 1914 or 1915. The leader of this group of minor landowners is the protagonist, but there is another main character, who is an intellectual ideologue, and it is character contrast rather than plot that is the main focus of a series of powerful, loosely connected episodes. Most of the revolutionaries die violently, the ideologue shows that he is a hypocrite and the leader goes home to die a symbolic death. Guzmán is less heavy-handed than Azuela in dealing with similar subject matter. Instead of an unknown leader, Guzmán focuses on the notorious *caudillos*: *El águila y la serpiente* shows Guzmán's ambivalence vis-à-vis Pancho Villa, while Venustiano Carranza is faulted for his greed and ambition. What this novel lacks in drama it makes up for with elegance of style and cool analysis. It is more detached and far longer than *Los de abajo*, but also episodic in structure. Guzmán continued throughout the 1930s and 1940s to work on Villa, publishing a fictionalized biography in *Memorias de Pancho Villa* and a political novel, *La sombra del caudillo* (1929), which deals with the background to the assassination of General Obregón, an act of betrayal that has come to epitomize the corruption of the Revolution.[24]

The episodic format was now imitated by many others; it was as if the Revolution were too chaotic and unmanageable to be told otherwise. Two of the best works are also concerned with the north and with Pancho Villa; these are by Rafael Muñoz and Nellie Campobello. Muñoz's *Vámonos con Pancho Villa* (Let's Ride with Pancho Villa) portrays the excitement of the Revolution and the attraction of Villa's charismatic figure, but it leads to a sad outcome: six country boys who sign up with Villa meet their end. In her memoirs, *Cartucho* (1931) and *Las manos de mamá* (1937), Campobello provides anecdotes and vignettes grouped around three topics: 'Men of the North', 'Victims of Execution' and 'Under Fire'. These are told with the candour and innocence of a young girl, and in the first person, but they also give an idea of the views and feelings of the adults who were with her. Campobello was one of few women writing at the time.

The literary champion of the rebellion in the south, which was much more of a peasant revolt and did not decline so dramatically into violence and banditry, was Gregorio López y Fuentes. He wrote novels focusing on groups rather than individuals, novels that were of indifferent quality but strong on message, including *Campamento* (1931), *Tierra* (1932) and *El indio* (1935). Here was another author who used the episodic structure. The unifying element in *Campamento* is a group of people who come together one night, in *Tierra* it is an *hacienda* and in *El indio*, as the title indicates, the Indian community. Though direct treatments of the Revolution's armed phase dried up by the mid-1930s, this last novel heralded later expressions of concern about the plight of the Indians. Mauricio Magdaleno's *El resplandor* (1937) makes a more sophisticated contribution to *indigenista* writing, mystifying the Indians but also delving into psychology.

In theatre, the early part of the century had seen a number of developments that helped consolidate the sort of infrastructure that few Spanish American

[24] That same event also inspired Rodolfo Usigli's play, *El gesticulador* (censored by government officials for a number of years). Indeed, when a film version of Guzmán's novel was finally made in 1960, it suffered from government censorship for the next thirty years.

countries enjoy. However, it must be said that Mexican theatrical history has been a tale of ups and downs, a history fraught with financial and political difficulties, and that evidence of its continuing woes is not hard to find. In the early years of the century there were initiatives designed to consolidate healthy theatre and secure its infrastructure. For example, in 1919 the government founded the Teatro Folklórico with the explicit mission of providing popular theatre based on indigenous themes. That was followed by the Teatro de Murciélago (1924), whose repertoire was predominantly one of lyrical, folkloric indigenous rituals. Thirdly, the Secretaría de Educación Pública established a touring company in 1929 called Teatro del Periquillo, to take theatre out into the provinces. Provincial theatre now took on an especially vital character in Yucatán, where there was in any case a tradition of Mayan theatre. During the second decade of the century theatre activity in Yucatán reached such a level that Mérida came to have more theatres than Mexico City.

In contrast with the indigenous and social biases of such companies, a group that came to be called the 'Grupo de los Siete' tried to foster serious cosmopolitan theatre; their nickname, revealingly, was 'The Pirandellos'. Invoking not only the Italian example but also people like Chekhov and Strindberg, they produced a convincing manifesto, but not very much in the way of plays; however, they were an important counterbalance to the government-sponsored ethos. In 1923 some of them helped establish the Unión de Autores Dramáticos. The main writers among the Seven were José Joaquín Gamboa and Víctor Manuel Díez Barroso. Díez Barroso was the most productive; he wrote about psychological states, playing with theatrical techniques and perspectives; among his best plays are *Véncete a ti mismo* (Overcome Yourself, 1925) and *El y su cuerpo* (He and His Body, 1934). Francisco Monterde, another member of the group, also wrote plays but distinguished himself for his efforts to promote the theatre, as a critic, an historian, a teacher and as president of the Academia Mexicana de la Lengua. Another Mexico City-based theatre company during the 1930s was called Teatro de Ahora, led by Mauricio Magdaleno and Juan Bustillo Oro, both of whom went on to careers in the film industry. A play by Bustillo that deserves comment is *San Miguel de las Espinas: Trilogía dramática de un pedazo de tierra mexicana* (San Miguel de las Espinas: a Trilogy about a Mexican Plot of Land, 1933). Like many of the plays from this group, this is a piece of social realism with a message, but it is remarkable for its grand scale, its very conscious theatricality and the inventiveness of its technique.

There were two major and somewhat dissimilar literary groups that took shape, the *Estridentistas*, who in typical vanguard fashion set out to marry socialism, literature and technological progress, and the *Contemporáneos*, who favoured no particular ideology. *Estridentista* authors published manifestos and produced some poetry and novellas, whose primary effect was to shock. Manuel Maples Arce (1900–81) was the founding father. *Estridentismo* was quite ephemeral: from the point of view of the social realists its authors were too arcane and from that of more cosmopolitan people they were too naïvely proletarian, even strident. However, Maples Arce's poems in *Urbe* (1924) were well-received and were translated by the American novelist John Dos Passos. The *Contemporáneos* were far less programmatic, championing the kind of cosmopolitan literary culture espoused by the *Modernistas*, but also showing respect for the social benefits of a humane culture. Several of the members of the *Contemporáneos* group worked under Vasconcelos; Jaime Torres Bodet is an example, being at the Ministry of Education for many years.

This was the era when mural painting and the indigenist music of Carlos Chávez were in the public eye and ear; Mexico was actively constructing an image of its national culture. The *Contemporáneos* thought of themselves as directly opposed to the flashy nationalism of people like Rivera, whose work they found patronizing, and instead they combined affectation with bohemianism; indeed, some people thought them dangerously effeminate. For one thing, they were against the macho image of the revolutionary hero. The *Contemporáneos* were individualistic intellectuals, most of whom, having grown up with the Revolution's chaos and witnessed the disillusionment that followed it, were sceptical about social reforms. They preferred more aesthetic pursuits and put most of their energy into producing magazines, including the one that bore their name and appeared from 1928 to 1931. In that magazine their work appeared together with that of major international figures of all persuasions. Among the *Contemporáneos* Carlos Pellicer was one of the leading poets, Jorge Cuesta channelled his energy into the voluminous *Poemas y ensayos* (1964 and 1981), while theatre was the tramping ground for Xavier Villaurrutia, along with Salvador Novo and Celestino Gorostiza. Some of the writers produced novels that were more psychological, more of an aesthetic construct than a social tract. A good example is Torres Bodet's *Primero de enero* (1934). 'Canto a un dios mineral' (1942), by Cuesta, and 'Muerte sin fin' (1939), by José Gorostiza, are also key representative works of the *Contemporáneos*. 'Muerte sin fin' is transparent and readable, but 'Canto a un dios mineral' seems almost incomprehensible, pushing language to its limits. Some critics think that Villaurrutia's poems in *Nostalgia de la muerte* (1938) are better because they have something of the surrealistic character of much *Contemporáneos* poetry, but avoid its worst excesses.

The development of theatre was further influenced by Ulises, a group founded by Salvador Novo and Xavier Villaurrutia; they and others in the group, such as Gilberto Owen and Celestino Gorostiza, were members of the *Contemporáneos*. Their theatre was provocative, unconventional, disrespectful and a little arrogant. Although Ulises itself did not last long, many of those involved in it went on to involvement with Gorostiza's government-backed company Teatro de Orientación (1932–38), which slowly built up a significant following for its highbrow theatre. The repertoire expanded; there was more experimentation and they looked abroad and to the future, rather than homewards and to the past. Translations of foreign plays (Sophocles, Shaw,

Shakespeare, Chekhov) gave way to original plays, such as Villaurrutia's *Parece mentira* and *¿En qué piensas?* After Gorostiza had moved on to run Bellas Artes, Teatro de Orientación was left in the hands of Villaurrutia, Rodolfo Usigli and Julio Bracho. During the 1930s Bracho, who was also a filmmaker, had founded his own companies, with a more Mexican orientation: Escolares del Teatro, Trabajadores del Teatro and Teatro de la Universidad. Experimentalism, however, did not provide a good living so, while these people did keep quality alive, in an era of crass commercialism they found themselves having to turn to the kind of realism they preferred to avoid.

Witness the theatre of Villaurrutia (1902–50), whose works of the 1940s were intended for the commercial theatre and were less aggressively experimental than others he wrote. Among his most important early experimental works were *Parece mentira* (Whoever Would Believe It?) and *¿En qué piensas?* (What Are You Thinking About?). The first of these is a humorous play with a realistic setting but it is full of unknowns; even the characters are anonymous types. Villaurrutia suggests here that the conventions and suppositions of ordinary life are volatile and untrustworthy, perhaps anticipating later intellectual preoccupations with the status of language. *Invitación a la muerte*, written in 1940 but not premièred until 1947, is a personal, Mexican adaptation of *Hamlet* that explores the idea of the double, and deals with incest, things that would reappear in Villaurrutia's comedies *El pobre barba azul* (1947) and *La tragedia de la equivocaciones* (1950). Gorostiza (1904–67) said that Villaurrutia's characters led 'mathematical lives'.[25] Like Villaurrutia's, his own theatre evolves from avant-garde experimentalism to realism. *El nuevo paraíso* (The New Paradise, 1930) portrays Adam and Eve as victims of convention and self-deceit; *La escuela del amor* (The School of Love, 1933) centres on a group of people who take refuge in dreams and illusions because they cannot deal with reality; *Ser o no ser* (To Be or Not to Be, 1934) is another development of the Faust theme. Gorostiza struck a sensitive vein in the Mexican psyche with a box-office hit in 1952, *El color de nuestra piel* (The Colour of Our Skin); though quite a conventionally conceived drama, it deals with a *mestizo* family who try to hide their ancestry, only to become victims of their own kind of prejudice. He would become increasingly didactic in his later plays. Like others of his generation he also dealt with indigenous themes, particularly in his last, somewhat melodramatic *La Malinche* (1958): Cortés is helped to overcome mere greed by the higher moral qualities displayed by Malinche. Gorostiza was a director and promoter of theatre who occupied some influential posts, not least that of director of the Instituto de Bellas Artes, as mentioned. He it was who invited the US dancer and choreographer Waldeen to create Mexico's first modern dance company, the Ballet de Bellas Artes.

Villaurrutia's friend Salvador Novo (1904–74) was another poet turned dramatist. Novo was a great deal besides: translator, theatre director, writer

25 'El teatro de Xavier Villaurrutia', in *Cuadernos Americanos*, XI, 2 (1952).

about society and even official chronicler of the capital (under President Díaz Ordaz), winner of the Premio Nacional de Letras, and in charge of theatre at Bellas Artes. Villaurrutia would step from reality into the area of the personal; Novo preferred satire and later turned to classical and pre-Hispanic matters. Novo's *Divorcio* (1924) claims to be in the style of Ibsen but is so only in its subject matter; it makes fun of social and theatrical conventions in an avant-garde manner. *El tercer Fausto* (The Third Faust) is an early play, like *Divorcio*, but publication was delayed because Novo felt that Mexico was not ready for it at the time; its protagonist appeals to the Devil for help in becoming a woman because he is in love with his male friend; after the change, however, it turns out that the male friend is in love with the original (male) protagonist. After a twenty-five year hiatus starting in 1924 Novo came back to writing for the theatre, as did Gorostiza. Novo now wrote brief, sardonic and anachronistic *Diálogos* involving people such as Adam and Eve, Sor Juana and Malinche, but *La culta dama* (1951) is a full-length work of social criticism, and quite realistic in style. His work began to show signs of the influence of the structure of Greek tragedy, and the style of Anglo-American drama, and he became more of a sceptic. In *Yocasta, o casi* (Yocasta, Well Almost, 1961) he writes: 'La gente no advierte hasta qué punto todos los mitos siguen vivos, latentes, reiterados como la corriente metálica y subterránea de nuestra cotidiana vulgaridad.' (People don't realize how far all those myths are still alive, latent, reiterated in the underground, metallic current of our daily commonness.)[26] *Cuauhtémoc* (1962) marks a turn towards indigenous themes. Novo even wrote a comic opera first performed in 1972, not long before his death: *In Ticitezcatl o El espejo encantado* (The Enchanted Mirror) is a parody of a Greek-style tragedy set in Teotihuacan; it has an anachronistic cast of tourists and Indian deities and the rhyming language is preposterous.

On the fringe of Ulises and Teatro de Orientación was to be found the most distinguished of modern Mexico's dramatists, Rodolfo Usigli, whose plays are more varied and much better-known outside the country than are those of his contemporaries. Drawing on the examples of Ibsen and Shaw, Usigli considers the flaws and contradictions of human nature; in fact one of his most famous plays, *El gesticulador* (The Impersonator, 1937), shows the influence of the Norwegian. This satire on politics proved to be such sensitive material that Usigli had to wait ten years before seeing it performed. The problem was that the Partido Revolucionario Institucional assumed it was the target of criticism (after all, the play does speak of compromised ideals), but in fact the target is a broader one that encompasses corruption, personal relationships, and various kinds of deception. This was not the only case of censorship weighing in on Usigli. *Corona de sombra* (Crown of Shadow, written in 1943), his most celebrated play, was closed down only two nights after its première in 1947. It deals with the brief reign of Maximilian and is one of three Usigli plays to focus on

26 *Yocasta, o casi* (Mexico City: Los Textos de la Capilla, III, 1961), p. 118.

significant periods in the history of Mexico. Usigli presents *Corona de sombra* as an 'antihistory' and says his aim is to explore how certain historical moments have contributed to shaping the national consciousness. Sandwiched between scenes that occur in the Brussels of 1927, as Carlota nears her death, is Mexico under Maximilian. The set is divided in such a way that, as the actors cross the stage, they pass from one time frame to another. The other crowns in the trilogy, *Corona de fuego* and *Corona de luz*, deal respectively with the conquest and with the appearance of the Virgen de Guadalupe. By contrast, *Noche de estío* (Midsummer Night, 1933), is one of what Usigli called 'three impolitic comedies'. For all his denials that these comedies were based on real people and events, *Noche de estío* obviously alludes to the presidency of Plutarco Elías Calles. In fact, scarcely anyone emerges unscathed from this particular piece of buffoonery. Another farce is *La mujer no hace milagros* (Women Don't Perform Miracles, 1939), a play full of stock misunderstandings and heavy-handed jokes, that comes complete with clowns and dimwitted lovers. After the Second World War social criticism was more visible in Usigli's plays. *La exposición* (1955) is about art exhibitions but also exposes the foibles of the art world in Mexico. Driven by the events of 1968, Usigli wrote *Buenos días, señor Presidente* (1972), but his vision there is of a future in which young people take over and then turn to fruitless in-fighting.

Like Novo, who was his friend until they had a falling out, Usigli was more than just a dramatist and did a great deal to encourage theatre. One person who studied under him was Luisa Josefina Hernández (b. 1928). A teacher at the Universidad Nacional Autónoma and a writer of thirteen novels, she is nonetheless known for her thirty-odd plays, which concern human relationships, social injustice, and mysticism. Emilio Carballido, a Novo protégé, was to become a prolific dramatist, capable of writing anything from allegory to farce. *Un pequeño día de ira* (A Small Day of Wrath, 1962), a play about provincial life, won him the Casa de las Américas prize. *El relojero de Córdoba* (The Clockmaker of Cordoba, 1960) is a farce on a colonial theme, and *Medusa* (1960) is based on mythology. *El censo* (The Census) was written expressly for the working-class audience at the theatres of the Social Security Administration and is a piece of social realism; *Yo también hablo de la rosa* (I, Too, Speak of the Rose, 1966) is a piece of metatheatre. If there is a unifying thematic thread in all this it is probably Carballido's condemnation of falseness and his respect for spontaneity and creativity.

Not even playwrights as good as these could stave off a mid-century slump as the theatregoing public's appetite turned to foreign works, flashy spectacles and melodrama. There were personal tensions and political difficulties, and commercialism was again taking its toll on serious theatre, which went through another lean period before there were signs of new life in the 1970s, thanks in part to the tutelage of Hernández, Leñero and Carballido. And yet the new generation of dramatists seemed often to be at pains to reject both parents and teachers. We shall return to the theatre shortly, after considering some mid-century developments in other genres.

The 1940s had seen the end of the presidency of Lázaro Cárdenas and the start of a style of government that encouraged modernization by means of capitalism. Before then, the Revolution had seemed to demand that writers take a visceral, partisan stance; now they no longer found themselves driven into adopting ideological postures, and aesthetic aims seemed more compatible with social concerns. But it also became evident that idealism had given way to disillusionment as institutional stability and corruption became facts of life. Many intellectuals also reacted against the Americanisation of the 1940s, believing that it was undermining national values. Also indicative of these changing times was the publication of works that attempted to deal with the 'filosofía de lo mexicano'. Among these, the two most famous were by Samuel Ramos and Octavio Paz. Ramos had published *El perfil del hombre y la cultura en México* in 1934, criticizing the nation's provincialism and cultural dependence and controversially talking of a Mexican inferiority complex. Paz was more ready than was Ramos to embrace the popular culture. In his much-quoted meditation *El laberinto de la soledad* (1950 and 1959), he suggested that the solitude that characterized Mexico distinguished it from its powerful neighbour to the north and he argued that the true heritage of Mexico was one of repeated cycles of conquest and violence. Whereas others tended to see assimilation of the Indian into the process of modernization and 'westernization' as the only way forward, Guillermo Bonfil Batalla, an anthropologist, spoke of a 'México profundo', a 'deep Mexico' that was comprosed of the Indians, the *mestizos* and the urban poor, all of whom had a heritage that was essentially Mesoamerican. In later years the key works of the 'filosofía de lo mexicano' were attacked by writers such as Roger Bartra, for their sweeping generalizations and speculations, and it was suggested that they served to bolster stereotypical ideas of what Mexicans were.

In a different vein, Rosario Castellanos (1925–74) is one of the most engaging figures to emerge at about this time. She was born in Mexico City to rich landowning parents but grew up in Chiapas, in the care of an Indian nanny, an experience that is crucial for her largely autobiographical novel *Balún Canán* (1957). There she sympathetically describes the life of Indians and deals with the question of land rights, a fact that is particularly interesting when one bears in mind that her own family had lost land following the Cárdenas policies of redistribution. Castellanos' parents favoured her younger brother over her. These things help explain her interest as a writer in two aspects of a shared problem: ethnic and gender discrimination. Castellanos' technique was basically a realistic one but *Balún Canán* has some interesting structural features too; it is also valuable as a reflection of the sort of conditions that led to the Chiapas uprising some forty years later. Another important contribution to indigenist writing is Castellanos' *Oficio de tinieblas* (1962), where her portrayal of Indian ways is almost ethnographic, and yet she manages to give her characters individuality and psychological depth. The position of women is the subject of the essays in *Mujer que sabe latín* (1971) and of her play *El eterno femenino*

(1975), while the title of her poetry collection *Poesía no eres tú* (1972) implies a deliberate rejection of the sugary romanticism of Bécquer. Much of her work reflects the bitterness of her struggle for intellectual respectability; the famous short story 'Lección de cocina', for example, portrays an intelligent woman trying to get to grips with the expectations placed upon her by society and marriage, but it is laced with irony and self-awareness, and its protagonist knows that she cannot simply blame her woes on others. The voice of Rosario Castellanos is an intelligent one that has found sympathetic ears among feminist critics of our time. Her essay 'La liberación del amor' (1972), however, is a merciless attack on the superficiality of feminism. Although she was quite successful in her time, her life was marred by a good deal of unhappiness and it ended with an accident that took place in Israel, where she was her country's ambassador.

While a number of significant poets emerged during the 1940s and 1950s, Castellanos among them, none can compare with Octavio Paz (1914–98); indeed, no writer in modern times can do so. Paz, thanks in part to his Nobel Prize, awarded in 1990, has in a sense come to stand for modern Mexican literature and criticism. However, his international visibility has had the effect of isolating him from other Mexican writers and inevitably his influence has declined over the years. Paz was a prolific and chameleonic writer over a period of some seventy years, one whose formative experiences were the Spanish Civil War and the period following the Second World War, with its Stalinist purges. In this he was not alone, since many intellectuals of the time were deeply influenced by these events. In 1937, along with Neruda and other prominent Latin American writers, Paz attended the anti-fascist writers' conference that took place in Spain, in Valencia. He recalls that experience, his disquiet at the doctrinaire attitude of several leading figures and his horror at the way in which André Gide was excoriated during the proceedings, in *Itinerario* (1993), an account of Paz's political evolution.

He was always primarily a poet, even if he is better known for his essays. For Paz, poetry was a transcendental art; in composing it he drew on a huge range of sources, including Surrealism, the classics, the Mexican tradition, pre-Hispanic civilizations and oriental philosophy. At first, he defined himself in contrast to the *Contemporáneos*, who were perceived as an apolitical group; in the 1930s he produced poems committed to international socialist and revolutionary causes. But that was a relatively shortlived phase, and significantly, almost all the early political poetry was eliminated from editions of his 'complete' poetic works; one of few such poems to survive is called 'Elegía a un compañero muerto en el frente'. Paz's interest had shifted to the power and potential of language, and despite his repeated references to worldly elements – earth, wind, water and fire – he was essentially an idealist, a visionary. In his view it is through words that the mystery of life can be explored and harmony with creation achieved. Thus the title of *Libertad bajo palabra* (1949, 1960, 1968), one of his most important collections, suggests that by means of the word one can transcend the awfulness of reality. Paz delights in abstraction and reduction, in oppositions and paradoxes.[27] In two of his most famous poems 'Piedra de sol' (1957) and 'Himno entre ruinas' (1949), both of which appeared in what is perhaps his crowning poetic achievement, *La estación violenta* (1958), he is elusive and haunting. 'Himno . . .' speaks of a mystical instant when the sun is at its peak and reality is perceived in all its stark significance. The poet looks back through the ravages of history; now a new ritual is in progress on the top of the pyramid at Teotihuacan, involving a group of guitar-wielding, marihuana-smoking youths. 'Piedra . . .' is based on numerical principles from pre-Hispanic cosmology, with the last verse repeating the first, as if to set the cycle in motion again. In his later works Paz can be earthy, hermetic and boldly experimental. *Ladera este* (1969) reflects the influence of his encounter with India, where he was ambassador until his resignation at the time of the Tlatelolco massacre.

Paz was by no means the only prominent intellectual to protest over Tlatelolco, but José Revueltas, long a political activist and Communist Party member, became its most visible martyr, and his imprisonment for having been one of the organizers of the 1968 demonstration provoked loud protests at home and abroad. Yet Paz's resignation received greater attention because of his reputation: Paz was the cosmopolitan intellectual, in some ways an establishment figure. Revueltas by comparison was marginal, and thus he became a countercultural hero.

Revueltas was to be one of the writers who most influenced the development of the novel, together with the more respectable Agustín Yáñez. These writers managed to deal with what was characteristically Mexican without giving in to stereotypes; they added psychological depth to their characters without losing sight of the broad historical context. Revueltas' siblings included an actress, Rosaura, a muralist, Fermín and a composer, Silvestre, much the most famous of the three outside Mexico. But at home José is something of a modern legend. His works are based on an unusual amalgam of Christianity, utopianism and Marxism, but also show his interest in human will and his personal despair at the imperfections of society. Critics complain about his longwinded moralizing; they also find him self-contradictory and heavy-handed, too often tempted to overstep the mark. His first novel, *Los muros de agua* (Walls of Water, 1941) is based on his own experience and concerns the fate of a group of political prisoners, and in his last, *El apando* (Solitary, 1969) he treads similar ground, dealing with human degradation in prison. *El luto humano* (Human Mourning, 1943) brought him greater critical acclaim than his first novel; using flashbacks and interior monologues it seems to be in search of Mexico's soul, at once denouncing social injustices and seeking redemption. Though often said to be his best novel, *Los días terrenales* (Life on This Earth, 1949) was unavailable

27 His account of his poetics can be found in *El arco y la lira* (1956).

for many years because Revueltas himself went round removing it from bookshops after it had been criticized by the Party.

In 1947 Yáñez, who by contrast was a respectable bureaucrat, published one of the most important novels to appear before the Boom period, *Al filo del agua* (The Edge of the Storm, 1947). In it he brought a new level of sophistication to the genre in Mexico, both in terms of technique and of social analysis. Set in pre-revolutionary days, this novel explores the morals and the social dynamics of a closed provincial community whose self-satisfied ways are gradually affected by contact with the outside world. Yáñez plays with time, point of view and allegory, dipping into the minds of his characters by means of interior monologue and stream of consciousness. Subsequent novels of his include *La creación* (Creation, 1959) and *Las vueltas del tiempo* (The Twists of Time, 1973).

Other leading lights of the 1950s were Rulfo, Arreola and Garro, not to mention Carlos Fuentes. Juan Rulfo and Juan José Arreola were both from Jalisco, both were perfectionists, and neither wrote much. Arreola revised and regrouped his fictions over the years – witty, philosophical and sometimes whacky pieces that were often very brief, although he did also publish a short novel. Known too as an actor (he spent some time with the Comédie Française), he held workshops for aspiring writers, and also hosted a culture programme on television. Important works of his are *Varia invención* (1949) and *Confabulario total* (1962), one of several 'Confabulations' that he published as he revised and augmented his collected short fictions. They are not easy to characterize, largely because of their variety: some are merely playful, others satirize technology and commercialism, some wax philosophical, some deal with human relationships. One can perhaps see hints of Cortázar and Borges in them, and of Monterroso, to compare a writer closer to home.

Whereas Arreola was a visible, social being, and one with a fine sense of humour, Rulfo was a gloomy introvert whose secretive ways generated an aura of mystery. He first worked selling tyres, then as a bureaucrat at the Instituto Nacional de Antropología e Historia, and these jobs helped him become more closely acquainted with provincial life. Rulfo's complete works consist of a short collection of stories, a short novel and a filmscript, the first two being the most significant. He spoke for years of another novel in preparation (his working title for it was *La cordillera*), but it never materialized. *Pedro Páramo*, the published novel and *El llano en llamas*, the collection of stories, both portray the harsh realities of peasant life in dry lands during the post-revolutionary period. The stories are spare, elliptical and joyless. The novel, while hardly more upbeat, is structurally interesting, challenging the reader with several narrative voices (which speak from the grave, as he discovers only halfway through), and giving distinctly Mexican subject matter a universal dimension. It is set during the Cristero Rebellion (1926–28), a violent backlash against government anticlericalism, and it portrays a downtrodden rural community dominated by a ruthless landowner and let down by religion. This novella and to a lesser extent the stories are the basis for Rulfo's reputation as a crucial figure in the development of fiction; in the novel his narrative technique and style invite comparisons with writers of the Boom.

Josefina Vicens was in some ways like Rulfo – lonely, laconic, the author of a couple of respected works, both of them brooding and metafictional. That said, she does not enjoy the same prominence and indeed those novels, *El libro vacío* (The Empty Book, 1958) and *Los años falsos* (False Years, 1982) are not widely known. Much better known is Elena Garro, whose acclaimed novel *Los recuerdos del porvenir* (Recollection of Things to Come, 1963) is acknowledged by García Márquez to have been an influence upon him. Furthermore it has a certain amount in common with *Pedro Páramo*. Somewhat like Rulfo's novel, this one is set in an imaginary small town during the Cristero Rebellion. It is concerned with the different fates of two women who live in this stiflingly conservative and macho society, the tale being enriched by the use of sophisticated techniques, which include a collective narratorial voice (the town) and much playing with point of view and time; historical reality is juxtaposed with myth, rather as one finds in the works of Fuentes. This is undoubtedly a fine piece of literature, but Garro is at least as famous for her public attacks on her former husband, Octavio Paz.

If Paz is the towering poet and essayist of the twentieth century, then Carlos Fuentes (born in 1928) is the towering novelist, his success assured by the consecration of his *La muerte de Artemio Cruz* as one of the key novels of the Boom of the 1960s.[28] Paz was already established by the time Fuentes' reputation grew, and the works that made Fuentes famous are entirely in tune with Paz's thinking as expressed in the seminal *El laberinto de la soledad*. Both men acquired stellar international reputations, and so it was perhaps inevitable, though a little ironic, that they became rivals, even antagonists. Sometimes it has seemed that their supporters have been more at odds with each other than have the two writers themselves, and generally the whole business has smacked of envy, disloyalty and petty-mindedness, things that are not unknown on the Mexican cultural scene.

Carlos Fuentes had a comfortable, cosmopolitan upbringing that equipped him to move with ease from one culture to another. Having lived and studied in several countries and being from a family of diplomats, he is fluent in French and English. He himself was once a diplomat in Switzerland and France. His short stories in *Los días enmascarados* (The Masked Days, 1954), provide early evidence of the use of a blend of the historical and the mythical to interpret history that would become Fuentes' trademark in later years. His first novel, *La región más transparente* (Where the Air is Clear, 1958), applies elements of the mythical past to an understanding of present-day realities in Mexico City, and in that book he deploys several techniques: allegory, symbolism, interior monologue, fragmented time, metaphor, and vivid visual imagery. One of Paz's acolytes, Enrique Krause, seized on Fuentes' narrative panoply as justification

28 Fuentes is a nephew of the film director Fernando de Fuentes.

for calling his fiction showy and insubstantial. In *La muerte de Artemio Cruz* (The Death of Artemio Cruz, 1962), Fuentes traces the history of Mexico from the latter part of the nineteenth to the mid-twentieth century, concentrating especially on the period of the Mexican Revolution. The most important moments in the life of Artemio are reviewed over the course of the twelve hours prior to his death. Here are the triumphs and failures of the Revolution, and here the lost ideals. These, as we have seen, are topics that had been rehearsed *ad nauseam* in the works of the novelists of the Revolution; what is different in this novel is the narrative strategy. First-, second- or third-person narratives respectively tell of the narrator's thoughts in the present, the future, and the past. In the yet more adventurous and metafictional *Cambio de piel* (A Change of Skin, 1967) Fuentes lays a present reality beside others from different times and places, and point of view shifts with ease; it could be said that the novel's structure reflects the human struggle to make sense of the absurd and the tragic. But it is *Terra Nostra* (1975) that most critics see as his masterpiece, a big book in every sense. In it Fuentes once again takes liberties with historical chronology as he juxtaposes European and Mexican history and myth in an account that encompasses two continents and some seven centuries. The protagonist, Señor Don Felipe, is building the El Escorial palace; this is not Philip II but a fictional amalgam of several early colonial monarchs who epitomizes the rigid intolerance of imperial Spain. Fuentes has published plays that also aim to understand Hispanic culture on both sides of the ocean, the best-known being *Todos los gatos son pardos* (All Cats Are Grey, 1970), about the encounter between Cortés and Montezuma, mediated by Malinche. Thereafter Fuentes shifted his focus to the relationship between Mexico and the United States, in *Gringo viejo* and especially *Cristóbal Nonato* (Christopher Unborn, 1987). In the latter, which, like many works before it, is a very self-conscious piece of fiction, gone is the 'suave patria' of which López Velarde wrote. In its place there is a filthy, polluted and degraded land that has lost or squandered its natural resources, is mired in foreign debt, has a government that diverts attention from the truth and a population that speaks not Spanglish but 'Anglatl', rather as if the Hispanic input has been brushed aside.

Two prominent groups in the 1960s were *Onda* and *Escritura*, whose names came from a publication entitled *Onda y escritura en México*. Neither group had much time for the nationalistic preoccupations of earlier generations, but it could be said that *Onda* was, thematically at least, a little closer to the realities of contemporary life. The *Escritura* group consisted largely of people born in the 1920s and 1930s, many of them protégés of Octavio Paz, who in the 1960s found themselves collaborating on a number of significant literary journals, particularly the *Revista de la Universidad de México*, and the *Revista Mexicana de Literatura*. They are sometimes known as the *Revista Mexicana de Literatura* group. Their emphasis was philosophical, writerly, highbrow and experimental. Both Paz and Fuentes were associated with *Escritura*, which the rival group declared was dominated by a literary mafia that controlled access to publication and limited opportunities for other writers; Luis Guillermo Piazza went so far as to thematize this in a novel about the politics and personalities of the 1960s literary scene.

The *Onda* group, on the other hand, was full of young upstarts whose works often reflected the language and lifestyle of young city-dwellers. While the *Onda* fiction writers were happy to exploit the techniques that had become so characteristic of the Boom – point of view, narrative voice, temporal displacements, and so on – they were open to popular culture as well. These were noisy and irreverent writers who were in tune with the protest movements of the 1960s, the anti-war movement, the drug culture and the sexual revolution.

Salvador Elizondo (b. 1932) had immense success with his first and most important novel, *Farabeuf* (1965). It is a technical *tour de force*, a Mexican *nouveau roman* that involves violent, erotic and arcane practices. After that novel Elizondo's work became still more experimental, impenetrable and somewhat sterile, but it always kept its cult following. As a novelist, Juan García Ponce (1932–2003) steadfastly pursued a mystic quest for a new morality. He was a fine essayist, and much involved with art criticism. He and Elizondo were once thought shocking, but their notoriety faded as others took centrestage. Sergio Pitol (b. 1933), who first became popular in Spain, returned to Mexico after some years in the diplomatic service in Europe and then took off as a writer. Among his works are the self-conscious *El tañido de una flauta* (The Sound of the Flute, 1972), *El desfile del amor* (1984; The Parade of Love) and *Domar a la divina garza* (To Tame the Divine Heron, 1987), into which he introduces elements from detective fiction. José Agustín (b. 1944) and Gustavo Sainz (b. 1940) created even more of a furore in the 1960s, and their works sold well. Sainz's first novel, *Gazapo* (Tall Tale, 1965) made such an initial impression that it was promptly reprinted and translated into several languages. In *Gazapo* the troubled world of the adolescent is portrayed through recorded conversations, letters, diaries and telephone calls, the tape-recorder serving as the means whereby the protagonist reinvents the past, escapes the restrictions of the present, and explores his fantasies. The structure is fragmentary, the language strikingly varied. Colloquial language also is prominent in Agustín's *La tumba* (The Tomb, 1964) and *De perfil* (In Profile, 1966), which reflect the frustrations of youth and attack class values. Agustín also published three provocative, experimental plays, including *Abolición de la propiedad* (Abolition of Property, 1969). In an entertaining story called '¿Cuál es la onda' (What's up?, in *Inventando que sueño*, 1968), he revels in wordplay, free associations and references to pop culture, in what is arguably the text that best epitomizes *Onda* writing. That writing is, as the current American expression goes, 'full of attitude', so some people have dismissed it as immature. Agustín's *Se está haciendo tarde (final en laguna)* (It's Getting Late [Blank Ending], 1973) serves as an epitaph to the *Onda* generation; while both he and Sainz carried on publishing, they never matched the impact of their early works.

Other significant writers of the 1960s and 1079s were Vicente Leñero, Jorge Ibargüengoitia and Fernando del Paso. Del Paso (b. 1935), who lived in England for several years and worked for a while at the BBC, kept his distance from the literary world of Mexico City, though he is sometimes thought of as one of the *Onda* writers, largely because of his irreverent style. Since his works are large-scale and quite complex, he has as much in common with writers of the Boom. *Palinuro de México* (1975) is a comic and erotic compendium of episodes in which characters stolen from other works of literature feature prominently. The events of 1968 provide the climax for this novel. Previously, del Paso had focused on Tlatelolco in *José Trigo* (1966), comparing a workers' strike there with the conquest of the Aztecs. Ibargüengoitia (1928–83) might chronologically be thought of as one of the *Escritura* group, but since instead of turning his back on things Mexican he put them at the core of his work, he sits apart from writers like Elizondo and García Ponce. Ibargüengoitia, who was blessed with a lively sense of humour, used several different styles to deal with popular Mexican subject matter, and some of his works seem to herald the Post-Boom. Here and there he used detective fiction, a documentary style, direct speech and interior monologue. *Los relámpagos de agosto* (1964), a parody of the novels of the Revolution, was one of his major successes. Leñero (b. 1933), one of the most influential dramatists of the 1960s and 1970s, is also known for the novel that won him Spain's Premio Biblioteca Breve, *Los albañiles* (1963), which later became a film directed by Jorge Fons. It was also rewritten by Leñero for the stage, winning him the Ruiz de Alarcón prize in Mexico. At bottom, the novel is an attempt to come to grips with urbanization. The investigation of a murder at a building site casts suspicion on workers who have migrated to the capital from the provinces, but in the end questions society itself. Leñero is a pioneer of the documentary novel and of fact-based theatre; and the critical eye he turns on the establishment and on certain national symbols has got him into trouble, despite his reputation abroad. For example, *Martirio de Morelos* suggests that Morelos, one of the leaders of the drive for independence from Spain, was an honourable man who buckled under torture, rather than the heroic martyr of the history books. Morelos' martyrdom in the play is being obliged to hear official accounts of his exploits, which leave him dumbfounded. This would not do as far as the authorities were concerned: attempts were made to suppress the play, there was a public outcry and eventually a face-saving compromise. Performances of *Nadie sabe nada* (a play about corruption and collusion between government and the media) were held up until political censorship had deleted sensitive material from it and then allowed only on condition that the national anthem not be played ironically to mark disreputable political acts.

Now to three people who have managed to avoid dogma, party lines and destructive polemics, and who nevertheless have been critical commentators on the national scene. Elena Poniatowska was born in 1932, worked above all as a journalist and truly came to the fore after Tlatelolco, with her testimonial collage documenting that experience, entitled *La noche de Tlatelolco* (1971, translated as *Massacre in Mexico*). Like many other observers, she sees Tlatelolco as a turning point in modern national history, the final proof of the bankruptcy of the Revolution and of years of deception. Paz, in *Posdata* (1970), had published his own assessment of the 1968 débâcle, showing sympathy with the protesters and reflecting that very view, but he also waxed critical of revolutionary movements in general and veered in his analysis towards the abstract, provoking much hostility because of it. Poniatowska, by contrast, brings together press clippings, formal interviews with important people, photographs, graffiti and accounts by eyewitnesses and victims. On the face of it, then, she seems to let the facts speak for themselves and writes rather little herself, but the truth is that there is quite a strong authorial hand at work. In her equally famous *Hasta no verte, Jesús mío* (1969, translated as *Until We Meet Again*), she writes a first-person narrative based on personal interviews; this time she portrays the life of a *soldadera* after the Revolution. She once again makes a documentary collage in *Nada, nadie: las voces del temblor* (Nothing, Nobody: Voices in Tremor, 1988), about the 1985 earthquake in Mexico City, its effects on individuals and communities, the community solidarity it drove, the good qualities it brought out in some people, and the incompetence and corruption in others. In *Querido Diego, te abraza Quiela* (Dear Diego, 1978), she creates imaginary correspondence between Diego Rivera and a lover, deflating the famous painter's aura. Poniatowska is famous for her straightforwardness and wit, her probing journalism and her in-depth interviews with prominent or unusual people. Other published works of hers include some collected interviews with Paz (*Octavio Paz: Las palabras del árbol* [1998]; Octavio Paz: Fruits from the Tree), a book about the avant-garde photographer Tina Modotti (*Tinísima*, 1992), and more recently *Paseo de la Reforma* (1996).

Some five years younger than Poniatowska, Carlos Monsiváis is also a product of the 1960s, though he has kept his independence from *Onda* and pointed out how much self-indulgent posturing and trendiness there was at the time. Monsiváis has dealt with many of the same issues as Poniatowska, but more acerbically, more flashily. Thanks to his lively and witty essays and speeches he has become a very visible cultural, social and political critic, has acquired a formidable reputation and is a star of the lecture circuit. One of his major contributions has been to insist on breaking down the divide between high and popular cultures and the popular, the subject of a lengthy magazine-article debate with Paz in the late 1970s. He has also done much to establish a new kind of journalistic chronicle of modern life that mixes inventiveness, style and serious comment, amounting to an updating of the old *costumbrista* sketch, and in the tradition of the work of Salvador Novo some thirty or forty years before him. *Días de guardar* (Days of Penance, 1970) is about 1968; *Entrada libre: crónicas de la sociedad que se organiza* (Free Admission: Chronicles of a Society in Movement, 1988), like Poniatowska's *Nada, nadie* . . ., is about local activism following the earthquake. Much of Monsiváis' work is scattered about in cultural magazines and the like, and has not been published in an orderly, coherent manner.

The brilliant public persona cut by Monsiváis has little in common with the quiet thoughtfulness of José Emilio Pacheco, who nonetheless has been similarly significant. Pacheco is a poet, novelist, short story writer and essayist. He has responded to the decline of highbrow poetry and the rise of mass media by making this and other aspects of modern society the subjects of his work, and without compromising his seriousness. His first novel, *Morirás lejos* (You Will Die Far Away, 1967) is highly poetic and experimental; there is, it seems to say, no one story, and we must consider the ethics of writing, our relationship with the idea of truth. This work is doubly interesting when one thinks of the documentary pretensions of those mentioned above. In Pacheco's early poetry one can see the influence of Paz. In later works like *Irás y no volverás* (You Will Leave and Not Return, 1973) and *Islas a la deriva* (Islands Adrift, 1976) he writes witty and original aphorisms, and sometimes makes fun of the apparent certainties of science. If not that, he is meditating on language or writing about environmental degradation or cultural imperialism, as in his novel *Las batallas en el desierto* (1981). In short, Pacheco has become the key representative of Mexico's spiritual conscience. He was, however, not alone in voicing concern at the way Mexico was going. Jorge Portilla's *Fenomenología del relajo* (1966) addressed similar issues. Gabriel Zaid (b. 1937), like Pacheco, is a poet, but he has also written essays about a wide range of topics, especially about the mindless pursuit of change, about urbanization and demographic displacements, and about social fads and consumerism. Zaid, iconoclastic and witty in style, rather in the manner of a latter-day Swift, is an industrial engineer from Monterrey, a man who is well aware of the border culture, and one whose perspective is somewhat different from that of writers in Mexico City.

Writers such as these, who were active in the 1960s in reviews such as *Nuevo Cine*, *Revista Mexicana de Literatura*, the *Revista de la Universidad* and *La cultura en México*, the supplement of the weekly *Siempre*, helped pave the way to the Post-Boom. In several ways they were leaving behind the high aestheticism of their predecessors and turning to social and ethical concerns. Indeed, it is often said that the Post-Boom brings literature closer to the people, and in a sense they did.

A generally recognized characteristic of writing of the Post-Boom is its tendency to assimilate popular cultural elements into narratives that are more straightforward than those of the Boom period. This shift may, of course, be seen as a predictable pendulum swing, a reaction against the grand literariness of earlier authors. Not that popular forms of fiction were lacking during the Boom period itself; the difference after it was that they were elevated to a new status, and in many ways became the bread and butter of fiction. While Fuentes and others like him were producing ambitious and complex works, Luis Spota (1925–84) had been making a good living by writing accessible bestsellers aimed at the masses and rich in *chismes* and scandal concerning famous people. Though his work was looked down upon at the time, present day interest in popular culture has led to his being the object of a certain amount of critical interest. One of his most successful novels was *Casi el paraíso* (1956). Spota also wrote a novel about Tlatelolco, called *La plaza* (1972). Poetry is not quite the abstruse, minority interest in Mexico that it has become in the English-speaking world, and so we find a popular poetic counterpart of Spota in Jaime Sabines (1926–99), a writer of accessible rather than hermetic poetry, which he collected as *Recuento de poemas*. His poems are emotional expressions of disappointment and tenderness that appeal to a wide readership, rather as did some of Neruda's work, though Neruda has greater depth.

A striking coincidence with the Latin American Post-Boom is the rise in prominence of women writers. In Mexico, we can date the start of that rise from the huge success of Angeles Mastretta's first novel *Arráncame la vida* (1985, translated as *Mexican Bolero*). She is Mexico's equivalent of Isabel Allende, both in terms of leading the national rise and in the controversy that surrounds her work. Add to her success that of Laura Esquivel with *Como agua para chocolate* (Like Water for Chocolate, 1991) and you have an inevitable discussion on whether such literature simply amounts to lightweight pandering to the masses, a charge that in any case is faced by many Post-Boom writers, women or not.

Arráncame la vida is a nostalgic revisiting of the novel of the Revolution, spiced up with a dose of soap-operatic interest in the lives of the rich and powerful; in some ways it follows the example of the commercial successes of Luis Spota. A young girl from the country is swept off her feet one day in Puebla when she meets the supremely self-confident Andrés Asencio. She marries him, only to find out that he has risen to power by virtue of his connexions and wiles, that he is an unscrupulous philanderer, and that he is capable of having his adversaries murdered. She finds solidarity with his children and love with a musician, but she never escapes the clutches of Andrés. How far is the heroine a woman of principle? How far is she manipulative? She is not so much submissive as astute. She may even be instrumental in the death of her husband, but if so, does his behaviour mitigate her guilt? It is the moral ambiguities surrounding the heroine, her refusal or inability to leave her patriarchal husband despite her awareness of his wrongdoings, that rescue this novel from the pile of pulp fiction: it is simple to read, but not simplistic. Mastretta has also published some engaging vignettes in *Mujeres de ojos grandes* (1991), where she amply demonstrates her ability to convey the characters and roles of women, using vivid, broad brushstrokes. *Mal de amores* (1996) is a long novel that has the Revolution as its main setting; here the daughter of a very progressive family struggles with life and love, becoming a *soldadera* and a sort of Florence Nightingale, though she has difficulty in reconciling the rival attractions of the two men in her life, the one a dashing adventurer and the other a respectable, elderly doctor. Esquivel's blockbuster novel, of course, has some comparable characteristics, though with the striking addition of magical real elements along the way.

Almost all the Post-Boom women writers address the social roles of women in some way. However, under this generality there lies a good deal of variation in their degree of concentration on that topic and their approach to the task of writing. In her first novel, *Mejor desaparece* (Better to Dissappear, 1987),

Carmen Boullosa (b. 1954) mixes narrative with reproductions of her own paintings as she recreates the childhood of the narrator and portrays her relationships with her siblings and father. The telling is fragmentary and the reading of it a challenge; in terms of form this book is a world away from the nostalgic romances of Mastretta and Esquivel. The story tells of the daughters of an authoritarian, hypocritical and moody father whom they grow to hate, along with their stepmother. One of the daughters turns to music, another to acting, and the third to wax. *Antes* (Before, 1989) is also a reconstruction – of the life of the child narrator before her death at the age of eleven – but it is less difficult to read. In *Llanto* (1992) there is nostalgia for the ordered world of the Aztecs: as the Aztec cycle comes up for renewal Moctezuma comes back to life and some women introduce him to the (incomprehensible) ways of the twentieth century. In this novel Boullosa has again turned to complexity and metafiction, and she wonders aloud how one is to go about writing an historical novel in our postmodern era. María Luisa Puga (b. 1944) is somewhere between the extremes of readability and difficulty illustrated above; her books are varied in technique but still accessible. Her first, *Las posibilidades del odio* (The Possibilities of Hatred, 1978) is not set in Mexico but is obviously relevant to it; it deals with the effects of colonialism in Kenya, with racism and cultural and economic imperialism. In *Pánico y peligro* (1983) she has a secretary who works in Mexico City reflect on her relationships, the secretary's notes being the 'chapters' of the novel. Some other women writers of today are Sara Sefchovich, Beatriz Novaro, Bárbara Jacobs and Silvia Molina.

Among male writers interesting work has come from Héctor Manjarrez (b. 1945) and Jorge Aguilar Mora (b. 1946). In *Lapsus* (1971), by Manjarrez, the characters revel in the alternative culture of the young, in perhaps a more sophisticated way than was the case in the *Onda* novels, and there is also some fun to be had here at the expense of literature itself. In *No todos los hombres son románticos* (1984), the counterculture is seen as fruitless and political activism takes its place. The works of Aguilar Mora – *Cadáver lleno de mundo* (1971) and *Si muero lejos de ti* (1979) – are more challenging and pretentious compositions. While both of the writers mentioned have a global perspective, Luis Zapata (b. 1951) and Armando Ramírez (b. 1950) limit their tramping ground to Mexico City and popular culture as manifested in radio, television and film. Yet they have made serious literature from this, rather as did Manuel Puig from similar material in Argentina. Zapata's *El vampiro de la colonia Roma* (1979) and *De pétalos perennes* (1981), and Ramírez's *Chin-Chin el teporocho* (1972) and *Violación en Polanco* (1980), are almost *costumbrista*-style accounts of certain sectors of modern society. Gay and lesbian writing has been further pursued by José Rafael Calva, Luis Arturo Ojeda and Sara Levy, while detective fiction has been revisited in the works of Paco Ignacio Taibo II and Rafael Ramírez Heredia. There has also been activity outside Mexico City (David Toscana [b. 1961] in Monterrey and Humberto Crosthwaite [b. 1962] in Tijuana, for example), together with a revival of indigenous writing in Chiapas, Yucatán and Oaxaca.

Highbrow fiction is represented by the 'Crack Generation', a name chosen to echo that of the Boom, rather than in reference to the drug. Perhaps intentionally, during the 1960s this generation raised some eyebrows with its public declarations. Its members are literary novelists and highly educated people, a fact reflected in the erudition that characterizes their work. Comparisons, not always sympathetic ones, have been made between them and predecessors such as the *Contemporáneos*. Their writing tends to be speculative and aggressively cosmopolitan, though it would be mistaken to suppose that they lose sight of Mexico. Jorge Volpi is the leading light of the Crack Generation, and his *En busca de Klingsor* (In Search of Klingsor, 1999) is the emblematic novel. Other members of the group are Ignacio Padilla and Eloy Urroz.

The two most outstanding dramatists at the start of the revival of theatre over the last quarter-century were Oscar Villegas and Willebaldo López, both of whom write about the destructive effects of society, though Villegas is more wordy and López more accessible. People in Villegas' plays are often victims of circumstance, and sometimes they are victimizers. *La paz de la buena gente* (The Peace of Good Folk) is typically full of short scenes and composed somewhat in the style of the theatre of the absurd. Villegas' characters could usually be anywhere, but López, whose approach is far more realistic, stresses the Mexican-ness of his. He turned to historical and cultural subjects after a period during which theatre itself was his subject, one he treated with a healthy dose of humour. Thus *Vine, vi y mejor me fui* (I Came, I Saw and I Thought it Better to Leave) brings his own technique under scrutiny, its leading character being 'The Dramatist'. In *Yo soy Juárez* a play about Juárez is being rehearsed, but once this work has been declared a slight on his reputation it has to be abandoned. One is reminded of Leñero's experience with the censored *Martirio de Morelos*.

Like his immediate predecessors, Gerardo Velásquez, who came to the forefront in the 1970s, wrote about human relationships, but he concentrated on women. *Toño Basura* (Tony Garbage) consists of four acts, each of which has associated with it certain motifs or symbols. We witness the rise and fall of the lead character, but this information does not come to us in an order that seems logical or that relates to a normal chronology of life. In other words, there is a deliberate puzzle effect that obliges the audience to arrange the information into a coherent pattern but also undermines certainty regarding facts and what they signify. Structurally, Velásquez's plays are generally inventive and demanding, in contrast to the didactic nature of many writers before him. Later dramatists build on Willebaldo López's experiments with historical themes, putting the believability of history in question. Sabina Berman, in another puzzle, *Rompecabezas* (Brainteaser), elevates doubt to its main theme; it is about the authorities' attempts to discover who was responsible for the assassination of Trotsky in 1940, but it gives contradictory accounts of the event and encourages confusion. The presumed assassin has five aliases, for example, and all the while a secretary is on stage transcribing, as if trying to make another version of the truth. Berman has demonstrated that dealing with Mexican subjects and being technically sophisticated at the same time are two quite compatible things. Her *Entre Pancho Villa y una mujer desnuda* (1993) enjoyed a long and successful run on the Mexican stage and she then adapted it for the movie of the same title. She has had success in the theatre to match those of writers like Esquivel and Mastretta in prose fiction. Other women have made their mark on theatre in recent years, among them Jesusa Rodríguez, whose provocative works include one-woman shows and an adaptation of Mozart's *Don Giovanni* for an all-female cast.

Women who live life vicariously through media stars are centrestage in Tomás Espinosa's *Santísima la nauyaca*. The title refers to a snake that becomes sanctified in the popular imagination and is said to be responsible for the death of a star called 'La María'. Then a 'real' woman whose name happens to be María Cruz assumes her identity and is rumoured to be able to walk on water. Another woman becomes identified with a crocodile. Through a glass partition (a TV screen?) the two main characters see it swimming to freedom, but not before they have symbolically brushed past a painting of The Last Supper.

Hugo Rascón Banda and Oscar Liera are social commentators and iconoclasts. Rascón sees the world in terms of a struggle between good and evil. From Liera's point of view, all the world's a stage. He became famous for the controversial satire *Cúcara y Mácara*, whose title characters are taken from a children's rhyme. Inspiration also comes from historical records of an unsuccessful attempt to damage the Virgen de Guadalupe. Liera sets out to show the extent to which the Church establishment is prepared to go to keep the image of the Virgen de Guadalupe untainted. He invents his own 'Virgen de Siquitibum', who appears before the title characters. The idea that the Virgin should appear to them rather than Juan Diego, as the tradition claims, is surely irreverent enough to cause indignation in certain quarters, but considering that this Virgin's name, 'Siquitibum', is normally a cry of encouragement that one hears at football matches and other sporting events, the insult is compounded. In his 'mythical' story of this other Virgin her shawl is destroyed and the Church goes to immense lengths to hide this fact from the faithful. Beyond its religious scepticism this is clearly a play about power and the control of information. It provoked a predictable furore, with criticism that it was not only irreverent but unpatriotic. Acting, ironically enough, rather like supporters at a football match, some indignant theatregoers would shout '¡Viva la Virgen de Guadalupe!' during performances; others, who simply thought that this was all a matter of trendy audience participation, joined in. During a 1981 performance some protesters even invaded the stage; most of the audience thought this was part of the play too, until the invaders physically assaulted the actors and the producer. By that time theatre in general was again prospering, and anything seemed possible in it.

One of Rascón Banda's plays, *Los ilegales* (1980), is about emigration to the US and the fate of Mexicans once there. Guillermo Sergio Alanís O., a border dramatist, looks instead at emigration's effects on those left behind. In his satirical *De acá, de este lado* (1986) what drives some characters is a wish to be prosperous but also a need for social and spiritual satisfaction; Alanís views these desires with sympathy but sometimes with black humour. The Mother character refuses to participate in national festivities and confines her children to the house, where they enact fantasies about the rosy future that awaits them; but they also lay bare the details of their somewhat murky family relationships, even to the extent of fantasizing about matricide. No doubt the Mother figure can be read as a metaphor for a repressive home country. Naturally enough, the preoccupations of border writers overlap to a large extent with those of *chicano* writers in the US.[29]

These are some of the many writers who are active in what is now a lively, healthy and extremely varied literary culture, notwithstanding fears in some quarters that modern media might seal its coffin, or at least the coffin of high-brow literature. Despite the fact that too many people in Mexico are still illiterate, despite the fact that books are too expensive for many pockets, despite competition from the media, literature in general has done well since the Boom, and partly because the Boom boosted the prestige of the writer. It is still the case that few writers can live on their royalties alone, but the Mexican reading public expanded a great deal during the twentieth century, the writer continues to enjoy considerable respect, and the publishing industry, albeit now largely a matter of international conglomerates, still sees Mexico as a hub rivalled only by Argentina.

Cinema

Mexico has been a major force in the field of cinema, and not only in Latin America. Even so, the industry has been through some periods when the quality of its products has been indifferent, and it has inevitably been at the mercy of market forces, uncertain financing and political pressures. Popular taste can change, and in any case does not always coincide with what critics regard as quality cinema. Moreover, the dynamics of private sector, state and foreign investment in the industry were always volatile. Yet as far as the Spanish-speaking market is concerned, in cinema Mexico's only real rivals have been Spain and Argentina.[30] Mexico has one of the strongest infrastructures for movie production in the world.

It helped that cinema as an art form worldwide was just finding its feet at the time of the Revolution, for the latter provided ideal material for the new

29 It is here in the borderlands and also in Yucatán that one finds the most vibrant signs of regional theatre; generally speaking, the dominance of Mexico City, with its stronger infrastructure, has tended to force dramatists to move there.

30 The same can be said of many aspects of cultural activity: Mexico and Argentina have been the Spanish-American powerhouses. In recent decades the Cuban film industry has risen in prominence.

medium. Later on there came a heyday, the 'Golden Age' of Mexican cinema, in the 1940s. One thing that helped boost the fortunes of Mexican cinema at that time was the fact that it could step into the breach during the Second World War years, when Hollywood production slumped. Mexico came to be regarded as a provider of Spanish-language alternatives to Hollywood fare. In fact, that was a role for it that was actively promoted during the 1940s, under President Alemán, who envisaged an independent Mexican industry making high-quality films. Indeed, the success of Mexico's industry has sometimes brought accusations that it has exerted its own sort of cultural imperialism, for undoubtedly it did corner the Spanish-American market and set the tone. Carlos Monsiváis argues that there was a time when it systematically defined a common set of ideas of what nation, family and society ought to be.[31] If so, then this is perhaps reflected in the fact that popularity and critical acclaim seemed very often to coincide during the Golden Age. After that time there came a lean period characterized by formulaic, lowbrow products, but more recently there has been a revival in the industry A good deal of contemporary cinema, unlike that of the Golden Age, questions national myths and re-examines the ways of society. This sometimes makes modern films unsettling to see, and moreover their complexity can make them quite demanding for audiences, so it may not be a coincidence that in modern times the gap between the box office appeal of commercial formula-films and the critical success of independent, experimental art films is quite wide. Much the same, of course, could be said of the modern industry elsewhere.

By the beginning of the twentieth century several cinemas had opened in Mexico City, and the taste for movies was spreading across the country. As in other parts of the world, the first movies made in Mexico were shorts of daily life and public events; *Riña de hombres en el Zócalo* (Men in a Scuffle on the Zócalo) is the illustrative title of one. Films began to make Mexicans more aware of their country, not to mention showing them what life was like abroad, and the fact that this new medium was able to reach a wide public was not lost on Porfirio Díaz, who took advantage to have himself filmed in flattering circumstances. Silent films from France came to cinema screens at first, then others from Italy, and finally those gave way to films from the United States.

Salvador Toscano, one of the most influential early entrepreneurs, made some of Mexico's first fictional films, but above all he produced documentary footage, only part of which survives today. In 1940 his daughter established an archive of his work, and some of it was brought together later in a full-length film called *Memorias de un mexicano* (1950). Here is the orchestrated pomp of Porfirio celebrating the anniversary of independence, and following that there is the outbreak of the Revolution, but together with these momentous historical events there are scenes of everyday life, sometimes filmed quite self-

[31] *A través del espejo*, 67–92.

consciously. An identifiably Mexican style and a surprising degree of narrative sophistication have been noticed in some of Toscano's films, such as *Viaje a Yucatán* (Trip to the Yucatán, 1906), which is about a visit made by Porfirio, and *La entrevista Díaz–Taft* (The Díaz–Taft Meeting, 1908). That was the year that saw the appearance of the first Mexican feature made from an original script, *El grito de Dolores*; it was an attempt to capture the highlights of the movement for independence, and yet it was not well received, being criticized instead as inaccurate, unrealistic and excessively complicated.

As noted previously, the Revolution provided dramatic material and charismatic personalities. Pancho Villa could be said to be Mexico's first film star, not simply because of the material provided by his notorious exploits but also because he performed some of them for the camera. In 1914 he signed a contract with the Mutual Film Corporation of the US, giving it the right to document and glorify his deeds. In a cooperative spirit, he would engage in battle at times when the light levels were good; and if the filmed results were unsatisfactory, he was willing to restage the battle. But other events associated with the Revolution provided the basis for what proved to be the key film of the silent era, *El automóvil gris* (The Grey Automobile, 1919), directed by Enrique Rosas. Members of Carranza's army had carried out a series of burglaries using a grey car as a getaway vehicle; following protests, some of the culprits had been arrested and executed. In this film, which is part fiction, part documentary (that is to say partly shot on location and partly compiled from newsreels), we have a re-enactment of these events in twelve episodes. *El automóvil gris* was re-edited more than once and eventually acquired a soundtrack; it is a sensational recreation of events that in some ways heralds the melodramatic style that became so characteristic of subsequent Mexican films.

The advent of the soundtrack forced Hollywood to reconsider its products, for now it could no longer count on being dominant in a market where all of a sudden language was a factor. But Hollywood's attempts to cater for the Spanish-speaking cinemagoer were less than successful. For example, Dolores del Río, the daughter of a wealthy Mexican family, was one of many people who had been drawn to the United States in the early years of cinema. Hollywood touted her as one of its discoveries and then marketed her as Spanish. Miscalculations such as this must have helped the advance of the Mexican industry. Be that as it may, in this changing scene Mexican actors and technicians who had been seduced by Hollywood and had honed their skills there came back home. Dolores del Río, the most famous of them, starred in her first Mexican film in 1943.

In the post-revolutionary environment, where culture was actively promoted by the state with the masses in mind, some moviemakers subscribed to the policy, some reacted against it and others kept their distance. As an example of a reaction against the prevailing political ethos we may take *En tiempos de don Porfirio* (1939), whose nostalgia for the stable days of the *Porfiriato* reassured those members of society who felt threatened by the Cárdenas reforms. At the other end of the spectrum are *Redes* and *Janitzio*, which, in focusing on the importance of Indians and poor people, were very much in harmony with post-revolutionary thinking, albeit critical of corruption and of failures to implement the promised reforms. These were the films that showed the greatest signs of the influence of international socialism and, as far as technique was concerned, of Sergei Eisenstein. Then there are the less committed but major films that were made by Fernando de Fuentes: *El compadre Mendoza* and *¡Vámonos con Pancho Villa!*

Eisenstein came to Mexico in 1930 after mixed fortunes in Hollywood; his relationship with the Russian authorities had its difficulties too. He had been sent by them to the West to find out about the latest movie techniques. After he had failed to get backing for his projects in California, Charlie Chaplin put him in contact with financiers who seem to have given him a very free hand as regards filming, but kept control of the editing stage: the plan was to make an epic about the Mexican Revolution, entitled *¡Que viva México!* Eisenstein was unable to see the project through to completion. In later years he spoke of the pressure he had been under from his backers and from the Mexican government, which found his approach uncomfortably radical. Finally, the backers pulled out. But some of Eisenstein's visual techniques, his slow-moving, carefully framed shots, did influence Mexican cinema, in particular the films of Emilio Fernández, such as *María Candelaria* (1943).

It was an adaptation of a popular turn-of-the-century novel by Federico Gamboa that became the first success of sound cinema: *Santa* (1931), a melodrama directed by Antonio Moreno. This was not the first film version, nor would it be the last.[32] The story is about an innocent country girl who is seduced by a soldier, flees in disgrace to a Mexico City brothel, and takes up with a bullfighter. Save for the selfless devotion shown her by a blind pianist, she is misused; she falls ill and dies. She is, in fact, an example of what would become an archetype of Mexican cinema: the fallen innocent. In addition, *Santa* contrasts rural virtue with urban decadence. It was a great commercial success, and it was made largely by Mexicans who had worked in Hollywood. Agustín Lara was one of the people working on the musical side, a man who knew a few things about playing pianos in brothels. A more polished urban melodrama, however, was *La mujer del puerto* (1933), directed by the Russian émigré Arcady Boytler and Raphael Sevilla. This is more sordid and atmospheric than *Santa*, but its storyline is not very different: the lead character kills herself after she realizes that the man with whom she has been sleeping in the brothel is her long-lost brother.

Though official Mexico was generally slow to see the potential of the industry, the Cárdenas government recognized that it could be used to foster education and social change. *Redes* (Nets, 1934), employed local villagers in the state of Veracruz as amateur actors as it set about recreating an historical incident involving workers' solidarity and resistance, and it was a film sponsored by

32 Paul Leduc's freely adapted *Latino Bar* of 1990 is the latest version.

the Secretaría de Educación. That film and *Janitzio* (1934) conveyed the revolutionary faith that injustices could be put right, that the rights of the common man, especially the Indian, could be vindicated. Both of these films were assembled by international teams, and both showed the influence of Eisenstein. *Janitzio* is the more melodramatic of the two, dealing with an Indian girl who is misunderstood, shunned and stoned by villagers, following which her fiancé carries her off in grief into the sunset. It is significant that Emilio Fernández played the part of the fiancé, for he was soon to become a major director in his own right and his *María Candelaria* of 1943 has more than a little in common with *Janitzio*.

The film-noir melodramatics of movies like *La mujer del puerto* and the social weight of films such as the two just described were offset by another Golden Age phenomenon that became known as the *comedia ranchera* and that propelled Mexican cinema to international popularity. *Allá en el Rancho Grande* (1936), directed by Fernando de Fuentes, was the prototype. This movie, which is packed with local colour, has an episodic structure and is frequently interrupted by song. If the festivities and socializing seem staged then so do the characters: the men are proud, noble and strong, the women blameless and beautiful. The plot involves misunderstandings and tensions but never delves below the surface, for this is a world that is comfortably uncontroversial and at bottom very artificial. *Allá en el Rancho Grande* was promoted by Emilio Azcárraga, who at the time was on the rise as a media mogul, and it met with huge success abroad – Gabriel Figueroa, the cameraman, won an award at the Venice Film Festival – a success that encouraged large numbers of Mexicans to go and see the film. It may have been corny, it may look extremely dated these days, but at least it was genuinely Mexican, and it was further proof of the world's interest in the country. Following this, Mexican film production steadily increased; about a half of the films made were along the lines of *Allá en el Rancho Grande*. Among the stock characters of the *comedia ranchera* was the singing *charro*, and that role made several people's careers, including that of Jorge Negrete (1911–53).

Fernando de Fuentes, the director of *Allá en el Rancho Grande*, became one of the driving forces of the Golden Age. Another of his films from the 1930s, *¡Vámonos con Pancho Villa!*, was made with generous government backing at the then state-of-the-art CLASA studios, despite which the government's own censors rejected the director's cut, demanding a more upbeat ending. The commercial failure of this film contributed significantly to future financial difficulties at CLASA, yet though the public of the time may not have liked it, critics have since found it interesting as an attempt to recast the narrative of the Mexican Revolution. It is not as if this film lacked talent: Xavier Villaurrutia, the playwright (and also one of Mexico's first serious film critics) helped write the screenplay and Silvestre Revueltas wrote the score. The story deals with a group of people who are swept along by the ideals of the Revolution and the charisma of its leaders; they join a revolutionary band soon after deserting the federal army, only to find their illusions exposed by the harsh chaos of reality.

(De Fuentes' ending had Pancho Villa ruthlessly slaughtering an innocent family, but that was the ending that was censored and only became public nearly fifty years later.) This film, then, was not just another piece of agenda-driven social realism, like *Redes*, but rather was trying to cast a critical eye on the realities of the Revolution; and of course it had almost nothing in common with urban melodramas and ranch comedies. De Fuentes' other film of note from the 1930s is *El compadre Mendoza* (1933). This time he looks into the moral questions raised by the Revolution and highlights the cynical opportunism of landowners. Mendoza is an *hacendero* who manipulates rival factions to his advantage and who betrays a man who has previously saved him from death. The word *compadre* in the title alludes cleverly to the theme of loyalty and betrayal.

These were the seminal movies from which the Golden Age blossomed, in the sense that they laid the foundations of the genres that would be at its heart. Yet even at the peak of the Golden Age in the 1940s, Hollywood products kept their edge at the box office: in 1930 about 2 percent of the films shown in Mexican cinemas were Mexican, and by the mid-1949s the proportion was nearing 50 percent. After the 1940s the stars began to fade and the formulae of Golden Age films began to seem tired. From a commercial point of view the industry had been churning out enough films of adequate quality to satisfy the market and make up for Hollywood. Despite the subsequent decline in quality, the Mexican industry did keep its foothold in later years.

One of the factors that had helped boost the Mexican industry, as we have noted, was the outbreak of the Second World War, which reduced Hollywood competition. Not only did Hollywood production diminish but both Spain and Argentina supported the Axis powers, and so US producers threw their full weight behind Mexico, increasing investment there and reducing supplies to the other two countries. In return, Mexico trumpeted the Allied cause and its solidarity with the United States, in propagandistic films like *Canto a las Américas* (Song to the Americas, 1942), and *Cadetes de la naval* (Naval Cadets, 1944). The PRI, following the presidency of the radical Cárdenas, was now led by people whose rhetoric was not very different from his but who in practice were more sympathetic to capitalism. One effect of this was to allay fears among investors that the industry might be nationalized. So the government turned to encouraging private initiatives while keeping control of part of the finances through its Banco Nacional Cinematográfico, which was established in 1942. Another form of control was through the official trade unions. The state-controlled Sindicato de Trabajadores de la Industria Cinematográfica (STIC) supervised all workers in the film industry from 1919 until the 1950s, but the stars were inevitably averse to being treated as equals of mere technicians, so they formed their own union, together with directors and cameramen: the Sindicato de Trabajadores de la Producción Cinematográfica (STPC). The government's willingness to tolerate the existence of this élite union may have seemed to contradict the talk of brotherly solidarity, but the fact was that the stars had friends in the right places.

The Golden Age had brought steadily improving production values and a system that aped Hollywood. Creative energy had been used to make films that had a wide appeal, which now slotted predictably into a few categories: the ranch comedy, the urban melodrama, the Cantinflas comedy and the allegory of national identity. Later, the *cine de arrabal* (a working-class melodrama) and the *cine de ficheras* (brothel melodrama) also became very popular, as a subclass of urban melodrama. But perhaps the key element in it all was the set of stars whom everyone recognized and wanted to see. Among these were Cantinflas the comedian, Jorge Negrete the singer, and the duo of Dolores del Río and Pedro Armendáriz. In films made by Emilio Fernández and Gabriel Figueroa, these last two actors were typecast: she was an archetypal, self-sacrificing Mexican woman with hints of the Virgen de Guadalupe and he was an honourable, decent man. Other stars who emerged later were Pedro Infante and María Félix. María Félix tended to play the feisty female, but she would succumb eventually to the male; Pedro Infante portrayed men who were humble and caring. When these stars were gone, the age was over.

Mario Moreno was the first actor with the kind of star appeal that could draw large audiences to the cinema, and he became an institution. The name he adopted, 'Cantinflas', was built upon 'cantina' and 'inflar', to convey the idea of a palterer, a person who would inflate his own importance, or at least let off a lot of hot air, while in a bar. Unlike many of his contemporaries, Cantinflas did not pass through Hollywood but instead worked his way up through the music hall; his first film roles were as a sidekick to Manuel Medel in two 1937 movies directed by Arcady Boytler. Cantinflas took a step up in his next film, *El signo de la muerte* (The Sign of Death, 1939), in that Salvador Novo and Silvestre Revueltas were contributors to it, but his reputation really dates from the time when he teamed up with Juan Bustillo Oro for *Ahí está el detalle* (That's the Thing, 1940). This is the quintessential example of Cantinflas' style: he is the fast-talking *pelado* who, after worming his way into a wealthy household, seduces the servant girl, empties the kitchen of food and by assuming a false identity lives at the expense of others. The most famous part of the film is the trial at the end, during which confusion reigns: Cantinflas generates much of the confusion himself, talking endlessly and quickly, but saying very little of substance. That was one of his hallmarks. Mexico can thank him for at least two additions to its everyday vocabulary, the verb 'cantinflear' and the noun 'cantinflada'. The film was a huge success, but after it, Cantinflas gradually lost his edge. Starting with a spoof of the police, *El gendarme desconocido* (The Unknown Policeman, 1941), he turned away from the mischievous and resourceful *pelado* to play more ambiguous working-class characters, and his humour became more and more predictable. In all he made over fifty films, acquiring an international reputation. His main rival in the field of comedy was Germán Valdés (otherwise known as 'Tin Tan'), who was equally prolific, but started his career somewhat later and based his image on a *pachuco* operating in the borderlands, no doubt reflecting increasing public awareness of what was happening in that part of the country. Valdés' humour is laced with liberal doses of Spanglish. If Cantinflas' talk had been full of double-entendres, Valdés was more explicit in his references to sex, and when he appeared he was often surrounded by show girls. A typical film of his, with a suggestive title, is *Calabacitas tiernas* (Tender Little Pumpkins, 1948).

1943 saw the production of an outstanding film adaptation of Rómulo Gallegos' novel *Doña Bárbara*, made by Fernando de Fuentes. Given that the author of that novel was Venezuelan, the filming of it seems to indicate that the industry was looking for a market that extended beyond Mexico itself. In all, this was a fine year for films, for it also saw Julio Bracho burst onto the scene with his *Distinto amanecer* (A Different Dawn), a sophisticated melodrama, and two major movies directed by Emilio Fernández, *Flor silvestre* and *María Candelaria*. The Fernández movies, after taking prizes in Europe and establishing his reputation in the United States, opened the way for him to collaborate with John Ford.

Emilio Fernández made about forty films in as many years, not all of them of the same quality, his best period undoubtedly being the 1940s, when he worked with the cameraman Gabriel Figueroa. Drawing together the essentials of previous Mexican films, Fernández married melodrama with lyricism and socio-historical criticism. He had been born to an Indian mother and came to be known as 'el Indio'; perhaps for that reason, one of his films would be *Soy puro mexicano* (I'm A Mexican Through and Through, 1942). Fernández had played small parts in the Californian industry during the 1920s, and he returned to Mexico 1933 determined to make films with Mexicans, for Mexicans and about Mexicans. He had a flair for self-promotion to compare with Rivera's, once even declaring that he *was* Mexican cinema. Like Rivera, he presented a stylized, artificial view of life and with Rivera he shared much the same view of the function of art; in fact both were criticized for dancing too readily to the political tune. Fernández and Figueroa drew heavily on a set of stereotypical Mexican images: the people tended to be nobly *mestizo* or Indian, the landscapes were generally dry, with a blue sky, and were punctuated by churches, cactuses and ancient ruins. Visually, their work is dramatic, carefully composed, and satisfying. In fact the technical features of their films are more interesting than their laboured content and usually indifferent acting.

Flor silvestre (1943), a Fernández–Figueroa masterpiece, tells a story of impossible love coupled with political drama. Dolores del Río is a widow who is telling her son, a military cadet, the tragic story of the brave and principled father he never knew. That story is presented in flashbacks. It is set, as others would later be, in a rural environment dominated by a landowner, one in which everyone knows everyone else. The ideals of the Revolution are offset by its failures, and, curiously, it is the children of the prosperous who are seen as the repository of hope that society might improve in the future. *María Candelaria* was an even greater success. This time Dolores del Río is the virtuous daughter of a prostitute, unjustly spurned by her community in the floating gardens (*chinampas*) of Xochimilco, where she tries to sell flowers from her boat. She is denied the quinine that the local strongman hands out to others, and soon after we see her bitten by a mosquito, a portent of her death. Only the local priest and her loyal husband (Pedro Armendáriz) give her support. The themes are thus social prejudice and injustice. The acting is generally ponderous and the music cloying, but the visual qualities are strong. This film may be largely simplistic but it does have an interestingly ambiguous character whose uncomfortable reminiscences preface the main action; he is a painter who has done a portrait of María's emblematic Mexican beauty, who seems to be sympathetic and protective of her, but whose unthinking self-interest has been the cause of her dishonour and death.

Other films made by Fernández's during the 1940s are more ideological, but less sentimental. *Enamorada* helped make María Félix a star. As the opening shots of this carefully constructed film reveal, it is she, the daughter of wealthy Cholula family, who will fall in love and the man with whom she will do so is a tough yet principled revolutionary leader (Pedro Armendáriz). For all her shrewishness, in the end she becomes a *soldadera*, marching behind her horse-riding man. *Río Escondido* is a visual exercise that shows off the team's techniques but also toes the party line; here María Félix is schoolteacher charged (a trifle improbably) by the president himself with taking education to rural areas and counteracting the sinister forces that oppose the Revolution. During her arduous journey she falls victim to a heart condition and is saved by a medical student who has been sent on a similar mission. Once she reaches her destination she has to deal with a cruel local strongman; she stands up to him, uses his desire for her to secure support for her social and educational reforms, yet keeps her honour all the while.[33] The peasants having been duly educated and their consciousness aroused, she now confronts the strongman, is raped by him and shoots him, only to succumb thereafter to her ailing heart. From her deathbed she reports back to the president, who declares her a national heroine. As can be deduced from this summary, melodrama is never far away. One of the last Fernández films of the 1940s was *Salón México* (1948), in which the melodrama is played out in an urban setting.[34] This film, set in a dance hall, is an example of a subgenre that would be heavily exploited in the ensuing decade, *cine caberetera* or *cine de ficheras*; *fichas* were tokens used to book girls. Here again, in *Salón México*, one finds a noble friendship destined for tragedy; a kind-hearted policeman tries to save a fallen young woman from abuse and dishonour, and succeeds in doing so, but he is left with his love unrequited.

Bracho, who was mentioned earlier, came from a far more prosperous background than Fernández and was a relative of Dolores del Río. In *Distinto amanecer* his actress sister played opposite Pedro Armendáriz in a story that

[33] In real life she was less virginal: it is well known that María Félix had affairs with Negrete, Lara and even President Alemán.

[34] Aaron Copland would use the same title for one of his musical pieces. There is a 1996 remake of *Salón México*, by José Luis García Agraz, starring María Rojo.

covers a single night in Mexico City; in this atmospheric film a chance meeting with a friend from student days leads to the bored couple becoming enmeshed in crime and political intrigue. Here the acting is of a higher level and the treatment of urbanization, moral decadence and alienation pulls no punches. From a present-day perspective this film seems not only to speak of post- revolutionary disillusionment but also to anticipate the disaffection of the 1960s. Bracho also made *La sombra del caudillo* (The Shadow of the Dictator, 1960), based on a novel by Martín Luis Guzmán, a film found so controversial that it was suppressed for almost thirty years.

It was during the 1940s that melodrama prospered. At first it focused on the lives of the middle class to which many Mexicans wished to belong; it dealt in feuds, jealousy and scandal, in the way that soap operas would later. An early hit was Juan Bustillo Oro's *Cuando los hijos se van* (When the Children Leave the Nest, 1941), which later became a television soap-opera. Alejandro Galindo managed to address tricky social issues and yet not lose his popular base. His *Una familia de tantas* (A Family Like So Many Others, 1948) deals with an authoritarian patriarch who is out of touch with modern times, but, since his daughter's heart is won over by a salesman, the film alludes to tensions generated by (American) commercialization. US–Mexican relations are the nub of several other popular and critically acclaimed films of his, such as *Campeón sin corona* (Champion Without a Title, 1945), a chronicle of the rise of an inner city boxer who finds himself out of his depth in the United States, and *Espaldas mojadas* (Wetbacks, 1953), about the fate of Mexican immigrants to the US.

As melodrama shifted its focus from the middle class to the urban slums there arose another subgenre, the *cine de arrabal*, of which Ismael Rodríguez became the prime exponent. He made a trilogy that, though scarcely known outside the Spanish-speaking world, made Pedro Infante a star. *Nosotros los pobres* (We, the Poor, 1947), together with *Ustedes los ricos* (You, the Rich, 1948) and *Pepe el toro* (Pepe the Bull, 1952), were watched by millions. *Nosotros los pobres* deals with intrigue, betrayal and deception, but these things are outweighed by compassion and solidarity, and at bottom we are given a slightly sanitized version of reality. Pepe el Toro, the humble carpenter whose life is chronicled in *Nosotros los pobres* is generous, sincere, compassionate and steadfast in his faith in people. Its popularity suggests that this movie struck a sympathetic chord with the Mexican people. Later, its director made *La cucaracha* (The Cockroach, 1958), bringing in both Dolores del Río and María Félix, together with Emilio Fernández, once again in an acting role. It was meant to be the *magnum opus* of revolutionary cinema, but it did not live up to expectations.

Though the number of films made during the 1950s did not decline, their quality – and taste – did. The fact that society and its values were changing was reflected especially in the *cabareteras*, the most popular genre of the 1950s. The prostitutes no longer had hearts of gold, were no longer simply victims of circumstance. Also popular were movies that exploited dance crazes, not only reflecting passing fads in Mexico but also trying to appeal to a broader

Spanish-American audience at a time when Hollywood was back in business. There are two *cabareteras* that should be mentioned for their quality: *Sensualidad* (Sensuality, 1950) and *Aventurera* (Adventuress, 1949), both directed by Alberto Gout. In both, the Cuban actress Ninón Sevilla plays a prostitute in a society whose corrupt public officials and local élites keep the shadier side of life going and profit from it. There are hidden secrets, families at risk and people capable of sordid and vicious acts. Faced with competition from television, some moviemakers also turned to nudity in an attempt to attract audiences, in films like *La fuerza del deseo* (The Power of Desire, 1955), and *La virtud desnuda* (Naked Virtue, 1955). Society's standards were to undergo radical changes in the 1960s and such films would then come to be seen not as signs of moral decadence but as heralding new freedoms.

Against the background of general decline in the wake of the Golden Age, the work of Buñuel is like a beacon. Even films such as *El bruto* (1952), ostensibly very much in the Mexican melodramatic tradtition, and, as if by way of proof, starring Pedro Armendáriz, are unmistakably Buñuel's. Judicious lighting and camera angles give Armendáriz a brutish, lumbering air for his title role as a butcher contracted by a miserly plutocrat to evict poor tenants from his property. All the beautiful women, including the plutocrat's young wife, are attracted by the animal qualities of this brute, who, in his own words, 'thinks slowly'. But he reveals his more sensitive side and chooses the noblest of the women before meeting his end. If that film has been largely forgotten, the same cannot be said for another that Buñuel made at about the same time: *Los olvidados*. This is a film that invites comparison with *Nosotros, los pobres*: the Buñuel film is a visceral, honest and unpatronizing view of the lives of street children in Mexico City's poorest neighbourhoods, whereas *Nosotros . . .* is a sentimental sublimation of poverty. Buñuel's masterpiece, made with actors who were not known stars, won him the prize for best director at Cannes in 1951, but it troubled moviegoers and government officials alike; like some other films before it, it had to be well-received by foreign audiences and critics before it was accepted in Mexico.

A refugee from Franco's regime, Buñuel had arrived in Mexico in 1946, and had come by way of the United States. By that time he was already a well-known director. During his time in Mexico he made a large number of films – some twenty, including the masterful *El ángel exterminador* – and then he returned to Europe in the 1960s. Chauvinistic critics have argued that Buñuel overshadowed his contemporaries in Mexico and that he did not really show an understanding of its people and society, even in those of his films that have an explicitly Mexican setting. Whether or not such a charge can be justified, Buñuel must certainly be given credit for keeping Mexico on the international cinematic map and for bringing a new creative energy and professionalism to the industry. Artistic achievements apart, he kept to budget, delivered the goods on time and did not compromise his integrity. If no more is said about him here, that is simply because so much has been said about him elsewhere.

By contrast, further signs of the decline of the Mexican industry were to be seen in an endless series of superhero films that began in 1961 with *Santo contra el cerebro diabólico* (Santo Versus the Evil Brain). It seems that Mexican cinema had little to say about Mexico and was out of touch with international cinematic developments, to boot; it was making cheap downmarket products, in addition to which its administration and finances were in disorder. These things were symptoms of a wider social malaise, as Tlatelolco would demonstrate. However, in the early 1960s a few experimental films came from outside the cinematic establishment, from independents, a number of whom had been at the UNAM. In the early 1960s there appeared a new if shortlived magazine called *Nuevo cine*, with which a number of people who later became influential in cinema were associated. Among them, Emilio García Riera became Mexico's leading film historian, Carlos Monsiváis one of the country's most acute critics, and Manuel González Casanova the first director of the Centro Universitario de Estudios Cinematográficos (CUEC), founded in 1963. They were all fully cognizant of Buñuel's contribution and of the need for Mexico to stop looking at its navel and become more cosmopolitan in outlook, so that they viewed expressions of nationalism in art, such as Muralism and the films of Fernández and Figueroa, as old hat. Instead, they advocated dealing with universal themes in adventurous, experimental ways. In doing so they trod on several toes, sometimes accusing the old guard of colonial dependency, and probably impervious to their own, insofar as they wanted to imitate foreign trends. The first major product on film was Jomi García Ascot's *En el balcón vacío* (On the Open Balcony, 1961), which evokes a woman's traumatic childhood memories; it was scripted by his wife and based on her experiences while being brought up in Spain and later as a Civil War exile. Distributors did not like it, but people at the Locarno Film Festival did.

At a 1964 film competition organized by the breakaway STPC union, the top prize was awarded to an inventive compilation of offbeat images by Rubén Gámez, called *La fórmula secreta, o Coca-Cola en la sangre* (The Secret Formula, or Coca-Cola in Your Blood, 1964). Gámez uses text by Juan Rulfo that is read by Jaime Sabines, the poet. Rather like Rulfo, after this film Gámez became something of a legend, while producing nothing for years. The transfusion of Coca-Cola that is given to a patient at one point obviously alludes to slavish imitation of the US lifestyle and to the ravages of imperialism, but much of the film amounts to a parody of Mexican stereotypes, a critique of a people whom Gámez saw as lacking initiative and imagination. The second prize winner was *En este pueblo no hay ladrones* (There Are No Thieves in This Town, 1964), directed by Alberto Isaac, and with brief appearances by a host of important cultural figures of the time. These included Rulfo and García Márquez (on whose short story the film was based), José Luis Cuevas, Leonora Carrington, García Riera and Monsiváis, the film's own director and another aspiring director called Arturo Ripstein. It was he, Ripstein, who made *Tiempo de morir* (A Time to Die, 1965), which was also based on a García Márquez story.[35] Both films deal with isolated communities and buried passions. The increasing interaction between literature and film was further evident in Rulfo's screenplay for the veteran Roberto Gavaldón's *El gallo de oro* (The Golden Cockerel, 1964), and in Carlos Velo's less felicitous adaptation of Rulfo's novel *Pedro Páramo* (1966).

Tlatelolco poured cold water on a number of initiatives, but it inevitably became a topic that engaged filmmakers in the longer run, albeit to a lesser degree than it engaged writers. Paul Leduc and others made a documentary of the Tlatelolco events, *El grito* (The Shout, 1968), edited from film shot between July and October of 1968, and including an eyewitness account by the Italian journalist Orianna Fallaci. *El cambio* (The Change, 1971) and *Crates* (1971), another student product, portrayed the disillusionment and alienation of young people. But Felipe Cazals' *Canoa* (1975) was the best film to be inspired by the Tlatelolco events, in fact almost the only one, until Jorge Fons released *Rojo amanecer* in 1990. *Canoa* is again based on fact. It tells about some employees at a university in Puebla, one that at the time was known for its radicalism, who set off on a hiking trip but are driven by the weather to stop in San Miguel Canoa; though their activities have been harmless, their lives become endangered by a mob of locals, incited by the parish priest. Interestingly, *Canoa* was produced by CONACINE, an organization that had been established by the Echeverría government after Tlatelolco; this film might thus be seen as proof of the government's new tolerant line, but the references to Tlatelolco in it are quite oblique, and most importantly the wounded and battered students are just saved from a lynching by the arrival of federal troops, both of which might suggest the government's image is being rehabilitated. *Canoa* was remastered in the 1990s but, thankfully, otherwise left unchanged; it does have its faults, among them some dead wood and uneven pacing, but it still serves as an important text in the history of Mexico and its cinema. One of its most interesting features is that it is constructed on several levels: there is documentary material of the facts on which the story is based, a fictionalized pseudo-documentary about the community, with a cynical local informant acting as narrator, and thirdly the narrative of the young workers during their ill-fated trip. *Canoa* still commands respect, and thanks to it and two other movies of the 1970s, *El apando* (1976) and *Las Poquianchis* (1977), Cazals has a solid reputation. These last two films are also fact-based, revealing other aspects of the darker side of Mexican life. José Revueltas, the novelist and activist, wrote a novel about his experiences in prison that provided the basis for *El apando*. *Las Poquianchis* draws on a notorious traffic in young country girls who were being bought from poor families and destined for a slave-like existence in urban brothels. Cazals slides from one time frame to another, from one place to

35 During the 1980s the Colombian author, long a Mexican resident, would be officially made the czar of Mexican cinema, in an attempt to revitalize it and give it direction.

another, making reading this sombre film quite difficult, though his condemnation of the abuse is clear enough.

CONACINE was not the only initiative taken by the Echeverría government in its attempt to be conciliatory after Tlatelolco and to improve the international reputation of the industry. An official film school, the Centro de Capacitación Cinematográfica (CCC), was set up and premises were found for a Cineteca Nacional (National Film Institute). State support for the industry increased, with the Banco Cinematográfico being restructured. There was unprecedented freedom, allowing filmmakers to deal frankly and critically with sensitive socio-political issues. Some film historians, however, are cynical about the motivation behind all these changes and also wonder how effective they were: quality film production and international recognition were not much in evidence, even after the changes. García Riera (1998: 323) gives some figures for film production during the 1970s; they show that in 1971 private producers financed 77 films but by 1976 that number had dropped to 15. Conversely, state-financed films for the same period rose from 5 to 35. Figures for independent movies were stable (5 and 6).[36]

The same old genre films were still appearing, added to which the new permissiveness led to the production of some soft porn (for example, Gabriel Retes' *Fin de fiesta*, 1971). A film called *Tivoli* (1974), a nostalgic take-off of the 1950s cabaret scene, started a new, slang-ridden and more sexy round of *cabaretera* films. Frank and explicit films such as *Noches de cabaret* (Cabaret Nights, 1977) and *Muñecas de medianoche* (Midnight Dolls, 1978) established a new set of stars like Sasha Montenegro. Many of these films were directed by people who had made reputable films during the Golden Age. The 'narcofilm' also made its appearance; this was usually set in a stereotypical borderland dominated by drug barons and their henchmen, with corrupt officials, undercover US agents, hard men and women, and a lot of violence. Narcofilms became a very profitable line. *Lola la trailera* (Lola the Lorrydriver, 1984) is an example: made for US $150,000, it took in $3,500,000 (more than half of which came from tickets sold to Mexicans living across the border.) However, the Mexican industry, which now, under Echeverría, was more or less a nationalized one, did allow independent filmmaking to make progress, encouraging the work of directors already mentioned and others such as Luis Alcoriza, Jaime Humberto Hermosillo, Alfonso Arau and later Nicolás Echevarría, Alberto Cortés, Alfonso Cuarón, María Novaro and Guillermo del Toro.

Somehow, the industry managed to weather the financial crises of the second half of the twentieth century. President López Portillo (in office 1976–82) made the catastrophic appointment of his inept sister as director of Radio, Television, and Cinema. Since López Portillo's government was less enthusiastic about state aid for quality filmmaking than Echeverría's had been, there were now incentives to attract foreign producers and directors to Mexico. There was also

36 Interestingly, Paz kept his distance from the Echeverría government but Fuentes actively defended it; he even became its ambassador to France.

favouritism and scandal. As if that were not enough, a fire destroyed the Cineteca Nacional and with it one of Latin America's most extensive film collections. The next two presidents, Miguel de la Madrid (1982–88) and Carlos Salinas de Gortari (1988–94), generally favoured privatization but also understood it would be disastrous to stop state aid to the film industry. De la Madrid created the Instituto Mexicano de Cinematografía (IMCINE) in 1993, and it gave some support to productions during the 1980s and 1990s. TELEVICINE, created in 1978 as the film division of the Azcárraga empire, has exploited international Spanish-language markets, especially in the US, producing family-oriented films that could be put out on television, such as *El chanfle* (The Soccer Boot, 1978) and *La ilegal* (The Illegal Immigrant, 1979). The latter stars a female pop idol, as do many such films, but TELEVICINE's biggest successes were with 'la India María' (María Elena Velasco), an earthy and resourceful character somewhat in the Cantinflas mould, who emerged from a variety show on television and who became very popular through farces such as *La presidenta municipal* (The Municipal President, 1974) and *Ni de aquí, ni de allá* (Neither from Here nor There, 1987), in which she plays an illegal worker in Los Angeles. During the 1990s TELEVICINE added some artistic films to its commercial fare. The onset of NAFTA did not help the fortunes of the Mexican industry because it sabotaged rules that required that 50 percent of the films screened in Mexican cinemas be Mexican. Moreover the state-owned distribution monopoly lost its sway and international interests weighed in. The Mexican industry faced serious challenges.

Among the directors mentioned previously, Alcoriza must be given credit for keeping serious filming alive in some of the darkest days of the industry. Alcoriza began as an actor and then became an assistant to Buñuel, working with him on many of the scripts for his Mexican films, including *El bruto* and *Los olvidados*; like Buñuel, he was a refugee from the Spanish Civil War. He made some symbol-laden satires, carrying Buñuel's torch. *Tiburoneros* (Sharkhunters, 1963) explores the effects of modernization in both town and country; its protagonist leaves behind his family and busy life in the city to become a shark hunter. In *Mecánica nacional* (National Workshop, 1971), he turns his critical eye on the new Mexico, its vulgarity and lack of moral fibre, a Mexico that, in its rush to progress, has lost its way. On their way to watch the end of a car race on the outskirts of the city, people caught in a traffic jam pull off the road and settle into a dusty area where national characteristics are revealed by their interactions. The men regale each other with their opinions on the woes of the nation and on football. One gun-toting macho, accompanied by a curvaceous redhead, on finding that his aggressive style makes no impression on the others switches to an elegant homily about the virtues of Mexican hospitality. Standing in the dust and a sea of gaudy cars, a group of Spaniards launches nostalgically into 'Asturias, patria querida'. The central figure of the film is the significantly named Eufemio, a mechanic who has taken his family along for the day. Things do not go well for him: by the end his daughter has lost her honour to her fiancé, his wife has tunelessly but successfully been serenading another man, he has taken a drug given him by an American girl, and his mother has died. The old lady dies of overindulgence, of 'congestion', as the doctor puts it when the television cameras stage a suitably pious scene of mourning around her, in order to fill in time before the arrival of the racing cars. The dead woman, to whom no-one has paid much attention prior to her death, is promptly sanctified (a photo of the Virgen de Guadalupe is placed on her bloated belly); all gather to pay homage until the cars are heard in the distance and people gradually peel away, leaving the body abandoned. At the end, the emergency services hurry home in order to avoid having to work and the dead woman has to be manhandled back into the family car, to be transported back to Mexico City accompanied by an escort of police motorbikes with sirens blaring, as if she were someone important, as her son observes, like a politician. Halfway through the film an American girl is heard saying 'There's nothing Mexican here'; this is no doubt intended by the director to be seen as an ironic observation, but one also wonders whether the American is lamenting the absence of the usual stereotypes she might expect to see. Alcoriza makes sure the viewer realizes that his title has national implications by clothing his mechanic in a loud baseball cap and a jacket with 'Mexico' across the back. All this hardly has the bite of Buñuel; *Mecánica nacional* was no doubt thought daring and on target at the time, but it now comes over as laboured, longwinded and obvious, despite some amusing moments. A more excoriating national satire was Gustavo Alatriste's *México, México, ra, ra, ra* (1974). The star of both, Héctor Suárez, also appeared in the gentler commercial comic success, *El milusos* (The Jack of All Trades, 1981) and *El milusos 2* (1983), about the life of provincial immigrants to Mexico City, and he went on to make satirical sketches for television.

Paul Leduc had been one of the leading lights of the *Nuevo cine* group. His first major film was *Reed: México Insurgente* (1971). In this, use of hand-held camera and false sepia tones leave the impression that one is watching a documentary about the Revolution; in fact Leduc had drawn on the photos in the Archivo Casasola (see page 95). He won a number of international awards for *Frida, naturaleza viva* (Frida, A Vibrant Still Life, 1984), no doubt in part because of its subject. Whereas *Reed . . .* feigns documentary realism, *Frida . . .* is an almost silent film that is subjective and fragmentary, consisting of slow, poetic scenes filmed with an ever-changing camera angle. Scenes of the pain-wracked painter in later life are interspersed with flashbacks, some of them in black-and-white, but these are not in chronological order. The painter's life, the defiant challenges she poses in her art, her suffering, her political activities, her relationships with her husband Rivera and with Trotsky and her love of things Mexican are all evoked in this collage. Its title is, of course, ambiguous, suggesting both a contradiction of still life ('naturaleza muerta') and the lively nature and intelligence of Frida Kahlo; but the phrase itself was not Leduc's, since María Izquierdo, a contemporary of Kahlo, had called some of her own paintings 'naturalezas vivas'. Leduc's films are distinctive, and one of their most characteristic distinctions is that dialogue is often sparse, if not absent. In his version of Alejo Carpentier's novella *Concierto barroco*, which becomes simply *Barroco* (1989), it is music that speaks. *Latino Bar* (1990) is a loose adaptation of the old *Santa* story, and waxes critical of society. *Dollar Mambo* (1993) uses a rape by US soldiers, dating from the time of the Panama invasion in 1990, to explore the broader issue of the role of the US in Latin America.

Another interesting case has been that of Arturo Ripstein, whose family history in the industry (his father was a producer) may well have helped him get backing at difficult financial moments. He has made some very successful films, and has insisted all along that his aim is to move audiences, not to convey any message. His early films treated the themes of isolation and subjection to controlling forces. In *El castillo de la pureza* (The Castle of Purity, 1972), a man locks up his wife and children so that they will not be contaminated by the outside world, yet he makes a living by selling rat poison; *Cadena perpetua* (Life Imprisonment, 1978) is about a small-time robber who fails to escape the web of urban crime and corruption. Some of Ripstein's films have been large-scale revamps of the established genres of Mexican cinema. Another literary adaptation, of José Donoso's *El lugar sin límites* (A Place Without Limits, 1977), for which the Argentine writer Manuel Puig wrote the screenplay, won critical plaudits and helped bring Mexico back into the international arena. After some indifferent work during the years of the López Portillo government, Ripstein came back with *El imperio de la fortuna* (The Realm of Fortune, 1985), based once again on Rulfo's screenplay for *El gallo de oro*, a film that is too long but cleverly structured. He also had a commercial hit with an urban family saga called *Principio y fin* (Beginning and End, 1993). More recently he has returned to the themes of obsession and entrapment with *Profundo carmesí* (Deep Crimson, 1996), in which a gigolo enters improbably into a relationship with an overweight single mother and together they make their way towards disaster. 1999 saw the release of Ripstein's faithful but slightly dull adaptation to a Veracruz environment of García Márquez's *El coronel no tiene quien le escriba* (No-one Writes to the Colonel).

By contrast, Jaime Humberto Hermosillo has directed more modest and understated films; these are sometimes a little burdened by dead weight, and they can be rather bleak, but they are generally gentle comedies of human relationships, often with women as the main focus. Though only distributed in 1991 (when it did quite well at the box office), *La tarea* was a remake of an early film. Here María Rojo, an actress who by this time was appearing in a great number of films, is setting up a hidden video-camera for a student project, apparently in order to film a sexual encounter with a former lover. Slow pacing and a weak plot help foster the impression that this is thinly veiled soft porn, or perhaps the unpolished student project the title suggests, but then the whole thing is turned upon itself and shown to be quite a clever exercise in filmmaking. There are several comic touches along the way, including a hilarious scene of lovemaking in a hammock. *María de mi corazón*, once again taking its story from García Márquez, is one of Hermosillo's most successful films, and it is one of several that portray women who are trapped. Now María Rojo is with a former lover who is a petty thief and she makes a living as a children's party entertainer. She charms the man away from his errant ways and he becomes her assistant, but their life falls apart when she is mistakenly taken into a mental institution and made prisoner. Although Hermosillo's films are inclined to ramble and their content can be depressing, they are not heavy-handed or moralistic, and he is sympathetic to his characters, all of which places him rather apart from the general cynicism of films at the time. *Doña Herlinda y su hijo* (Doña Herlinda and Her Son), a mildly amusing treatment of homosexuality, only came out in 1991 but was made years before; once again, officials were reluctant to distribute it until they began to feel the pressure of its international success.

In 1976, Jorge Fons made his first feature film, *Los albañiles* (The Stonemasons), based on the novel by Vicente Leñero. A long time elapsed before his second, *Rojo amanecer* (Red Dawn), released in 1989, that is to say some twenty years after the massacre at Tlatelolco, on which it is based. People wondered whether Fons had to make concessions to government censors in order to get the film distributed, though it treats the Tlatelolco massacre more uncompromisingly than any film before it. *Rojo amanecer* won several Ariel awards (the Mexican 'Oscars') and has come to be regarded as a modern classic. The action takes place in a flat overlooking the square, and the focus is on the effects of the 1968 events on members of a typical middle-class family, whose personal tensions give way to solidarity as they become aware of what is happening outside. Critics have voiced reservations about this film, ranging from the observation that it does not have the documentary weight that one might have expected in a film appearing so long after the massacre, to complaints about the stiltedness of the dialogue. But the aims of *Rojo amanecer* are not documentary; it sets out to give a human angle on the events, and its ending is no compromise, evidently not out to paper over any cracks. Fons based his film on Poniatowska's account of the massacre in *La noche de Tlatelolco*.

As in literature, in cinema women have been making more of a mark as directors and among the ranks of the powerful. Matilde Landeta and Marcela Fernández Violante are rather exceptional in that they had important roles at a time when running the industry and making films was largely a male preserve. Landeta directed a few films in the late 1940s and early 1950s and then returned to the industry after years of absence with *Nocturno a Rosario* (A Nocturne for Rosario, 1990). Fernández Violante, known primarily for her 1975 film *De todos modos Juan te llamas* (Whatever You Do It Makes No Difference), was made Director of CUEC in 1985. *De todos modos . . .*, says Fernández Violante, 'asks what combinations of power lead an apparently idealistic person to betray his or her goals' (Burton: 198). Fernández Violante lacked money to make the film she would have wished, but with the backing of the university she managed to avoid censorship while attacking both the Church and the military establishment. She went on to make *Cananea* (1977) and *Misterio* (Mystery,

1980). The latter is a critique of TELEVISA, the television monopoly, and is a film that mixes melodrama and farce, but one that has a serious subtext. *Misterio* was withdrawn from cinemas in Mexico after only a week, and generally not well-received by critics at home, though it took several Ariel awards and also did well with critics abroad.

Since the 1970s, cinema has frequently questioned machismo and the patriarchal society, concentrating on women's issues and perpectives instead. By the 1980s women film directors were increasingly in evidence, not simply feminists but directors who have enjoyed exploring the intuitive and magical dimensions of filmmaking. Busi Cortés gave us *El secreto de Romelia* (Romelia's Secret, 1988), an adaptation of a Rosario Castellanos text about three generations of women in a single family, but with added political overtones. Critics have compared Dana Rothberg's *Angel de fuego* (Angel of Fire, 1992) to the work of Alejandro Jodorowsky, a Chilean director who was active in Mexico in the post-*Onda* era. Certainly Rothberg's film has a rambling, oneiric quality, as seems fitting for a film that traces experiences of a young girl who is a fire-eater at a circus called the Circo de la Fantasía. She falls under the influence of 'La Patrona', a woman who stages puppet shows of the story of Abraham's sacrifice, a woman who has a sado-masochistic relationship with her son, Sacramento, and who undertakes to 'purify' the fire-eater, who is pregnant by her own now-deceased father. The girl aborts, receives the sacrament, that is to say makes love to Sacramento, and the latter kills himself prior to the Angel of Fire destroying herself and the whole circus by fire. A Buñuelian film indeed, as Rashkin claims (203): a 'highly aestheticized tragic narrative with a documentary-like critique of social reality'. But the importance of the portrayal of poor people should not be overstated: if Buñuel is our point of comparison, this is a film to compare with *Viridiana* rather than with *Los olvidados*, as Rashkin does. More comparable with *Los olvidados* is Gerardo Tort's unsettling modern portrayal of street people in Mexico City, *De la calle* (Street Lives, 2001).

The woman director who has established the most solid reputation is María Novaro, most of whose films have screenplays she wrote together with her sister Beatriz. *Lola* (1989) deals with the situation of a single mother who makes a living by selling black-market clothing at a street stand in Mexico City, is overcome by her circumstances, abandons her daughter, but later comes to terms with her responsibilities. The single mother in Novaro's second film, *Danzón* (1991), a telephone operator, is looking for personal fulfilment through ballroom dancing; this film suffers from a certain amount of sentimental corniness. *Danzón* could be read as a response to the tradition of the *cabaretera*. The *danzón* was at the heart of the Emilio Fernández classic *Salón México*; thus this dance, which has Caribbean roots, became associated not only with dance halls but with prostitution. As far as Julia, the protagonist, and her friends are concerned, the dance is a way of escaping the drab routines of life, but the opening images of the film, with their fixation on feet and shoes, might suggest otherwise: are these people going anywhere, or are they condemned to going round and round? Besides, it seems that once the shoes are off and ordinary life resumes its sway, the character of people changes. The driving force for the plot is the disappearance of Julia's dance partner and her obsessive search for him. Margo Glantz writes that it is rather as if Penelope were abandoning her sacred place and going in search of Ulysses.[37] Her journey takes her to another sacred place, Veracruz, the Mecca of the *danzón*, and there she feels at ease. The fact that once there she is persuaded to teach a transvestite to dance the female role and the fact that she takes the lead in a brief fling with another man seem to suggest that she is indeed finding her feet and going against tradition (though the film does not allow us much information about her Mexico City life outside the dance hall and prior to her journey). At the end of the film Julia returns home as if from a holiday, and her dance partner reappears of his own accord, as if to suggest that the quest was unnecessary.

Novaro's *El jardín del Edén* (The Garden of Eden, 1994), continues to explore the theme of women's search for meaning and identity, this time in the disorienting, disorderly borderland environment of Tijuana, and via an ensemble cast. There are several key female characters: a single mother trying to make ends meet and deal with her recalcitrant son, a Mexican-American who has imperfect Spanish but has brought her daughter to Mexico as part of her search for her Mexican roots, and a dumb American blonde who initially is looking to re-establish contact with her reclusive brother but who ends up becoming involved with a Mexican who wants to cross the border. This film explores the complex relationship between the Mexican and US cultures, but also points to the diversity that is Mexico. Is there a paradise, as signs in front of sleazy bars and hotels on both sides of the border claim? These characters find some purpose in their interactions with one another, but the final scenes suggest that any paradise is much further south, and perhaps a chimera: the *güera* (the blonde), captivated by the sight of an Indian woman with a birdcage, and still showing signs of naïveté, seems about to follow her on the bus to Tabasco. In all, this is one of Novaro's most interesting films, though like others by her it has been accused by some critics of dealing in shallow stereoptyes.

Entre Pancho Villa y una mujer desnuda (Between Pancho Villa and a Naked Woman, 1994) is a film that manages to go some way towards bridging the divide between commercial viability and quality, though like so many films it rather overstays its welcome. It is an adaptation of Sabina Berman's stage play, done by herself and co-directed by Isabelle Tardán. At the start we see two executive women and their male subordinate; they are trying to set up a *maquiladora* deal – to betray the country, as the leading male character puts it. He is the lover of one of the women, and he is writing a book about Pancho Villa. Berman gives the writer a hard time, its effects on the viewer mitigated by some humour: he likes to think of himself as a Don Juan but in fact is very insecure, and looks to Pancho Villa, a kind of *alter ego*, for support. Villa puts in appearances at key

37 '*Danzón*: Los pies de las mexicanas', in *Nitrato de Plata*, 17 (1994), 18–21.

moments to cheer him on when his spirit is flagging, but Villa's image is sabotaged by being portrayed as dominated by his mother. The writer's lover, however, is also none too secure in her independence, sometimes succumbing to the legendary masculine image. Thus the film deals with a macho myth and with the changing roles of women (who in the male view would presumably be seen as betraying the country in another sense). There are a number of political and social asides along the way, but the main focus is on modern love relationships, which are anything but simple.

With the increasing recognition of the importance of the Hispanic population in the United States, not to mention the popularity of things 'Latin', Mexican stars and moviemakers have once again been attracted to Hollywood, by its material benefits, including more liberal and less bureaucracy-ridden financing. Alfonso Arau's *Como agua para chocolate* (Like Water For Chocolate, 1993) was the first blockbuster to result from this phenomenon. Based on Laura Esquivel's novel, it is the story of star-crossed lovers trapped by stifling traditions: since convention dictates that the eldest daughter of a family must be the first to marry, the younger one cannot consummate her love. The concentration on a household of women might seem to suggest that this is to be a feminist film, but these women barely challenge tradition. All is well for the lovers in the end when they finally find each other's arms amid flames and fireworks. Depending on one's viewpoint this is nauseating or wonderfully over-the-top. All along the film makes use of magical realism – as do many novels of the 'women's boom' – and there are some funny, exaggerated touches in that style, but for the most part the attitudes are stereotypical, the characters are two-dimensional, and there is no real delving into issues. A recipe, one might say, for success at the box office. That success led to Arau making an insipid Hollywood film with a similar formula, *A Walk in the Clouds* (1994).

Younger directors have gone across the border and beyond, or come to Mexico across it, making genre films that have enjoyed a cult following. Drawing on the narcofilm genre, a *chicano* filmmaker, Robert Rodríguez, made *El mariachi* (1992) on a paltry budget but it met with great commercial success, even making something of a critical hit. In the borderlands, an itinerant musician gets caught up in drug wars but manages to win the girl and stand up to the drug barons. Rodríguez went on to Hollywood, with mediocre results. A cult grew around a horror film directed by Guillermo del Toro, *Cronos* (1992), in which an elderly antique dealer discovers an ancient device that gives vampire-like immortality. Del Toro was promptly given thirty million dollars by Miramax to make *Mimic* (1997). Later he made a movie set at the end of the Spanish Civil War, *El espinazo del Diablo* (2001), more of a film with a ghost in it than a ghost story, as he himself describes it. It has been compared with the Chilean director Alejandro Amenábar's *Los otros*, which came out at about the same time. In fact the ghost element in *El espinazo* . . . does seem incidental and perhaps unnecessary; the film's best quality is its atmospheric evocation of the period and of the traumatic effect of war on children. *El espinazo* . . . was produced by Pedro Almodóvar, has the veteran Argentine actor Federico Luppi as one of its stars, and was of course filmed in Spain (as was *Los otros*), all of it evidence of how the modern film industry is an international business.[38]

Back in Mexico, moviemakers of the new generation have given us some interesting and commercially sucessful products, despite the renewed pressures from abroad. In the wake of NAFTA, faced with the loss of protective regulations and government backing, they have been resourceful in obtaining finances from a variety of sources and have often produced films that manage to please a cinemagoing public that is perhaps becoming more sophisticated. The formulaic low-end films are still being made but so too are films of considerable quality. Some examples are Alberto Cortés's *Amor a la vuelta de la esquina* (Love Around the Corner, 1985), Carlos García Agraz's *Mi querido Tom Mix* (My Dear Tom Mix, 1991), Carlos Carrera's *La mujer de Benjamín* (Benjamin's Wife, 1991), and Alfonso Cuarón's *Sólo con tu pareja* (Only With Your Partner, 1991). *Del olvido al no me acuerdo* (From Forgetting to Not Remembering, 1999), by Juan Carlos Rulfo, the famous writer's son, is a fine documentary. Cuarón's *Y tu mamá también* (And Your Mother, Too, 2002), and, more deservingly, González Iñárritu's *Amores perros* (Love's a Bitch, 2000), both received wide international distribution following their success at film festivals. Ricardo Benet's first full-length feature film, *Noticias lejanas* (2005) deftly tells of a young man's attempts to break the sterile cycle of poverty in which his family is trapped.

A good example of resourcefulness is Nicolás Echevarría with his *Cabeza de Vaca* (1990). This was planned as an IMCINE production during the 1980s, but for unexplained reasons the state withdrew financial support. However, given time and a great deal of determination, Echevarría gathered together a cluster of international backers, including Channel Four and a Spanish television company, and in the process ensured that his film would be well distributed. *Cabeza de Vaca* is loosely based on one of the major biographical texts of early colonial times, which tells of the experiences of a member of an expedition under Pánfilo Narváez to the coast of Florida that ended in shipwreck, in 1527. The film recounts his wanderings across what is now the southern United States and his chance encounter, after eight years, with another Spanish expedition. Echevarría had experience with documentaries but this film is very subjective and not a little hermetic; the imagery is inventive, the action sometimes mysterious and the dialogue intermittent and often incomprehensible. Alvar Cabeza de Vaca took up with Indian tribes and became a shaman before rediscovering his own people and facing a new period of disorientation as a result. It is by sharing that feeling of disorientation that the viewer gets a sense of Cabeza de Vaca's experience and perhaps also some idea of the culture shock experienced by the Indians when they found themselves face to face with the Spaniards; Echevarría's film has an heuristic quality in that the viewer, trapped in an experience that mimics that of the protagonist, must try to make sense of things.

38 Luppi had also starred in *Cronos*. Critics have mistakenly called both Amenábar and Del Toro 'Spanish' directors.

The opening and closing scenes, in which we see Spaniards interacting with Spaniards, are the only really transparent ones; in the first, the shipwrecks look to the cross for salvation, while in the last a group of conquistadors is seen marching some Indians across a barren plain, bearing an immense silver cross, the symbol of the Spanish cause. There is some ambiguity in this film, since the cross is a constant motif in it, and since Cabeza de Vaca once or twice assumes Christ-like characteristics. At the end, facing reintegration with the Spaniards, he states that there will be some lying to be done; we soon see him, torn from his acquired culture, declaring that here is only one true faith and that all the lands belong rightfully to Spain. Other rescued Spaniards are heard bolstering the myths of discovery, with talk of golden cities and three-breasted women.

There have been other revisionist films dealing with early Mexico, several of them carefully planned so that their release would coincide with the Quinto Centenario, the quincentenary of 1492. Juan Mora Catlett's *Retorno a Aztlán/In Necuepalitzli in Aztlán* (Return to Aztlán, 1990) is visually a stunning movie that tells a magical tale of the origins of the Aztecs; it has dialogue in Nahuatl and music played on what are supposed to be pre-Hispanic instruments.[39]

Turning back to Mexico City and the portrayal of modern times, in 1994 Jorge Fons used a screenplay by Leñero, based on a novel by the Egyptian Naguib Mahfouz, for *El callejón de los milagros*, another film that has done quite well abroad (in English-speaking countries, under the title *Midaq Alley*). If Novaro's *Danzón* was in some way indebted to the *cabaretera* tradition, Fons's film revisits that of the *cine de arrabal* and comes with Salma Hayak as a bonus. The inhabitants of an old working-class area of Mexico City cross paths in a sophisticated but largely predictable soap-opera. This is an anthology of dreary lives alleviated by gossip; the only escape routes open to the younger generation are crossing the border or turning to prostitution. More positively, the film gives a good idea of how, in the huge conglomeration that modern Mexico City now is, certain *barrios* retain their own identities and community spirit. Furthermore the consecutive focus on different protagonists enriches the film by giving several perspectives on shared experiences.

A shared experience is at the core of Alejandro González Iñárritu's *Amores perros*, based on a screenplay by the novelist Guillermo Arriaga. The movie is structured around the well-worn narrative device of lives brought together by chance; in this particular case the contact is fleeting, for they meet only when a car crash takes place at, symbolically, a crossroads. The narrative moves in and out from the nexus of the crash, exploring the stories of the people affected. A young man from the working class loses the fighting-dog on which his hopes have depended, and his life falls apart; some professionals who set up house together find their glamorous lives ruined; but an alienated man, who was once an activist and a prisoner and has become a hired assassin, rescues the dog, and eventually his own life. The convincing representation of different social strata

[39] There have also been some militant films encouraged by the 1994 Zapatista rebellion in Chiapas.

and their strengths and weaknesses is managed without resorting to moralizing.[40] The model whose professional and emotional life is destroyed by the accident is Spanish (and a blonde, to boot), a woman whose beautiful image appears on billboards in the background in stark contrast with what the viewer knows is her current, ruined state; here there is surely a reminder of how a certain Mexico idolizes what is foreign, and also a lesson in superficiality. This observation may be related to the possible implications of the film's closing images, which show the reformed assassin (as proof, he is clean shaven and has had a haircut) selling off a luxury vehicle and heading with his faithful dog across a wasteland to an unclear destination. Setting the faithfulness of dogs apart, human love is a bitch, the film seems to say: its human relationships – sexual, fraternal and parental – have come to grief, and the assassin turns his back on it all, perhaps also on the Mexico that engenders them. González Iñárritu, too, has crossed the border since *Amores perros* met with such success; his second film, *21 Grams* (2004), based, like the ealier one, on a screenplay by Guillermo Arriaga, is set in Memphis and again uses the shattering effects of an accident as its axis. Analogously, the narrative is also shattered into fragments that have to be composed like a jigsaw, which makes for an exhilarating and challenging piece of virtuoso filmmaking, though the experience is marred a little by the ending.

Two films written and directed by Carlos Reygadas, his first full-length feature *Japón* (2002 and set, despite its title, in rural Mexico) and the subsequent *Batalla en el cielo* (2005) have divided the critics and alienated quite a few Mexicans, although everyone praises the movies' strong visual and sound qualities. This is *auteur* cinema somewhat in the style of Tarkovsky or Kiarostami. It is a longwinded cinema of sight and sound that has an authentic, documentary feel about it but lacks clear character definition and narrative strength; tighter editing, a less hermetic style and greater narrative drive might be what is needed to appeal to a wider public.[41] Surely such features partially explain the success of *Amores perros*: here is a film that can be enjoyed on several levels and appeals to audiences of differing degrees of sophistication. And there are other films of the modern era, such as those of Hermosillo, Novaro and Ripstein, that seem further to justify a feeling that the gap between serious and popular cinema can be successfully bridged. A key to understanding what makes for such success may lie in identifying what most modern films are not. Discounting the generic potboilers, nowadays one is generally faced with films that are not agenda-driven (as were many films of the past, such as those of Fernández and Cazals), not a deliberate contribution to the national narrative, not about issues as such. On the whole the archetypes and stereotypes have been

40 Not that the film is representative of the true ethnic mix that is Mexico, for *mestizos* and Indians are not much in evidence.

41 *Japón* is a title that seems to bear no relation to the film it fronts. Presumably, for practical reasons Reygadas felt that he had to give his film some title and saw this one as neutral.

left behind, or have become the butt of parody, and what one finds instead is a personal cinema, a cinema about individuals, a cinema with a degree of subtlety. Plenty of books are still being published in Mexico, but in our visual age it seems especially important for such films to engage the interest of all sorts of people.

6

Closing Words: Language

As is well known, the marriage of Ferdinand and Isabella in the middle of the fifteenth century paved the way for the unification of a reconquered Spain and the dominance of Castilian among its languages. Castilian was a language that would serve the Catholic Monarchs as an 'imperial instrument', as Nebrija put it. Such was the allure, such the administrative importance of Mexico that large numbers of Spaniards came to it after the conquest. However, it must be borne in mind that in the early days of colonization the linguistic unity of the peninsula was still in the making. Settlers and soldiers with other dialects and languages also made their way to the New World: people came not only from Castile but especially from Andalucía and Extremadura. Among these people, some, such as the missionaries and the administrators, were well-educated, but there were also substantial numbers who were neither educated nor from the upper social strata. In all, a variety of language practices came to Mexico, some refined, some popular, and these varieties made contact with the Indian languages, especially with Maya and Nahuatl.

These, then, were the key early colonial ingredients. A later one was the importation of slaves from Africa, but it was to become less of a factor in the linguistic development of Mexico than it was in some other countries, such as those of the Caribbean. In Mexico, the African presence was most noticeable in the Veracruz and Acapulco areas, both large ports; there, one still finds vestigial cultural and linguistic influences, though generally the Africans were quick to assimilate and mix with other races, with the result that it is difficult to identify their influence on the modern language very discretely. There were other foreign-language influences upon nineteenth-century Mexico, despite which the country never received the kind of large-scale waves of immigration that left such an imprint on some other countries, particularly Argentina. The single most important influence in modern times is clearly that of the United States; its proximity, its chequered history of interaction with Mexico, the power of the media and the ever-increasing flow of Mexicans across the border, which gathered pace in the second half of the twentieth century, have meant that the influence of US English on Mexico's language has been considerable and increasing.

A surprising number of Indian languages were spoken in Mesoamerica; they have been classified by linguists into more than a dozen groups, the most extensive of which they call Uto-Aztecan. Within that group the most important language is Nahuatl, which, as we have seen, was the *lingua franca* of the Aztec empire that was dominant at the time of the Spaniards' arrival. Nahuatl is thus the Indian language that has had greatest impact on Spanish, and through it on other languages such as our own. Nahuatl is still spoken in the central highlands and in the state of Guerrero. Not that it is by any means the only language to have survived into the present day. For example, Mixtec and Zapotec are found in Oaxaca, and various languages of the Maya family in the southeast, but whereas the Aztecs were imperialists, most of the other peoples were relatively sedentary, so that their linguistic influence outside their own communities has been less marked. Nowadays there are more than a million speakers of the main indigenous languages (Nahuatl, Maya, Zapotec, Mixtec, Tzotzil and Tzeltal). In all, more than fifty indigenous languages, reflecting a similar number of ethnic groups, are still used by at least a few speakers; some sixteen of these languages are found in one state alone, Oaxaca.

The influence of Indian languages on Spanish was an early and considerable one, still particularly noticeable for its effects on the lexicon. Indeed, Indian languages have provided some words that have become standard in Spanish the world over, and some of them have made their way via Spanish into English: *tomato*, *chocolate*, *coyote*, for example, all derived from Nahuatl. But a great many more terms have become standard in, and largely exclusive to Mexican Spanish, many of them relating to natural or local products, for example, *metate*, *zapote*, *molcajete*, *pozole*, *huipil*, *cuate*, *guajolote*, *tianguis*, *escuincle*, *comal*, *tlapalería*, *huarache*. By far the greatest number of words of Indian origin are from Nahuatl. Indian-language influence on the grammar of Spanish seems to be very little. One or two distinctive phonological characteristics of Mexican Spanish, however, have been ascribed by some linguists to the Indian substrate. One of these is the marked insistence (at least in non-coastal areas) on sibilants, especially unvoiced sibilants in word-final position.[1]

The dialects of spoken Spanish are largely distinguished by phonological features. The Spanish of the borderlands is highly influenced by English; that *norteño* speech (the singsong variety one associates with Cantinflas) starts in the state of Durango and extends north into the United States. For geographical and historical reasons the Spanish spoken in southern areas of the country, such as Chiapas and Yucatán, has as much in common with the language of neighbours to the south as with that of compatriots to the north. For a start, the southern areas were part of the Capitanía General de Guatemala and therefore administratively linked to areas further south. Secondly, the Indian influences here were different from those that affected Spanish in the central valley and to the north. Then there are the coastal areas, some of which, in particular the Veracruz and Tabasco areas, but also parts of the Pacific coast, have characteristics that place them closer to Caribbean dialects of Spanish. This reflects the fact that both Veracruz and Acapulco were major slave-trading areas, but also a far more general, indeed continental difference between highland and lowland

1 Some linguists believe that this may have medieval Spanish roots.

speech patterns. The rest of the country is broadly classifiable as a single dialect zone. Some observers speak of the distinctive linguistic characteristics of Mexico City, but there is not a great deal of agreement about how far out of the city such characteristics extend; in any case, immigration from the provinces is so voluminous that any such distinctiveness is under pressure.

One could argue that Mexican Spanish is conservative in that it has kept alive certain forms of usage that have long since disappeared in Spain. Examples are *Se me hace* (*Me parece* in peninsular Spanish [I have the impression]), *¿Mande?* (equivalent to the peninsular *¿Diga?* or *¿Perdón?*), *¿Qué tanto?* and *¿Qué tan?* (e.g. *¿Qué tanto duele?* [How much does it hurt?] and *¿Qué tan largo es?* [How long is it?]), *Dizque* (apparently) and the use of *Donde* in conditional clauses (*Donde se lo digas, te mato* – [If you tell him, I'll kill you]). By the same yardstick – comparison with modern Spain – there are also many antiquated lexical items, some of them shared by other Spanish-American countries, such as *prieto* (black) and *pararse* (to stand). A further sign of conservatism, and no doubt also of lingering influence of the indigenous heritage, is the insistence in modern society of formulaic courtesies. To take an obvious example, while 'Usted' is rapidly losing ground in the peninsula, in Latin America it is very much alive, and nowhere more so than in Mexico. This and other linguistic formalities among Mexicans are important reflections of a society that is generally courteous.

Disregarding fashionable trends and specialist jargon, the main characteristics of modern Mexican Spanish can be summarized as follows:

Lexicon

As noted, there are many Hispanicized loan words from Indian languages and also a number of archaisms, of which some examples have already been given. In addition, a host of terms and usages are specific to Mexican Spanish; examples are *rebasar* (to overtake), *güero* (blonde), *charola* (tray), *burro* (ironing board), *pinche* (damned/bloody), *joto* (queer, gay). *Siempre* may mean 'definitely' ('siempre no voy con él'); *mero* is used to denote precision, for example in 'en el mero centro' (right in the centre) and 'ayer mero' (just yesterday), or, paradoxically, to indicate approximation, as in 'ya mero llegamos' (We're almost there); *¿Ese?* can mean *Why?*; *¡órale!* and *¡ándale!* are exhortatives or indicators of agreement (OK/ There you go! etc.); *¡Híjole!* expresses amazement (Wow!); *¿Qué onda?* (used above all by the generation that came of age during the 1960s and 1970s, and by younger people) and *¿Quihúbole?* (*Qué hubo + le*, similarly used, but primarily by men) are both ways of saying 'What's up?'; the ubiquitous *chingar* is roughly equivalent to peninsular *joder* (to screw). Words attributable to US English influence are rife and many of them are not used in other parts of the Spanish-speaking world: *mofle* ('muffler', i.e. silencer), *clóset*, *pai*, *lonchería*, *rentar*, *suiche*, *elevador*, and so on. In publications dating from the 1970s Del Rosario and Lope Blanch commented that one might expect the influence of English to be greater; Rosario thought its influence in the Caribbean and in Central America greater than in Mexico. Perhaps they would revise these opinions these days.

Morphology and syntax

Vos is used as a pronoun in Chiapas, an area that linguistically, as already noted, has much in common with Central America. This usage is accompanied by a shift in stress in verb forms and the loss of diphthongs, producing for example *mirás*, *tenés*, as happens in other dialects that use *voseo*.

The word *hasta* is often used in elliptically negative utterances, for example, *Abrimos hasta las nueve* (standard Spanish would be 'No abrimos hasta . . .' [We don't open till nine]).

There is redundant use of possessives, as in 'su coche de Juan' rather than 'el coche de Juan' (Juan's car).

¿Qué? can be used to anticipate a question (rather like the French tag *Est-ce que* . . .), for example, in *¿Qué, no vino?* (Didn't he come?); *¿A poco . . .?* functions in much the same way, or can be used in isolation to express surprise or doubt (Really?).

Lo can be used pleonastically, as in 'lo compramos el guajolote' (We bought the turkey).

Le is commonly added to command forms as an intensifier; thus *pásale* for what in Spain would be *pasa, pasa*, to encourage someone to come in.

Se, with a plural command, can become, for example, *váyansen*, the final 'n' presumably being a compensatory device to indicate plurality in the embedded verb. This phenomenon may in turn lead to loss of the previous 'n', thus giving *váyasen*.

Gustar is regularly used transitively, as is the English verb 'to like': *Lo que usted guste* (Whatever you like); *¿Gusta Usted otra cerveza?* (Would you like another beer?).

The liberal use of the diminutive *-ito* often renders it meaningless (*ahorita mismito*)!

Superlative forms may be constructed using *mucho muy* + adjective.

The verbs *andar* and *ir* are used a great deal for aspect, as in *Voy acabando ahorita* (I've just finished) and *¿Qué andas haciendo?* (What have you been up to?).

Phonology

Some of the distinctive features are these:

A groove fricative sound can be heard in place of /y/ and (perhaps especially in women's speech) in place of the trilled /rr/. A syllable-final /r/ is often made voiceless.

In addition to the striking emphasis on final sibilants mentioned earlier, there is a tendency to reduce final vowels occurring before them, especially /e/, even to the point of elimination.

In contrast to the firmness of /s/ in the central region, in the rural northwest /s/

is reduced and sometimes aspirated. In Jalisco it may be nasalized, in Yucatán and the coastal areas it is often reduced or lost.

Another striking feature of central valley educated speech is the very deliberate articulation of [ð], even as a replacement for initial [d].

In Yucatán, a final /n/ may be realized as [m]. /y/ may be elided. Stressed vowels tend to be markedly lengthened. The plosives /p/, /t/, /k/ are often aspirated, while their intervocalic fricative counterparts /b/, /d/ and /g/ may become plosives, especially before stressed vowels. Here and on the coasts the velar /x/ is reduced to a weak aspirated [h], as in the Caribbean.

Conclusion: One nation?

Mexico is a puzzle, a paradox that raises all sorts of important questions. Take, for example, the position of the Indians. Prior to the conquest, the Indians did not think in terms of private property, and even these days they consider themselves as members of communities as much as they see themselves as individuals; yet many of them (indeed much of the country in general), are now desperate to acquire private means and possessions, aping US consumerism. A concomitant factor is increasing faith in the power of linear progress through change, something that is in marked contrast to the traditional Indian worldview, according to which life is cyclic. At present some of the Indians cross cultures, for example by looking first to the services of a *curandero* (a faith healer) before turning to a doctor, or by wearing no shoes during the week in the country and putting them on to go to town for weekend market. In the longer run, have the Indians of Mexico, living in this globalizing world and faced with such powerful commercial pressures from outside, any choice other than to keep the shoes on and march in time with the prevailing tune?

At several points during this study there has been evidence of the tension between traditionalism and a drive towards modernity, a tension that has not only affected the Indians. Consider the nineteenth-century *criollos* who, while proud of the newly independent Mexico, continued to cling to Spanish traditions and later sought refuge in things French, prolonging their cultural dependence even while advocating modernization. Or consider the post-revolutionary era, when there developed a somewhat schizophrenic wish to rescue and revitalize native traditions while at the same time celebrating technological advances and moving with the international times.

As we have seen, Mexican governments, particularly those of the post-revolutionary era, have been at pains to project an image of national unity, and ordinary Mexicans have predictably closed ranks when faced with the need to mark off their territory, to identify themselves as different from members of other nations: Mexico is neither Spain nor the United States, nor is it to be confused with the rest of Spanish America. Then what does make it different? Linguistically, one of the most distinctive features of Mexican Spanish is a lexicon that boasts a large number of items that derive from the Indian substratum. Other aspects of the culture that can be attributed to the Indian heritage also serve as proof of the country's distinctiveness. Yet the very people who proudly call attention to that distinctiveness often choose to adopt European and US lifestyles and look down on Indians in everyday life.

The truth is that for every sign of unity one can find another that suggests contradiction, diversity and division, whether regional, ethnic, linguistic, topographical or economic. The land itself makes for diversity and regionalism: much of it is arid, much of it mountainous, but there are relatively fertile valleys between its mountain ranges, and steamy tropical zones on the Gulf coast and in the south. Most of the major cities are located in the central *mesa*, between the two main ranges that run north to south. It is here that Mexico City sits, at an altitude of some 2,000 metres, the main locus of power since the days of the Aztecs; but in opposition to central power there have long been strong regional interests, in many ways matching the geographical diversity just described. The colonial habit of granting titles to land and labour encouraged the creation of large *haciendas* that became societies in their own right, resulting in the emergence of the *caudillos* who played key and often antagonistic roles in nineteenth- and twentieth-century politics. During the twentieth century, power depended to a large extent upon alliances that the PRI made with local strongmen. Seeing it from the other side, so to speak, one might argue that opposition to central power has been regionalism's *raison d'être*. Clearly the north has tended to rival the south, and both have resisted the authoritarian centre; it is a little as if things have not changed much since the time of the uneasy Aztec federation.

There are also economic factors that interlace with social and cultural contradictions. Experts on Mexican culture have tended to speak of the delicate co-existence of two Mexicos, one comprising the majority, whose culture can be traced, at least in part, back to pre-Hispanic times, and the second comprising an élite, outward-looking minority that has sought to modernize the country, often by imitating foreign ways, though at the same time, as we have noted, paying lip service to the Indian heritage. The facts are these: overwhelmingly, Mexico is a *mestizo* country, but for all its fusion of human types, despite the signature 'race', as Vasconcelos liked to call it, the country is fraught with divisions and distinctions between people. Economically speaking, masses of people face a daily struggle to eke out a living, begging is widespread, unemployment high, while at the same time a small privileged élite lives very well indeed, often impervious to the plight of the majority. Social divisions – and prejudices – are based not simply on race but equally on cultural and economic perceptions. Being 'Indian', for example, depends to a large degree on whether one is regarded (or sees oneself) as an Indian, and that in turn depends on how far one is in the swim, how far one has bought into the dominant culture, become part of the modern nation, as opposed to having traditional Indian cultural habits.

Cutting across these considerations is the question of language variety and ethnicity. In addition to differences between Mexican dialects of Spanish, many Indian languages are still spoken, especially in the south. Naturally, estimates vary, but the country's ethnic composition these days is roughly as follows: 60 to 75 percent of the people are *mestizos*, 15 to 30 percent Indian or predominantly Indian, and most of the rest are white. The black element has on the whole become fused with the *mestizo* group, but is still in evidence on the Gulf coast in the vicinity of the port of Veracruz, and on the Pacific coast in the states of Guerrero and Oaxaca. If the Indian population is defined strictly by language, however, it represents about 10 percent of the overall population. Modern communications, migration in search of work, and political pressures have inevitably undermined the separate identities of these groups and their languages, but some still exist in relative isolation, either by choice or owing to their marginalization from mainstream society. When the Spaniards came, the north had an Indian population that was scattered and nomadic; nowadays, *criollos* and *mestizos* are dominant there, while in the south, where the Indian population was more concentrated and more highly organized, Indians or *mestizos* are more common.

The interaction between north and south has not been great and this, together with the proximity of the United States, has led to marked disparities; by all sorts of yardsticks – income, education, and literacy among them – the north is more advanced and modern. It is also more individualistic. And yet Mexico is both the community-minded Indian of Chiapas who lives a life apart from the Hispanic mainstream and at the other extreme, both geographically and culturally, the US-oriented inhabitant of Tijuana who, there, in a city of two million people on the busiest border in the world, sells visitors Bart Simpson spin-offs and Osama Bin Laden *piñatas*, before retiring to his makeshift shack.[1] Mexico is also the prosperous *criollo* family of the main conurbations of the *mesa*, whose offspring may well be educated abroad and who, in short, have relatively little in common with people in either of the regional groups previously described.

Mexico City itself, by some counts already the largest metropolis in the world (27 million?), depending on how the municipal area is defined, is surprisingly quiet and polite for such a chaotic, crime-ridden and polluted city, in which many people survive by hawking whatever comes to hand and where the infrastructure cannot cope with the constant influx of people from the provinces.[2] Much of the country at large is afflicted by erosion. Corruption in politics is on a scale matched in few Latin American countries. A large part of the economy is informal, not to say illegal. Drug trafficking is a major problem. Mexican factory workers receive miserable wages to produce goods that feed the gluttony north of the border. There is no sign of the flow of would-be immigrants to the US decreasing. So the litany of problems continues. Finally, it must be said that confidence in the government's ability to deal with national problems – the inequalities, the poverty and unevenness of public services, the loss

1 In 2005 the Mayor of Tijuana, a man with a shady past (inevitably, it would seem), ordered street vendors to wear traditional Mexican costumes when catering to the demands of people who had come across the border from the United States.

2 In March 2005 an international study reported that Mexico City was as dangerous as Bogotá. In his account of the conquest Bernal Díaz del Castillo writes of his surprise at the quietness of the *zócalo* at a time when it was teeming with Indians at market.

of revenues from the inefficient oil industry to foreign companies – is not high. In many respects Mexico is still Third World, yet – and here, perhaps is the greatest surprise of all – its people are above all stoical and proud of their country. 'Como México, no hay dos' – there's no place like Mexico.

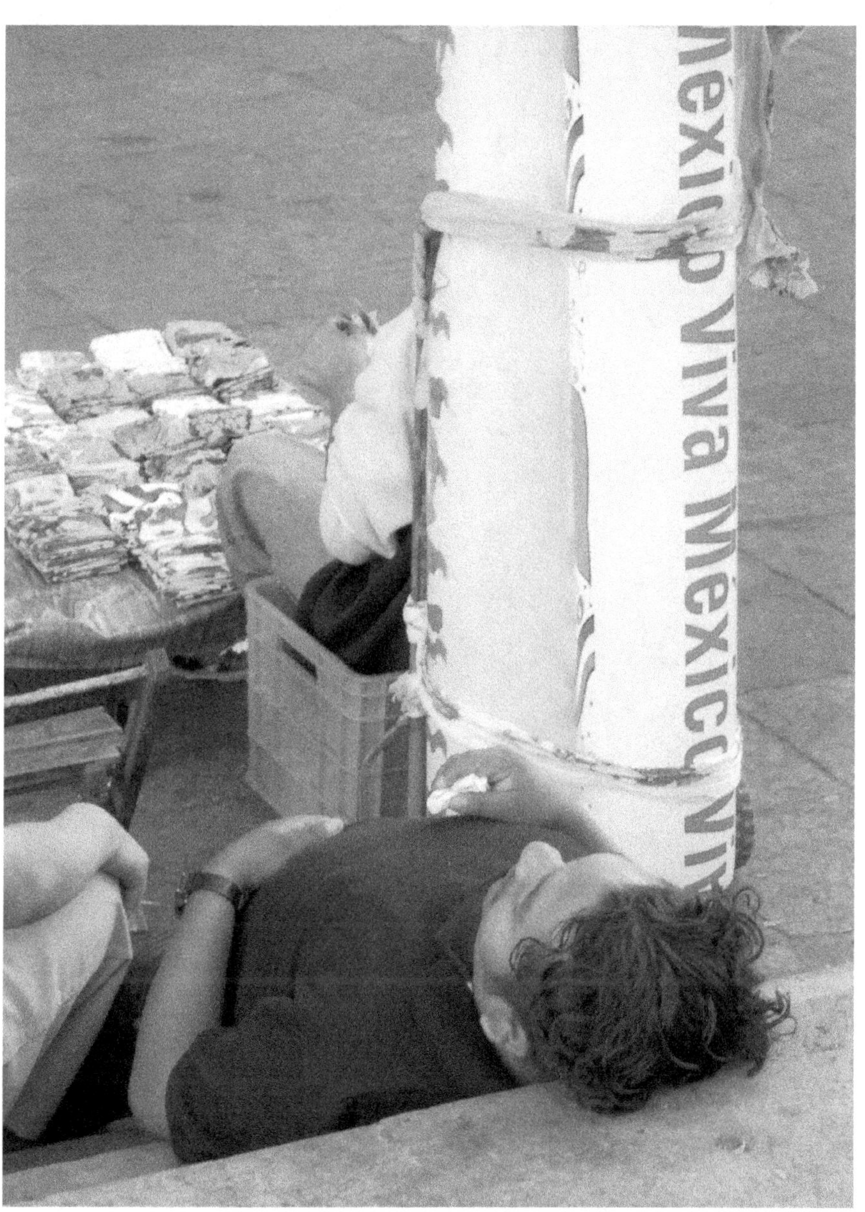
Viva México

CHRONOLOGY

50,000? BC First migrations to the Americas from Asia
12,000 BC Approximate date of earliest human remains found in Mexico
9,000 BC Beginnings of cultivation of maize
1,500 BC–AD 300 Formative Period of Mesoamerican civilizations
AD 300–900 Classic Period of Mesoamerican civilizations
900–1519 Post-Classic Period of Mesoamerican civilizations
1325 Foundation of Aztec capital, Tenochtitlan
1511 Spanish expedition shipwrecked on Yucatán coast. Jerónimo de Aguilar and Gonzalo Guerrero survive among the Mayas
1519 Cortés lands in Yucatán. Encounters Aguilar and Malinche.
1521 Siege of Tenochtitlan, Aztecs defeated
1521–42 Franciscan, Dominican and Augustinian orders begin to arrive (in that order). In 1523 the Franciscans are charged by the Pope with converting the natives
1522 Cortés named Captain General and Governor of New Spain
1527 Arrival of Mexico's first bishop, Juan de Zumárraga
1531 Virgen de Guadalupe appears before the Indian Juan Diego at Tepeyac, near Mexico City
1536 Colegio de Santa Cruz de Tlatelolco founded, for the education and indoctrination of the Indian nobility
1537 First printing press set up in New Spain (and the New World). Vasco de Quiroga begins to establish utopian communities in Michoacán
1542 Las Casas' *Brevísima relación de la destrucción de las Indias*
1553 The Real Universidad Pontificia (first university in the New World) starts classes
C. 1570 Diego de Landa writes *Relación de las cosas de Yucatán*
1571 Inquisition formally established in Mexico
1572 First Jesuit missionaries arrive
1577 Bernardino de Sahagún, a teacher at the Colegio de Santa Cruz, completes Spanish and Nahuatl versions of his four-volume *Historia general de las cosas de Nueva España*. Manuscripts thereof then lost for some 200 years
1597 First *corral de comedias* opens
1648 Birth of Juana Inés de Asbaje (later to become Sor Juana Inés de la Cruz)
1649 Puebla Cathedral dedicated
C. 1650 Indian population has by now declined from an estimated 20 million to about one million. It will begin to rise again from this time
1667 Mexico City Cathedral dedicated
1690 Carlos de Sigüenza y Góngora's *Infortunios de Alonso Ramírez*
1692 Popular riots in Mexico City; government buildings burned

1712 Indian uprising in Chiapas
1767 Jesuits expelled from Spanish America
1783 San Carlos Academy founded (Bellas Artes)
1805 First daily newspaper: *Diario de México*
1810 16 September: Father Miguel Hidalgo's 'Grito de Dolores' launches movement for independence from Spain
1811 José María Morelos takes up struggle for independence
1812 Fernández de Lizardi launches his first newspaper
1816 Lizardi's *El Periquillo Sarniento*, generally considered Latin America's first novel
1821 Independence from Spain. Iturbide leads victorious troops into Mexico City
1822 Iturbide crowned Emperor of newly independent Mexico; rules for 11 months. USA recognizes independence
1823 Central American Federation of territories declares independence from Mexico
1824 New constitution establishes federal republic. Iturbide executed. Guadalupe Victoria elected first President of the Republic
1829 Spaniards invade Tampico but surrender to Santa Anna. Slavery abolished
1830 Santa Anna assumes presidency for the first time; is in that office intermittently over next twenty-five years
1833 Valentín Gómez Farías leads attempts to secularize education
1836 Texas declares independence from Mexico
1838 In Yucatán there is increasing interest in the possibility of secession
1846–7 Mexican–American War. US troops invade Mexico City and Mexican government flees to Querétaro. World's first war photographs
1848 Treaty signed ceding half of Mexican territory to the United States, including California, Arizona, and New Mexico
1848–51 Caste Wars in Yucatán
1854 Liberals proclaim Plan de Ayutla and launch revolt
1855 Santa Ana abandons Mexico
1857 A new anticlerical constitution is promulgated
1858–61 War between liberals and conservatives, with two different governments claiming to have authority; Juárez, installed as president of the liberal government in Veracruz, promulgates Leyes de Reforma
1862 French troops arrive with support of conservatives. On 5 May, liberal forces defeat French at Puebla
1864 Maximilian of Habsburg is installed by Napoleon as new Emperor of Mexico. Chapultepec Castle, formerly a barracks, is rebuilt as official residence
1867 Liberal forces defeat troops loyal to Maximilian, and Republic is restored. End of French Intervention. Juárez elected president
1869 Ignacio Altamirano begins to publish *El Renacimiento*
1872 Benito Juárez dies
1877–1911 The 'Porfiriato', a long period under the dictator Porfirio Díaz. Renewed European influence
1877 National Conservatory of Music established
1880s *Modernismo* on the rise in literature
1887 José María Velasco's painting of Oaxaca Cathedral
1890s José Guadalupe Posada active as engraver
1896 First cinema opens

1910 *Regeneración* published in United States, advocates demise of Porfirio. Revolution begins. Díaz ousted. Pancho Villa dominates fighting in the north, Emiliano Zapata in the south
1911 Porfirio Díaz goes into exile; Francisco Madero becomes president
1913 Madero assassinated in coup led by Victoriano Huerta; Villa, Zapata, Carranza, Obregón and others return to arms. Manuel M. Ponce publishes *La música y la canción mexicana*
1914 Huerta flees capital and revolutionary factions march into Mexico City; at the *Convención de Aguascalientes* the revolutionary leaders fail to reach agreement
1915 Factions lead by northern landholders Carranza, Obregón and Calles gain the upper hand over the popular revolutionaries Villa and Zapata
1917 Carranza and the Congreso Constitucional promulgate new constitution that is nationalistic and anticlerical. Carranza elected president.
1919 *El automóvil gris*, the outstanding film of the silent era. Mexican Communist Party founded
1920 Rebellion by factions from Sonora led by Obregón and Calles. Carranza assassinated
1920–24 Presidency of Alvaro Obregón
1921 First radio broadcasts
1921–24 José Vasconcelos leads 'cultural revolution' as minister of education
1924 Carlos Chávez begins to dominate Mexican art music, Diego Rivera and the muralists its visual art
1924 Azuela's *Los de abajo*, previously serialized, is published as a book
1924–28 Presidency of Plutarco Elías Calles
1925 Vasconcelos publishes *La raza cósmica*
1926–29 Cristero Rebellion
1927 Presidential term extended to six years
1928 Mexican Symphony Orchestra founded. Obregón re-elected president but assassinated before taking office. *Maximato* begins
1929 Calles, running things from the wings, forms the Partido Revolucionario de la Nación (PRN) and establishes the populist government machine
1930 Radio station XEW begins broadcasting. Arrival of Sergei Eisenstein, the Russian film director
1930–50 Golden Age of radio and cinema
1930s Migration towards metropolitan area of Mexico City (DF) grows in significance (and increases in later decades)
1932 Formation of the *Contemporáneos* group
1934–40 Presidency of Lázaro Cárdenas, first Mexican president to campaign for office. Puts many of the ideals of the Revolution into effect
1935 Cárdenas establishes Confederación Nacional Campesina (CNC)
1936 Cárdenas establishes Confederación de Trabajadores de México (CTM)
1937 Rodolfo Usigli's play *El gesticulador*
1938 Cárdenas nationalizes oil industry. He changes name of party to Partido de la Revolución Mexicana (PRM)
1939 Conservative opposition party, Partido de Acción Nacional (PAN) founded
1940 *Ahí está el detalle*, Cantinflas' first hit film
1940s Mexico takes in refugees from Franco's Spain, including Luis Buñuel
1942 *Bracero* programme starts, allowing US employers to take on Mexican agricultural workers

1943 *Flor silvestre*, the first major film by Fernández and Figueroa. Goverment sets up national health, disability and pension systems, under Instituto Mexicano del Seguro Social (IMSS)
1946 Miguel Alemán elected; first civilian president of post-revolutionary period. Ruling party adopts the name Partido Revolucionario Institucional (PRI)
1947 Yáñez's novel *Al filo del agua* published
1948 Ballet Nacional de México established
1949–54 Ciudad Universitaria constructed, the campus of the Universidad Nacional Autónoma (UNAM), in Mexico City
1950 Buñuel's film *Los olvidados*. Octavio Paz publishes *El laberinto de la soledad*. Television transmissions begin
1950s *Ruptura* artists, such as José Luis Cuevas and Rufino Tamayo, break with dominant aesthetic of muralists
1953 Women win right to vote and hold elected office
1955 Publication of Juan Rulfo's novel *Pedro Páramo* .
1959 Ballet Folklórico founded
1959 Government-funded TV transmissions begin. Miguel León-Portilla publishes *Visión de los vencidos*
1960s *La Onda*
1961–62 *Nuevo Cine* published
1962 Carlos Fuentes' *La muerte de Artemio Cruz*
1964–65 *Bracero* programme suspended. Industrialization of border territory begins
1968 Tlatelolco massacre on 2 October
1970s Influx of political refugees from Chile and Argentina
1971 Luis Alcoriza's film, *Mecánica nacional*. Poniatowska publishes *La noche de Tlatelolco*
1975 Legal changes introduced protecting women's rights and allowing birth control
1976 Government orchestrates break-up of staff of *Excelsior* newspaper. New opposition papers are created (*Proceso*, *Unomásuno*) and Octavio Paz's literary monthly *Vuelta*. The peso suffers a 50 percent devaluation against the dollar
1981 Fall in oil prices triggers economic hardships
1982 The peso furthered devalued. President López Portillo nationalizes the banking industry
1985 Major earthquake in Mexico City. Protests against government corruption. Angeles Mastretta publishes *Arráncame la vida*
1987 Cuauhtémoc Cárdenas and Porfirio Muñoz Ledo, prominent politicians, publicly renounce their PRI membership
1988 PRI presidential candidate Carlos Salinas de Gortari defeats Cuauhtémoc Cárdenas. Massive protests against apparent fraud in state and federal elections ensue
1989–93 Salinas government carries out neoliberal economic reforms, privatizing several state-owned companies
1989 Establishment of socio-democratic opposition party, Partido de la Revolución Democrática (PRD), with Cuauhtémoc Cárdenas as leading figure. Jorge Fons' film *Rojo amanecer*, on the Tlatelolco massacre, is finally screened.
1993 Alfonso Arau's film version of Laura Esquivel's novel *Como agua para chocolate* (Like Water for Chocolate)
1993 The newspaper *Reforma* starts

1993 Second major commercial television network, TV Azteca, brings competition to Televisa empire. NAFTA established (i.e. TLC: Tratado de Libre Comercio)
1994 Ejército Zapatista de Liberación Nacional (EZLN), under Comandante Marcos, launches armed rebellion in Chiapas. Rash of political assassinations afflicts PRI
1995 President Ernesto Zedillo confronts another economic crisis and announces another 50 percent devaluation of the peso
1996 Zedillo introduces electoral reforms; autonomous Federal Elections Institute established
1999 Student strike shuts down the UNAM
2000 Elections bring Vicente Fox to power (PAN candidate). Seven-decade rule by PRI ends

GLOSSARY

Audiencia Colonial administrative agency responsible primarily for legal matters

Bolero A romantic song genre

Bracero Guest agricultural worker in the US (under a programme that operated for some years after 1945)

Cacique Regional strongman. A word of pre-Hispanic derivation

Capilla abierta An open church, sometimes with multiple naves, such that many people can be accommodated

Castas Colonial system for classifying people of mixed race

Caudillo A term of Arabic origin meaning 'leader' and applied in particular to charismatic, often dictatorial and military leaders of the kind that dominated nineteenth-century Latin America

Charro Stereotypical, traditional Mexican cowboy. Broad-brimmed hat, braided costume with short jacket and tight trousers, often in black (dress version)

China poblana Stereotypical, traditional young Mexican female figure. White embroidered blouse, full skirt

Chinampa Floating garden or raised cultivated area used by Aztecs in lakes of central Mexico

Científicos Term applied to the positivist advisers to Porfirio Díaz

Consejo de Indias Advisory body to Spanish Crown on matters relating to the New World

Corrido Narrative song ballad telling primarily of life in the northern region and/or exploits of the famous

Costumbrismo Artistic tendency involving the highlighting of local manners and human types, sometimes with a satirical purpose

Criollo\a Person of European descent but born in the Americas

Cristero Rebellion Anti-government and pro-Catholic war of immediate post-revolutionary era (1926–29)

Dedazo Political tradition in twentieth-century Mexico whereby the leader of the PRI would point his finger to identify his chosen successor. That identity then usually remained hidden (*tapado*) from the public until the moment of revelation (*destape*)

Ejido Communal land. The *ejido* system dates from pre-Hispanic times (the notion of private land ownership being foreign to the Indians) and was reinstituted under the land reforms of President Cárdenas

Encomienda Grant of land and Indian labour given to settlers by Spanish authorities, on condition that profits of labour be shared with Crown and Indians be cared for

Estípite A decorative architectural column that is usually wider at the top than at the bottom

Exvoto An object or artifact that is offered to a saint, Christ or the Virgin Mary, as public testimony and thanks for their intercession. Usually displayed at a church or shrine

Federales Armed militia of central government

Fotonovelas Printed spin-offs of television soaps

Gachupín Pejorative term of reference to a *peninsular*, a person from Spain

Gringo\a Refers primarily to a person from the US, though the term is frequently applied to non-Hispanic foreigners in general

Guadalupana Term applied to the cult of the Virgen de Guadalupe

Hacienda Large ranch or plantation worked by landless peasants but under control of a single owner, the *hacendado*

Historietas Comic books

IMCINE Instituto Mexicano de Cine, the Mexican Film Institute

INBA Instituto Nacional de Bellas Artes (National Institute of Fine Arts)

Indigenismo Artistic portrayal or advocacy of the Indian and Indian culture

Intendencia Colonial administrative agency with main responsibility for financial matters

Jarabe tapatío A dance form associated with Guadalajara: the 'Mexican Hat Dance'

Ladino\a Person outside the Indian community

Leyenda negra The tale of Spain's cruelty, used especially by the English to denigrate Spain's reputation

Limpieza de sangre Concern with 'purity' of blood, that is with having Spanish ancestors (and neither Jewish nor Moorish)

Malinchismo (Malinchista) In modern times this term is applied to a liking for (or to a person who likes) things foreign rather than Mexican. More broadly, Malinche, Cortés' mistress and translator, is associated with betrayal

Maquiladora Assembly (and sometimes manufacturing) plant located close to the US border

Maximato Period following assassination of President Obregón in 1928, during which former President Calles, known as the 'jefe máximo', maintained control behind puppet presidents, prior to the election of President Cárdenas

Mesoamerica Term used to refer to areas (parts of present-day Mexico and Central America) that were inhabited by ancient Indian civilizations

Mestizo\a Person of mixed European and Indian descent; during colonial times this usually meant having a Spanish father and an Indian mother

Mordida Bribe paid to official; such bribes are common

Norteño Music associated with the northern part of the country, particularly the US border region

Pachuco\a Person influenced by US culture

Pelado A broadly negative stereotype of the working-class Mexican, epitomized by the film star Cantinflas. A resourceful character who knows how to look after himself but whose self-confident exterior masks his insecurity

Peninsulares Native-born Spaniards

Porfiriato The period of authoritarian rule, political stability and economic and industrial modernization under President Porfirio Díaz (1877–1911)

PRI Partido Revolucionario Institucional, the Institutionalized Revolutionary Party, which held power for some seventy consecutive years during the twentieth century

Requerimiento Official summons to Indians requiring that they accept Christianity and declare allegiance to the Spanish Crown

Retablo Originally a series of decorative or didactic religious paintings, usually of saints or biblical scenes, displayed behind the altar of medieval Catholic churches. Today it also applies to small devotional paintings, such as *exvotos*

Rurales Rural police force used during the *Porfiriato*

Sexenio Six-year term of presidential office. No re-election allowed

Soldadera Female soldier during the Revolution

Telenovela TV soap-opera

TELEVISA Privately owned media empire and for many years a virtual monopoly. Also active in film production and in providing Hispanic television to viewers in the United States

Tlatelolco A place of meetings and celebrations since pre-Hispanic days and now incorporated into Mexico City. Its Plaza de las Tres Culturas was the site of a massacre that took place in 1968, as the Olympic Games were about to be held in Mexico

TLC The Tratado Libre de Comercio, i.e. NAFTA

UNAM Universidad Nacional Autónoma de México, the country's largest university

Zapatista Follower of Emiliano Zapata during revolutionary times or anti-government rebel in Chiapas at end of twentieth century

FURTHER READING

General

A useful bibliography is Florescano and Mijangos' *México en sus libros*, which is organized historically and by topic and deals primarily with matters social, historical and political; each of the six hundred-odd entries has a short descriptive paragraph accompanying it. Well-written topical essays by specialists are the basis of *The Oxford History of Mexico* (edited by Meyer and Beezley), an indispensable source of information, which also provides a good basic bibliography. The 2001 publication *Historia de México*, by Anna, Bazant, Kantz *et al.*, also consists of essays by specialists. The same goes for *Historia General de México*, published by the Colegio de México in 1981, a publication whose style and coverage are more like those of the *Oxford History* mentioned above. A reference work covering similar terrain, to which over eighty specialists contributed but which is addressed to a less specialist readership, is Vásquez's *Gran historia de México ilustrada*. The *Enciclopedia de México*, edited by Alvarez, has information on all aspects of the country and its history; its 1996 edition in fourteen volumes also includes census data and a copy of the constitution, and it is available on CD. The useful *Diccionario Porrúa . . .* has been updated by León-Portilla. Joseph and Henderson's *The Mexico Reader* is an invaluable compilation of extracts from primary sources relating to the history and culture; many extracts have been translated from Spanish, others are in the original English. More anecdotal but nonetheless useful information comes from the writings of many travellers to Mexico. Such accounts range from journalistic-cum-anthropological ones by people such as Oster and Toor through the work of creative writers such as Graham Greene and D.H. Lawrence, to the accounts left by missionaries and temporary residents, such as Fanny Calderón, the wife of Spain's first ambassador to the newly independent Mexico. Alan Ryan's *Reader's Companion . . .* is a useful selection of some of the impressions of a few such visitors. Alan Riding's *Distant Neighbors* is a well-informed introduction to the country written for the general reader. Floyd Merrell offers an authoritative introduction to Mexico's culture and to issues affecting it; he approaches the task in an unusual and stimulating way, but his style – he is trying to sell cultural awareness to American students – can be trying. In a more matter-of-fact vein, *Mexico: A Country Study* (Library of Congress, 1997) is a mine of information, especially useful for environmental and social data, as well as for its compact accounts of the various presidencies. Barry's *Mexico: a Country Guide* covers similar ground in a less detached, more combative style. For the country's overall history – and the material available on this is indeed voluminous – a few of the many authoritative sources are King, Bazant, Bethell, Cosío Villegas, Hamnett, Meyer *et al.* and Miller. Material on the Revolution is also too voluminous to detail here; Brenner and Leighton offer a fairly recent account, while Raat's bibliography is a useful stepping stone to others. The

Atlas nacional de México is an official and up-to-date publication. The country's natural resources and their exploitation are described by Bassols Batalla and others, the flora and fauna by Ramamoorthy *et al.* Benítez's *Los indios de México* is an invaluable source of information. Demographics can be approached via the publications of the Instituto Nacional de Estadística, Geografía e Informática, and the work of US anthropologists such as Eric Wolf. For an ambitious account of the effects of Mexicans abroad and of foreigners in Mexico, see González Navarro's *Los extranjeros en México* . . . Many writers have tried to address the question of Mexico's identity and the national image that has been projected by officialdom; for example, four essays on the subject make up *Espejo mexicano*, edited by Florescano. The work of Samuel Ramos and Octavio Paz as analysts of Mexican national identity has received a great deal of publicity; others such as Enrique Krause have broadly followed Paz's line of thinking. Roger Bartra, Guillermo Bonfil and Enrique Alduncín have been lively analysts from a different standpoint. Their theses have in turn been criticized by Claudio Lomnitz. Bartra has highlighted the interface of popular culture and power. Carlos Fuentes' *El espejo enterrado* can be considered part of the same debate. Néstor García Canclini (*Culturas híbridas* . . .) is one of the most interesting analysts of the meeting of US and Mexican cultures.

Cinema

Overviews of Latin American cinema include King's *Magical Reels*, which has a very good account of Mexico, and Hennebelle and Gumucio-Dagrón's wide-ranging *Les Cinémas de l'Amérique Latine*. Hart's *Companion* . . . consists primarily of descriptions and analyses of key films, a half-dozen of them Mexican; Deborah Shaw includes analysis of a couple of important Mexican films; Schnitman considers the vicissitudes and challenges of the continental film industry but has virtually nothing to say about the films themselves. Mexico does not particularly pepper the pages of Pick but they repay a peck through. Paranaguá parodies Porfirio's pronouncement for the title of his book, a good if brief outline of Latin American film. *Hojas de cine* . . . has historical and theoretical studies on the new cinema, as does Martin's *Latin American Cinema*. . . . Stevens' *Based on a True Story* . . . is about the relationship of film to history. Elena and Díaz López include useful discussions of some recent Mexican films. For an overview of Mexican cinema (at least until 1980), Mora's study has been the standby source in English: readable and reliable. The one chapter of Julianne Burton's book on Latin American cinema that deals with Mexico consists of an interview with Marcela Fernández Violante. More interviews are in Nevares Reyes' *Mexican Cinema*, but they are not very penetrating. The fullest and most up-to-date coverage of Mexican cinema is in Spanish, in works by García Riera. Paranaguá, Hershfield, and Maciel provide important collections of essays. Hershfield's *Mexican Cinema: Mexican Women* is an engaging study of the roles and portrayals of women at the height of the Golden Age; Tuñón covers similar ground. An interesting though none too fluid book is Susan Dever's, about melodrama as a vehicle for national expression and the projection of ideas of womanhood; this study moves from post-revolutionary Mexico across the border and into the modern era. The fullest account of women filmmakers and their rise in prominence in the last two decades of the twentieth century is by

Elissa Rashkin; moreover, this book has cogent things to say about recent trends in cinema. Other useful books for recent cinema are by Foster, Schaefer and Ramirez Berg.

Literature and Theatre in Spanish

Foster's 1992 bibliography is a good starting point. González Peña has long served as a traditional resource. Mexican literature is very competently surveyed by Steven Bell in a chapter of Foster's *Handbook of Latin American Literature*, and it naturally figures prominently in all the many discursive surveys of Latin American literature. The best and most complete quick general reference work on Latin American literature is Smith's compendious *Encylopaedia*. Authoritative essays on several periods and topics, by various hands, can be read in the *Cambridge History of Latin American Literature*. Foster's *Mexican Literature: a History*, one of the most complete and up-to-date books devoted solely to Mexico, is also a compilation of essays by different people, very useful but a little uneven in focus and readability. Jiménez Rueda is helpful regarding the nineteenth century. The **chronicles** may be approached via Murray or Pastor, and are widely available in reprints and translations. So also the **codices**; for example, the *Florentine Codex* can be read in a facsimile edition published by Mexico's Secretaría de Gobernación in 1979, and it has also been published in a twelve volume English edition by the University of Utah Press (1950–82). For the codices, see too Aguilera, Alcina Franch, Alvarez, Brotherston, Gutiérrez Solana, Lee and Nuttall. Velazco's *Visiones de Anáhuac* is especially useful for bicultural authors of the sixteenth and seventeenth centuries. (Suggestions regarding ancient literatures are given below, in the section covering Mesoamerica.) The **essay** of ideas is the focus of a book by Stabb, and of his contribution to Foster's *Mexican Literature* . . ., mentioned above. Paz's methodology is analysed by Aguilar Mora, in a book that represents the thinking of the next generation. A good general study of Paz's work is *Understanding Octavio Paz*, by José Quiroga. On the search for *lo mexicano*, see Schmidt, and Villegas; on positivism, Zea. Again in the Foster volume, one finds coverage of the literary reviews in an essay by Peña, a subject addressed in greater detail elsewhere by Carter and Martínez Peñaloza. General accounts of **theatre** include Dauster's *Historia del teatro hispanoamericano*, his *Perfil generacional* . . ., and works by Suárez Radillo. Olavarría y Ferrari's *Reseña histórica* . . ., a compendium of six volumes, covers the period from colonial times to the end of the Porfiriato. Also useful is Usigli's *Mexico in the Theatre*. For colonial theatre, see Arrom, the classic study, Arroniz, and Ravicz on the use of theatre for evangelization, also Williams and de Rojas. The period from independence to the Revolution is surveyed anecdotally by Reyes de la Maza. For popular theatre, see Weiss, and Frischmann. For a full description of theatre in the first half of the twentieth century, see Nomland, and for a less detailed one, Magaña Esquivel. Schmidhuber covers the period 1922–38 and Mendoza López 1928–41; the former's is the more professional piece of work. For post-Tlatelolco theatre, Burgess. Regional theatre in Yucatán is dealt with by Muñoz. Teatro de México is the subject of a solid study by Unger. Another useful source of information is the *Latin American Theater Review*. Now to **poetry**. Sor Juana has been the subject of numerous studies, including the famous one by Paz; other important book-length studies of her work are by Merrim, Pfandl, and Sabat de Rivers. There is an anthology of her work in English translation by Alan Trueblood. Buxó deals with Góngora's influence on seventeenth-century poetry. Méndez Plancarte has a useful two-volume edition of colonial poetry. For Romantic poetry a starting point is Millán. For *modernismo*, see the Jrade and González essays in the *Cambridge History* and the latter's *Companion to Spanish American Modernismo*. For a wider view, Blanco's *Crónica . . .* is a fine piece of criticism. Books by John Brushwood have long served as standard works on the **novel**; others among the many that focus on narrative are by Azuela, Duncan, Langford, Magaña Esquivel, Navarro, Sommers, Torres, and Warner. Teichmann offers interviews with writers, while *Los narradores ante el público* is an interesting two-volume collection of lectures sponsored by Bellas Artes and given by a total of thirty-three contemporary authors. Women writers of the twentieth century are the focus of many recent studies, including those of Franco, Ibsen, Steele, and Taylor. Ocampo's is a major study of the *Onda* generation. Leal's *Aztlán y México . . .* is a comparative study of Chicano and Mexican cultures. López González *et al.* approach the same subject via women writers of both countries. Villanueva's is a useful anthology of Chicano writing and was published in Mexico.

Media

Carlos Monsiváis has been one of the liveliest and most frequent commentators on the role of the modern media. Trejo Delarbe's publications have to do with the powers of the media in modern Mexican society. General studies include those of Fernández Christlieb, Hayes, Lombardo, and Noriega; Hayes is particularly useful but limited in the period it covers. For a more exclusive focus on the evolution of radio, see Romo; for television, Sánchez de Armas; for the press, Ochoa Campos, Orme, and Reed Torres. Websites for various publications and media companies provide access to a wide range of information; a useful source for such information, based outside Mexico, is newslink.org. *Telenovelas* are dealt with by Cueva, comics by Hinds and Tatum, and Rubenstein.

Mesoamerica

The Indian civilizations have captured the imagination of countless people, including a great many scholars; only a small selection of book-length studies can be mentioned here. A number of books that were first published long ago are still respected as essential sources of information. One such is Sylvanus Morley's *The Ancient Maya*, first published in 1946. It has been through at least five editions, the most recent involving considerable revisions (by Robert Sharer), and it has a full bibliography. In general, it is important to rely on the latest edition of such works, or other new and recent publications, because in the last fifty-odd years our understanding of Mesoamerican civilizations has advanced very significantly, and some of the old assumptions have been shown to be wrong. Authoritative writers on Mesoamerican civilizations include Adams, Benson, Berdan, Boone, Brumfield, Carrasco, Culbert, Matos Moctezuma, Schele, Smith, Stuart, and Wolf. For a general account of the indigenous past, one that gives unusual prominence to northern regions, see López Austin's *El pasado indígena*. Duverger's *Mesoamérica*

. . . emphasizes the continuities and similarities between Mesoamerican cultures and has four hundred colour illustrations. Cline's *Handbook of Middle America Indians* is a major work for bibliographical and manuscript sources. Alcina Franch is very useful for information about the codices. The origins of the Mesoamerican ballgame, together with its vestigial influence on the modern *pelota*, are the subject of the essays gathered by María Teresa Uriarte in *El juego de pelota en Mesoamérica*. Soustelle's *Los olmecas*, published in 2000, is a thorough account of that civilization and of current research on it. Baudez and Becquelin provide a finely illustrated introduction to the Mayas (in French). Michael Coe's *The Maya* is a very useful general survey (and much revised since first published in the 1960s), as also are his *Mexico: From the Olmecs to the Aztecs* and his more specialized account of the history of the decipherment of the Maya code. Ayala Falcón gives a readable account of progress in deciphering the Maya hieroglyphics. A clear account of astronomy is provided by Aveni, one of the calendar by Harris and Stearns, one of the numerical system by Lounsbury, and one of the hieroglyphs by Montgomery. Maya cosmology is covered by Freidel, Schele, and Parker. For the pantheon of gods, see Miller, and Taube. León-Portilla regards Toscano's *Arte precolombino . . .* as the first real attempt to take a comprehensive look at Mesoamerican art and to apply adequate aesthetic and scholarly apparatus to it; first published in 1944, Toscano's work has been updated in later editions by Beatriz de la Fuente. Miller's *Art of Mesoamerica* is a wide-ranging discussion, while Berlo offers an annotated bibliography on Mesoamerican art. Also for art, see Reents-Budet on the Mayas, Baquedano and Pasztory on the Aztecs; Pasztory also has a book on Teotihuacan. For a study of the Toltec heritage and its significance in later years, see Davies. A short glossary of common terms in Nahuatl is to be found in Michael E. Smith's general account of *The Aztecs*, along with a very long bibliography. Those interested in tackling the language itself are advised to look at Andrews' *Introduction to Classical Nahuatl*, at the *Foundation Course* by Campbell and Karttunen, at the latter's dictionary and at Sullivan's grammar. For the role of Tlaxcala, see García Cook and Merino. *Crónica mexicana*, by Fernando Alvarado Tezozómoc, is an account of Aztec history by a man of Mexica ancestry; his account should be balanced by a reading of others by Alva Ixtlilxochitl, Chimalpahin, Muñoz Camargo, and Zapata (see Velazco). Clendinnen bases *Los aztecas: una interpretación* on a close study of the *Florentine Codex*. The Aztecs after conquest are the subject of a book by Lockhart, an author whose work is essential for an understanding of the Nahua culture and its survival strategies in the post-conquest era. *Transcending Conquest*, by Wood, illustrates the Nahua view of the Spanish occupation. Aspects of Aztec culture can be approached through a large number of modern secondary sources, in particular the work of León-Portilla and Angel María Garibay, who translated many original documents into Spanish. Garibay published *Epica Náhuatl*, *Veinte himnos sacros de los nahuas*, *Panorama literario de los pueblos nahuas* and especially *Historia de la literatura náhuatl*. León-Portilla's many contributions have sometimes been translated into English; thus *Visión de los vencidos* became *Broken Spears* and *La filosofía náhuatl* was updated as *Aztec Thought and Culture*. Both of the aforementioned works have essential bibliographies of primary and secondary sources. Theatre can be approached via Sell and Burkhart. Kissam and Schmidt offer English translations of Aztec poetry. The *Cantares mexicanos* were edited by León-Portilla and have also been fully annotated and translated into English by John Bierhorst, whose introduction is a sobering account of the difficulties inherent in dealing with a copied and transliterated manuscript based on an original in a remote language; published in 1985, Bierhorst's book has a full bibliography. There is a biography-cum-anthology of the work of Nezahualcóyotl, by José Luis Martínez. Horcasitas writes on Aztec theatre. León-Portilla's *Pre-Columbian Literatures of Mexico*, as its title indicates, deals with other cultures also. His 2003 book *Códices. Los antiguos libros del Nuevo Mundo* is authoritative. Dennis Tedlock has a useful edition of the *Popol Vuh*, expanded in its second (1996) edition; another is by Adrán Recinos. Tedlock's recent translation of *Rabinal Achí* offers a wealth of information, both about the process of translation and about the Maya performance tradition. See also Acuña for the *Rabinal Achí*. De la Garza's *Literatura Maya* is an essential sourcebook. See also Lee. Gutiérrez Solana gives detailed descriptions of the various Mexican codices. Edmondson's *Heaven Born* is about the Book of Chilam Balam.

Mexican Spanish

For general surveys of the Spanish of the Americas, see Lope Blanch (1968), Moreno de Alba, Del Rosario, Lipski, and Cotton and Sharp. The volume by these last two authors is structured rather like a course-book and contains information that might otherwise be thought outside the purview of its title; its chapter on Mexico, while good, veers off into Central America. Studies (mostly surveys) devoted to Mexican Spanish alone include Carreño, Hill and Hill, and Mejía Prieto. Much work on Mexican dialects is squirrelled away in journals, but for reasons of space only book-length studies are listed here and in the Bibliography. The work of a Spanish transplant to Mexico, Juan Lope Blanch, deserves mention; he has done much to document dialects and to encourage the work of others, and he is behind the ambitious atlas project, whose results have been slow to appear because of publication costs. For regional studies, see as follows: for Tabasco (Carrera, Gutiérrez Eskildsen, Williamson), Jalisco (Cárdenas), Sinaloa (Esqueda), Juárez (Hidalgo), Oaxaca (Garza Cuarón), México D.F. (Lope Blanch, Matluck), Yucatán (Patrón Peniche, Suárez). Santamaría's dictionary is an invaluable reference work for *mexicanismos* and the one by Sosa Pedroza *et al.* offers illustrations of regional usage.

Music and Dance

Among those writing in English, the most steadfast contributor to the history of music in Mexico has been Robert Stevenson, and the single most useful title of his is *Music in Mexico*. This however, was published some time ago. Mayer-Serra is authoritative and also provides a general survey, as do Morales, and Ortiz de Zarate. A closer focus on pre-Columbian music is available in the works of Castellanos, and Dájer; Saldívar is also useful on the pre-Columbian and colonial eras. For the twentieth century, see Malmström, and Garrido. Vicente Mendoza has been an active musicologist and written much on the popular forms that tradition has consecrated as Mexican, such as the *corrido*. Moreno Rivas has two important contributions, one on twentieth century classical music and one on popular music. Dallal and Ramos Smith are the two most prominent writers on dance. The African contribution is the subject of a book by Pérez Fernández.

Visual Arts

For general overviews of Latin American Art, see Ades *et al.*, Barnitz Castedo, Chase, and Baddeley and Fraser (though this last is a little tendentious). Justino Fernández's guide is among the most readable and comprehensive books on Mexican art, though it was published some time ago. Rojas also offers an overview, but it too was published some decades ago. Burke's *Mexican Art Masterpieces* has a good selection of reproductions representing artworks from pre-Hispanic times up to Neo-Mexicanism; these reproductions come together with brief but informative comments. Bradley Smith's *Mexico: A History of Art* is also useful, but it stops at the muralists. The publication that accompanied the 1990 anniversary exhibition at the Metropolitan Museum in New York, entitled *Mexico: Splendors of Thirty Centuries*, is notable for being dominated by Mesoamerican art. (Some suggestions for further reading on pre-Hispanic art were made above, in the section on Mesoamerica.) Manuel Toussaint's contribution to documenting colonial art is incomparable; it has been edited and translated by Elizabeth Weismann. See also Tovar de Teresa, and Early. The muralist tradition from pre-Hispanic times until the mid-twentieth century is given ample discussion by Edwards, backed by photographic contributions by Manuel Alvarez Bravo; it has only black-and-white illustrations. The Academia de San Carlos is the subject of books by Charlot and Weismann, both published by the University of Texas Press. Widdifield's *The Embodiment of the National in Late Nineteenth-Century Mexican Painting* is a fine study. There are countless studies devoted to the muralists, as a group or individually, for example Folgarait's *Mural Painting and Social Revolution in Mexico*, and studies by Reed, Rochfort, and Rodríguez, not to mention another book by Jean Charlot, one of the movement's participants. Goldman's 'time of change' is the transition from Muralism to *Nueva Presencia*; the opening pages of her book give a very good overview of the evolution of art after the Revolution. The twentieth century in Mexican art is covered by Sullivan *et al.*, Billeter *et al.*, and Del Conde. There is a fairly recent study of Surrealism by Rodríguez Prampolini. For graphic art, see Carrasco Puente, Fernández, and Haab. New tendencies at the end of the twentieth century are the subject of a lively little book by Rubén Gallo. Debroise gives one of the fullest and best overviews of photography and its evolution; other studies include Ferrer, Amor, Hooks (on Modotti) and Kismaric (on Manuel Alvarez Bravo). Sixteenth-century architecture is covered in Toussaint and Weismann, but also in Kubler (1948) and, together with the later colonial period, in Kubler and Soria (1959). The modern era in architecture is the focus of Cetto, González-Gortázar, Myers, Clive B. Smith, also Faber (on Candela).

BIBLIOGRAPHY

Such a wealth of material has been published concerning Mexico that drastic steps have had to be taken to keep the present Bibliography manageable. The principal strategy has been to confine it, with very few exceptions, to book-length studies and to those that deal primarily or exclusively with Mexico.

Acuña, René. *Introducción al estudio del Rabinal Achí*. México DF: UNAM, Centro de Estudios Mayas, 1975

Adams, Richard E. *Prehistoric Mesoamerica*. Norman: University of Oklahoma Press, 1996

Ades, Dawn (with Guy Brett, Stanton Loomis Catlin and Rosemary O'Neill). *Art in Latin America: The Modern Era, 1820–1980*. New Haven: Yale University Press, 1989

Aguayo Quezada, Sergio (ed.). *El almanaque mexicano*. México: Grijalbo/Proceso/Hechos Confiables, 2000

Aguilar Mora, Jorge. *La divina pareja: historia y mito*. México DF: Ediciones Era, 1978

Aguilera, Carmen. *Códices del México antiguo*. México DF: Instituto Nacional de Antropología e Historia, 1979

Aguirre Beltrán, Gonzalo. *La población negra de México*. México DF: Fondo de Cultura Económica, 1989

——. *Medicina y magia. El proceso de aculturación en la estructura colonial*. México DF: Fondo de Cultura Económica, 1992

Alcina Franch, José. *Códices mexicanos*. Madrid: MAPFRE, 1992

Aldrich, Richard. *Style in Mexican Architecture*. Coral Gables: University of Miami Press, 1968

Alduncín Abitia, Enrique *et al*. *Los valores de los mexicanos*. México DF: Banamex, 1994

Altman, Ida. *Emigrants and Society: Extremadura and Spanish America in the Sixteenth Century*. Berkeley: University of California Press, 1989

Alvarado Tezozómoc, Fernando. *Crónica mexicana*. Mexico DF: Leyenda, 1944

Alvarez, José Rogelio. *Enciclopedia de México*. México DF: Secretaría de Educación Pública, 1996

Alvarez, María Cristina. *Textos coloniales del Libro de Chilam Balam de Chumayel y textos glíficos del Códice de Dresde*. México DF: UNAM, 1974

Amor, Monica. *Five Decades of Mexican Photography*. New York: Throgmorton Fine Art, Inc./Mexican Cultural Institutes of New York & Washington, 1996

Andrews, J. Richard. *Introduction to Classical Nahuatl*. Norman: University of Oklahoma Press, 1975

Anna, Timothy, Jan Bazant, Friedrich Katz *et al*. *Historia de México*. México DF: Critica, 2001

Arrom, José Juan. *El teatro de Hispanoamérica en la época colonial*. Havana: Anuario Bibliográfico Cubano, 1956

Arrom, S.M. *The Women of Mexico City, 1790–1857*. Stanford: Stanford University Press, 1985

Arroniz, Othón. *Teatro de evangelización en Nueva España*. México DF: UNAM, 1979

Aveni, Anthony F. *Observadores del cielo en el México antiguo*. México DF: Fondo de Cultura Económica, 1991

Ayala Blanco, Jorge. *La condición del cine mexicano*. México DF: Posada, 1980

——. *La búsqueda del cine mexicano*. México DF: Posada, 1986

——. *La fugacidad del cine mexicano*. México DF: Grijalbo, 1996

Ayala Falcón, Maricela. *El fonetismo en la escritura maya*. México DF: UNAM, 1985

Azuela, Alicia. *Diego Rivera en Detroit*. México DF: UNAM, 1985

Azuela, Mariano. *Cien años de novela mexicana*. México DF: Ediciones Botas, 1947

Baddeley, Oriana and Valerie Fraser. *Drawing the Line*. London: Verso, 1989

Bantel, Linda and Marcus B. Burke. *Spain and New Spain: Mexican Colonial Arts in their European Context*. Corpus Christi: Art Museum of South Texas, 1979

Barkin, David. *Distorted Development: Mexico in the World Economy*. Boulder: Westview Press, 1990

Barnitz, Jacqueline. *Twentieth Century Art of Latin America*. Austin: University of Texas Press, 1998

Barrera Vásquez, Alfredo. *Estudios lingüísticos*. Mérida: Fondo Editorial de Yucatán, 1980

Barry, Tom (ed.). *Mexico: A Country Guide*. Albuquerque: Inter-Hemispheric Education Resource Center, 1992

Bartra, Roger. *The Cage of Melancholy: Identity and Metamorphosis in the Mexican Character*. Translated by C.J. Hall. New Brunswick, NJ: Rutgers University Press, 1992

Bassols Batalla, Angel. *Recursos naturales de México*. México DF: Nuestro Tiempo, 1997

Bataillon, M. and André Saint-Lu. *El padre las casas y la defensa de los indios*. Esplugues de Llobregat: Ariel, 1976

Baudot, Georges. *Utopía e historia en México: los primeros cronistas de la civilización mexicana (1520–1569)*. Madrid: Espasa Calpe, 1983

Bauer, K.J. *The Mexican War, 1846–1848*. New York: Macmillan, 1974

Bazant, J. *A Concise History of Mexico: From Hidalgo to Cárdenas, 1805–1940*. Cambridge: Cambridge University Press, 1977

Beardsell, Peter. *A Theatre for Cannibals: Rodolfo Usigli and the Mexican Stage*. London: Associated University Presses, 1992

Becerra Acosta, Manuel *et al*. *Prensa y radio en México (Comunicación y dependencia en América Latina)*. México DF: UNAM, 1978

Beezley, William H. *et al*. (eds.). *Rituals of Rule, Rituals of Resistance: Public Celebrations and Popular Culture in Mexico*. Wilmington, DE: SR Books, 1994

Béhague, Gerard H. *Music in Latin America: An Introduction*. Englewood Cliffs, NJ: Prentice Hall, 1979

Benítez, Fernando. *Los indios de México*. México DF: Era, 1991–98, 5 vols

Benítez, José María, Boyd G. Carter and Porfirio Martínez Peñaloza (eds.). *Las revistas literarias en México*. México DF: INBA, 1963

Benjamin, Thomas. *A Rich Land, a Poor People: Politics and Society in Modern Chiapas*. Albuquerque: University of New Mexico Press, 1996

Berdan, Frances *et al. Codex Mendoza*. Berkeley: University of California Press, 1997

Bergamo, Ilarione da, Fr. *Daily Life in Colonial Mexico*. Translated by William J. Orr. Norman: University of Oklahoma Press, 2000

Berlo, Janet Catherine. *The Art of PreHispanic Mesoamerica: An Annotated Bibliography*. Boston: G.K. Hall, 1985

Berumen, Humbert Félix. *De cierto modo: la literatura de Baja California*. Mexcali: Universidad Autónoma de Baja California, 1998

Bethell, Leslie (ed.) *Mexico Since Independence*. Cambridge: Cambridge University Press, 1991

—— (ed.) *The Cambridge History of Latin America*. Cambridge: Cambridge University Press, 1995

Bierhorst, John. *Cantares Mexicanos: The Songs of the Aztecs*. Stanford: Stanford University Press, 1985

——. *Codex Chimalpopoca*. Tucson: University of Arizona Press, 1992

Billeter, Erika (ed.). *Images of Mexico: The Contribution of Mexico to 20th Century Art*. Dallas: Dallas Museum of Art, 1987

Blancarte, Roberto (ed.). *Cultura e identidad nacional*. México DF: Fondo de Cultura Económica, 1994

Blanco, José Joaquín. *Crónica de la poesía mexicana*. México DF: Katún, 1977

——. *Esplendores y miserias de los criollos: la literatura de la Nueva España*. México DF: Cal y Arena, 1989

——. *Crónica literaria*. México DF: Cal y Arena, 1996

Bonfil Batalla, Guillermo. *México Profundo: Reclaiming a Civilization*. Translated by P.A. Dennis. Austin: University of Texas Press, 1996

Bonifaz Nuño, Rubén. *Ricardo Martínez*. México DF: UNAM, 1965

Borah, W.W. *et al. Historia y población en México: Siglos XIV–XIX*. México DF: Centro de Estudios Históricos, 1994

Brading, David A. *Prophecy and Myth in Mexican History*. Cambridge: Cambridge University Press, 1986

——. *La Virgen de Guadalupe. Imagen y tradición*. México DF: Taurus, 2002

Brandenburg, Frank. *The Making of Modern Mexico*. Englewood Cliffs, NJ: Prentice-Hall, 1964

Brenner, Anita and George R. Leighton. *The Wind That Swept Mexico: The History of the Mexican Revolution of 1910–1942*. Austin: University of Texas Press, 1984

Bricker, Victoria Reifler. *The Indian Christ, the Indian King: The Historical Substrate of Maya Myth and Ritual*. Austin: University of Texas Press, 1981

Brotherston, Gordon. *Mexican Painted Books*. Colchester: University of Essex Press, 1992

Brushwood, John S. *Mexico in Its Novel*. Austin: University of Texas Press, 1966

——. *La novela mexicana* (1972–1982). México DF: Grijalbo, 1985

——. *Narrative Innovation and Political Change in Mexico*. New York: Peter Lang, 1989

Bullock, W. *Six Months' Residence and Travels in Mexico*, London: John Murray, 1824

Burgess, Ronald D. *The New Dramatists of Mexico: 1967–1985*. Lexington: University of Kentucky Press, 1991

Burke, Marcus B. *Pintura y escultura en Nueva España: el barroco*. México DF: Azabache, 1992

——. *Mexican Art Masterpieces*. New York: Hugh Lauter Levin Associates, 1998

Burkholder, Mark A. and Lyman J. Johnson. *Colonial Latin America*. New York: Oxford University Press, 1994

Burton, Julianne. *Cinema and Social Change in Latin America*. Austin: University of Texas Press, 1986

Buxó, José Pascual. *Góngora en la poesía novohispana*. México DF: Imprenta Universitaria, 1960

Calderón de la Barca, Fanny. *Life in Mexico*. Edited by Howard T. Fisher and Marion Hall Fisher. New York: Doubleday, 1966

Camp, Roderic Ai. *Politics in Mexico*. New York: Oxford University Press, 1989

——. *Crossing Swords: Religion and Politics in Mexico*. New York: Oxford University Press, 1997

Campos, Rubén M. *El folklore musical en las ciudades*. México DF: Secretaría de Educación Pública, 1930

Canfield, D. Lincoln. *Spanish Pronunciation in the Americas*. Chicago: University of Chicago Press, 1981

Cárdenas, Daniel. *El español de Jalisco*. Madrid: Consejo Superior de Investigaciones Científicas, 1967

Cardoza y Aragón, Luis. *Pintura contemporánea de México*. México DF: Era, 1995

Carrasco, D. *Quetzalcoatl and the Irony of Empire: Myth and Prophecies in the Aztec Tradition*. Chicago: University of Chicago Press, 1992

Carrasco Puente, Rafael. *La caricatura en México*. México DF: Imprenta Universitaria, 1953

Carreño, Alberto. *La lengua castellana en México*. México DF: Imprenta Victoria, 1925

Carrera, Oscar. *Así hablan en mi tierra*. México DF: Consejo del Estado de Tabasco, 1981

Carroll, P J. *Blacks in Colonial Veracruz: Race, Ethnicity, and Regional Development*. Austin: University of Texas Press, 1991

Casasola, Gustavo. *Seis siglos de historia gráfica de México*. México DF: Editorial Gustavo Casasola, 1978

Castedo, Leopoldo. *A History of Latin American Art and Architecture*. New York: Praeger, 1969

Castellanos, Pablo. *Horizontes de la música precortesana*. México DF: Fondo de Cultura Económica, 1970

Cetto, Max L. *Modern Architecture in Mexico*. New York: Praeger, 1961

Chance, K. *Race and Class in Colonial Oaxaca*. Stanford: Stanford University Press, 1978

Charlot, Jean. *Mexican Art and the Academy of San Carlos, 1785–1915*. Austin: University of Texas Press, 1962

——. *The Mexican Mural Renaissance, 1920–1925*. New Haven: Yale University Press, 1963

Chase, Gilbert. *Contemporary Art in Latin America*. London: Collier Macillan, 1970

Clendinnen, Inga. *Los aztecas: una interpretación*. México DF: Nueva Imagen, 1998

Cline, Howard E. *Mexico: Revolution to Evolution, 1940–1960*. Oxford: Oxford University Press, 1963

—— (ed.). *Handbook of Middle America Indians*. Austin: University of Texas Press, 1972, several volumes

Cockcroft, James D. *Intellectual Precursors of the Mexican Revolution, 1900–1913*. Austin: University of Texas Press. 1968

——. *Mexico: Class Formation, Capital Accumulation, and the State*. New York: Monthly Review Press, 1990

——. *Diego Rivera*. New York: Chelsea House, 1991

Coe, Michael D. *Mexico: From the Olmecs to the Aztecs*. London: Thames & Hudson, 1994

——. *The Maya*. London: Thames & Hudson, 1999

Cook, Sherburne F. and W.W. Borah. *The Indian Population of Central Mexico, 1531–1610*. Berkeley: University of California Press, 1960

Cooper Alarcón, Daniel. *The Aztec Palimpsest: Mexico in the Modern Imagination*. Tempe, AZ: University of Arizona Press, 1997

Cope, Douglas R. *The Limits of Racial Domination: Plebeian Society in Colonial Mexico City, 1660 – 1720*. Madison: University of Wisconsin Press, 1994

Cosío Villegas, Daniel, *et al*. *Historia mínima de México*. México DF: El Colegio de México, 1983

——. *Historia general de México*. México DF: Colegio de México, 2000

Cotton, Eleanor and John Sharp. *Spanish in the Americas*. Washington, DC: Georgetown University Press, 1988

Cruz, Barbara C. *José Clemente Orozco*. New York: Enslaw, 1998

Cueva, Alvaro. *Lágrimas de cocodrilo: Historia mínima de las telenovelas en México*. México DF: Tres Lunas, 1998

Cumberland, Charles C. *Mexico: The Struggle for Modernity*. Oxford: Oxford University Press, 1968

Cypess, Sandra Messinger. *La Malinche in Mexican Literature: From History to Myth*. Austin: University of Texas Press, 1991

Dájer, Jorge. *Los artefactos sonoros precolombinos desde su descubrimiento en Michoacán*. México DF: Empresa Libre de Autoeditores/Fondo Nacional para la Cultura y las Artes, 1995

Dallal, Alberto. *El 'dancing' mexicano*. México DF: Oasis, 1982

——. *La danza en México en el siglo XX*. México DF: CONACULTA, 1994

Dauster, Frank N. *Xavier Villaurrutia*. Boston: Twayne, 1971

——. *Historia del teatro latinoamericano*. México DF: Ediciones de Andrea, 1973

——. *Perfil generacional del teatro hispanoamericano*. Ottawa: Girol Books, 1993

Davies, Nigel. *The Aztecs: A History*. London: Macmillan, 1973

——. *The Toltec Heritage*. Norman: University of Oklahoma Press, 1980

De Rojas, José Luis. *México Tenochtitlan*. México DF: FCE, 1986

Debroise, Olivier. *Fuga mexicana: un recorrido por la fotografía en México*. México DF: CONACULTA, 1998

Del Conde, Teresa. *Historia mínima del arte mexicano en el siglo XX*. México DF: Átame Ediciones, 1994

Dessau, Adalbert. *La novela de la Revolución mexicana*. México DF: Fondo de Cultura Económica, 1986
Dever, Susan. *Celluloid Nationalism and Other Melodramas: From Post-Revolutionary Mexico to fin de siglo Mexamérica*. Albany: State University of New York Press, 2003
Díaz-Guerrero, Rogelio. *Psychology of the Mexican*. Austin: University of Texas Press, 1975
Diccionario Porrúa de historia, biografía y geografía de México. México DF: Porrúa, 1995
Domínguez Michael, Christopher. *Servidumbre y grandeza de la vida literaria*. México DF: Joaquín Mortiz, 1998
Dr. Atl (pseud.). *Las artes populares en México*. México DF: Editorial Cultura, 1921
Drucker, Malka. *Frida Kahlo: Torment and Triumph in Her Life and Art*. New York: Bantam, 1991
Duncan, Ann. *Voices, Visions and a New Reality: Mexican Fiction Since 1970*. Pittsburg: University of Pittsburg Press, 1986
Duverger, Christian. *Mesoamérica: arte y antropología*. Paris: Landucci, 2000
Dwyer, Augusta. *On the Line: Life on the U.S–Mexican Border*. London: Latin American Bureau, 1994
Early, James. *The Colonial Architecture of Mexico*. Arlington: Texas A & M Press, 2000
Edmonson, Munro S. *Heaven Born*. Austin: University of Texas Press, 1986
Elena, Alberto and Marina Díaz López (eds.). *The Cinema of Latin America*. London: Wallflower, 2003
Elliott, David *et al*. *Orozco 1883–1949*. Oxford: Museum of Modern Art, 1980
Esqueda, Carlos. *Léxico de Sinaloa*. Culiacán: Editorial Culiacán, 1989
Faber, Colin. *Candela, the Shell Builder*. New York: Reinhold Publishing Corporation, 1963
Farriss, Nancy M. *Maya Society Under Colonial Rule: The Collective Enterprise of Survival*. Princeton: Princeton University Press, 1984
Fernández, Justino. *Litógrafos y grabadores mexicanos contemporáneos*. México DF: Editorial Delfin, 1944
——. *Prometeo: ensayo sobre pintura contemporánea*. México DF: Editorial Porrúa, S.A., 1945
——. *Orozco, forma e idea*. México DF: Editorial Porrúa, 1956
——. *Roberto Montenegro*. México DF: UNAM, 1962
——. *Arte mexicano de sus orígenes a nuestros días*. México DF: Porrúa, 1969
Fernández, Martha. *Arquitectura y gobierno virreinal. Los maestros mayores de la Ciudad de México*. Siglo XVII.
Fernández Christlieb, Fátima. *Los medios de difusión masiva en México*. México DF: Juan Pablos, 1985
Ferrer, Elizabeth. *A Shadow Born of Earth: New Photography in Mexico*. New York: American Federation of Arts/Universe, 1993
Flores Guerrero, Raúl. *5 pintores mexicanos: Kahlo, Meza, O'Gorman, Castellanos, Reyes Ferreira*. México DF: UNAM, 1957
Florescano, Enrique. *Memory, Myth, and Time in Mexico: From the Aztecs to Independence*. Austin: University of Texas Press, 1994
—— (ed.). *Mitos mexicanos*. México DF: Aguilar/Nuevo Siglo, 1995

—— (ed.). *El patrimonio nacional de México*. México DF: CONACULTA/ FCE, 1997

—— (ed.). *Espejo mexicano*. México DF: CONACULTA/FCE, 2002

Florescano, Enrique and Pablo Mijangos. *México en sus libros*. México DF: Taurus, 2004

Folgarait, Leonard. *So Far from Heaven: David Alfaro Siqueiros: The March of Humanity and Mexican Revolutionary Politics*. Cambridge: Cambridge University Press, 1987

——. *Mural Painting and Social Revolution in Mexico, 1920–1940: Art of the New Order*. Cambridge: Cambridge University Press, 1998

Foster, David William. *Mexican Literature: A Bibliography of Secondary Sources*. Metuchen NJ: Scarecrow Press, 1992

—— (ed.). *Handbook of Latin American Literature*. New York: Garland, 1992

—— (ed.). *Mexican Literature: A History*. Austin: University of Texas Press, 1994

—— *Mexico City in Contemporary Mexican Cinema*. Austin: University of Texas Press, 2002

Franco, Jean. *Plotting Women: Gender and Representation in Mexico*. New York: Columbia University Press, 1989

Frank, Patrick. *Posada's Broadsheets*. Albuquerque: University of New Mexico Press, 1998

Frischmann, Donald. *El nuevo teatro popular en México*. México DF: INBA, 1990

Fuentes, Carlos. *El espejo enterrado*. México DF: Fondo de Cultura Económica, 1992

Fuentes, Patricia de. *The Conquistadors: First-Person Accounts of the Conquest of Mexico*. Norman: Oklahoma University Press, 1993

Fusco, Coco. *The Bodies that Were Not Ours and Other Writings*. London: Routledge, 2001

Gallo, Rubén. *New Tendencies in Mexican Art*. New York: Palgrave MacMillan, 2004

García, Gustavo and Rafael Aviña. *Epoca de oro del cine mexicano*. México DF: Editorial Clío, 1997

García, Gustavo and José Felipe Coria. *Nuevo Cine mexicano*. México DF: Editorial Clío, 1997

García Canclini, Néstor. *Transforming Modernity: Popular Culture in Mexico*. Translated by L. Lozano. Austin: University of Texas Press, 1993

—— (coordinator). *Los nuevos espectadores: cine, televisión y video en México*. México DF: Consejo Nacional para la Culturay las Artes\IMCINE, 1994

——. *Consumidores y ciudadanos: conflictos multiculturales de la globalización*. México DF: Grijalbo, 1995

——. *Hybrid Cultures: Strategies far Entering and Leaving Modernity*. Translated by C. L. Chiappari and S. L. López. Minneapolis: University of Minnesota Press, 1995

García Cook, A. and B.L. Merino (eds.). *Tlaxcala. Textos de su historia*. Tlaxcala: Gobierno del Estado de Tlaxcala/Consejo Nacional para la Cultura y las Artes, 1991, 16 vols

García Riera, Emilio. *Historia documental del cine mexicano*. México DF: Universidad de Guadalajara, 1993–97, 18 vols

——. *Breve historia del cine mexicano: primer siglo (1897–1997)*. México DF: Ediciones Mapa/CONACULTA/IMCINE, 1998

García Rivas, Heriberto. *Historia de la literatura mexicana*. México DF: Textos Universitarios, 1971

García Silberman, Sarah and Luciana Ramos Lira. *Medios de comunicación y violencia*. México DF: FCE\Instituto Mexicano de Psiquiatría, 1998

Garibay Kintana, Angel María. *Historia de la literatura náhuatl*. México DF: Porrúa, 1992

Garrido, Juan S. *Historia de la música popular en México (1896–1973)*. México DF: Editorial Extemporáneos, 1974

Garza Cuarón, Beatriz. *El español hablado en la ciudad de Oaxaca*. México DF: Colegio de México, 1987

Genauer, Emily, *Rufino Tamayo*. New York: Abrams, 1974

Gerhard, Peter. *A Guide to the Historical Geography of New Spain*. Norman: University of Oklahoma Press, 1993

Gibson, Charles. *The Aztecs Under Spanish Rule*. Stanford: Stanford University Press, 1964

Glantz, Margo. *Repeticiones: Ensayos sobre literatura mexicana*. México DF: Universidad Veracruzana, 1979

Goldman, Shifra M., *Contemporary Mexican Painting in a Time of Change*. Austin: University of Texas Press, 1981

Goldwater, Robert. *Rufino Tamayo*. New York: Quadrangle Press, 1947

Gómez-Peña, Guillermo. *The New World Border.* San Francisco: City Lights, 1996

Gonzalbo Aizpuru, Pilar (ed.). *Familias novohispanas, siglos XVI al XIX*. México DF: Colegio de México, 1991

——. *Historia de la educación en la época colonial*. México DF: Colegio de México, 2000

González, Aníbal. *A Companion to Spanish American 'Modernismo'*. Woodbridge: Tamesis, forthcoming

González-Gortázar, Fernando (ed.). *La arquitectura mexicana del siglo XX*. México DF: CONACULTA, 1996

González Navarro, Moisés. *Los extranjeros en México y los mexicanos en el extranjero*. México DF: Colegio de México, 1993

González Peña, Carlos. *Historia de la literatura mexicana: desde los orígenes hasta nuestros días*. México DF: Porrúa, 1984

González-Echevarría, Roberto and Enrique Pupo-Walker (eds.). *Cambridge History of Latin American Literature*. Cambridge: University of Cambridge Press, 1996

Gutiérrez Eskildsen, Rosario. *Prosodia y fonética tabasqueñas*. México DF: Consejo editorial del Estado de Tabasco, 1978

Gutiérrez Solana, Nelly. *Códices de México: historia e interpretación de los grandes libros pintados prehispánicos*. México DF: Panorama. 1985

Gutmann, Matthew C. *The Meanings of Macho: Being a Man in Mexico City*. Berkeley: University of California Press, 1996

Haab, Amin. *Mexican Graphic Art*. New York: G. Wittenborn, 1956

Haight, Ann Lyon (ed.). *Portrait of Latin America as seen by Her Print Makers*. New York: Hastings House Publishers, 1946

Hale, Charles A. *The Transformation of Liberalism in Late 19th Century Mexico*. Princeton: Princeton University Press, 1990

Hamnett, Brian. *A History of Mexico*. New York: Cambridge University Press, 1999

Handelman, Howard. *Mexican Politics: The Dynamics of Change*. New York: St Martins Press, 1996

Hanke, Lewis. *The Spanish Struggle for Justice in the Conquest of America.* Boston: Little & Brown, 1965

Haring, C.H. *The Spanish Empire in America.* New York: Harcourt Brace, 1963

Harmony, Olga. *Ires y venires del teatro en México.* México DF: CONACULTA, 1996

Hart, Steven M. *A Companion to Spanish American Literature.* London: Tamesis, 1999

——. *A Companion to Latin American Film.* Woodbridge: Tamesis, 2004

Harvey, Neil. *The Chiapas Rebellion: The Struggle for Land and Democracy.* Durham, NC: Duke University Press, 1998

Hayes, Joy Elizabeth. *Radio Nation: Communication, Popular Culture, and Nationalism in Mexico, 1920–1950.* Tucson: University of Arizona Press, 2000

Hellman, Judith A. *Mexico in Crisis.* New York: Holmes & Meier, 1988

Helm, MacKinley. *Modern Mexican Painters.* New York and London: Harper Brothers, 1941

——. *Man of Fire: Orozco.* The Institute of Contemporary Art, Boston, New York: Harcourt, Brace and Co., 1953

Hennebelle, Guy and Alfonso Gumucio-Dagrón. *Les Cinémas de L'Amérique Latine.* Paris: Pierre L'Herminier, 1981

Herrera, Hayden, *Frida: A Biography of Frida Kahlo.* New York: Harper & Row, 1983

Hershfield, Joanne. *Mexican Cinema, Mexican Women, 1940–1950.* Tucson: University of Arizona Press, 1996

—— and David R. Maciel. *Mexico's Cinema.* Wilmington: Scholarly Resources, 1999

Hicks, D. Emily. *Border Writing: The Multidimensional Text.* Minneapolis: University of Minnesota Press, 1992

Hidalgo, Margarita. 'Language Use and Language Attitudes in Juárez'. Ph.D. dissertation, University of New Mexico, 1983

Hill, Jane and Kenneth Hill. *Speaking Mexicano:Dynamics of Syncretic Language in Central Mexico.* Tucson: University of Arizona Press, 1986

Hinds, Harold E. and Charles M. Tatum. *Handbook of Latin American Popular Culture.* Westport, CT: Greenwood Press, 1985

——. *Not Just for Children: The Mexican Comic Book in the Late 60s and 70s.* Westport, CT: Greenwood, 1992

Hodges, Donald C. and Ross Gandy. *Mexico 1910–1982: Reform or Revolution?* London: Zed, 1983

Holland, Gini. *Diego Rivera.* Austin: University of Texas Press, 1997

Hooks, Margaret. *Tina Modotti: Photographer and Revolutionary.* San Francisco: Harper, 1993

Hopkins, John H. *Orozco: A Catalog of His Graphic Work.* Flagstaff, AZ: Northland Press, 1967

Horcasitas, Fernando. *El teatro náhuatl, época novohispana y moderna.* Mexico DF: Instituto de Investigaciones Históricas UNAM. 1974

Hoyt-Goldsmith, Diane. *Day of the Dead.* New York: Holiday House, 1994

Hurlburt, Lawrence P. *The Mexican Muralists in the United States.* Albuquerque: University of New Mexico Press, 1989

Ibsen, Kristine. *The Other Mirror.* Westport, CT: Greenwood, 1997

Ingham, J.M. *Mary, Michael, and Lucifer: Folk Catholicism in Central Mexico.* Austin: University of Texas Press, 1986

Islas Escarcega, Leovigildo. *Dicccionario rural de México.* México DF: Editorial Comaval, 1961

Israel, J.I. *Race, Class, and Politics in Colonial Mexico.* London: Oxford University Press, 1975

Iturriaga, José E. *La estructura social y cultural de México*. México DF: FCE, 1951

Izquierdo, María. *The True Poetry: The Art of María Izquierdo.* New York: Americas Society Art Gallery, 1997

Jiménez Rueda, Julio. *Letras mexicanas en el siglo XIX.* México DF: Fondo de Cultura Económica, 1992

Joaquín Clausell y los ecos del impresionismo en México. México DF: Museo Nacional de Arte, 1995

Johns, Christina Jacqueline. *The Origins of Violence in Mexican Society.* New York:: Praeger, 1995

Johnson, H.L. 'The Virgin of Guadalupe in Mexican Culture'. In L.C. Brown and W.F. Cooper (eds.). *Religion in Latin American Life and Literature.* Waco, TX: Markham, 1980

Jorgensen, Beth E. *The Writing of Elena Poniatowska: Engaging Dialogues.* Austin: University of Texas Press, 1994

Joseph, Gilbert M. and Timothy J. Henderson. *The Mexico Reader.* Durham, NC: Duke University Press, 2002

Kandell, Jonathan. *La Capital: Biography of Mexico City.* New York: Holt, 1988

Karp, Lian. *Movimientos culturales en la frontera sonorense.* Hermosillo: El Colegio de Sonora, 1991

Karttunen, Frances. *An Analytical Dictionary of Nahuatl.* Norman: University of Oklahoma Press, 1983

Katz, Friedrich. *The Life and Times of Pancho Villa.* Stanford: Stanford University Press, 1998

Keen, Benjamin. *The Aztec Image in Western Thought.* New Brunswick, NJ: Rutgers University Press, 1971

Kicza, John E. *Colonial Entrepreneurs: Families and Business in Bourbon Mexico City.* Albuquerque: University of New Mexico Press, 1983

King, John. *Magical Reels: A History of Cinema in Latin America.* London: Verso, 1990

Kismaric, Susan. *Manuel Alvarez Bravo*. New York: Museum of Modern Art, 1997

Kissam, Edward and Michael Schmidt. *Flower and Song: Poems of the Aztec Peoples.* London: Anvil Press, 1977

Knight, Alan. *Mexico.* Cambridge: Cambridge University Press, 2002

Krause, Enrique. *Caudillos culturales en la Revolución mexicana.* México DF: Siglo XXI, 1994

——. *Mexico: Biography of Power.* New York: Harper Collins, 1998

Kubler, George. *Mexican Architecture in the Sixteeenth Century.* New Haven: Yale University Press, 1948

Kubler, George, and Martin Soria, *Art and Architecture in Spain and Portugal and their American Dominions, 1500–1800.* Baltimore: Penguin, 1959

La Botz, Dan. *Democracy in Mexico: Peasant Rebellion and Political Reform.* Boston: South End, 1995

Ladd, Doris M. *Mexican Women in Anahuac and New Spain*. Austin: University of Texas Press, 1978

Lafaye, Jacques. *Quetzalcoatl and Guadalupe: The Formation of Mexican National Consciousness*. Translated by Benjamin Keen. Chicago: University of Chicago Press, 1976

Langford, Walter M. *The Mexican Novel Comes of Age*. Notre Dame: University of Notre Dame Press, 1981

Leal, Luis. *Breve historia del cuento mexicano*. México DF: Ediciones de Andrea, 1956

——. *Aztlán y México: Perfiles literarios e históricos*. Tempe, AZ: Bilingual Press, 1989

Leander, Brigitta. *In xochitl in cuicatl. Flor y canto. La poesía de los aztecas*. México DF: Instituto Nacional Indigenista, 1991

Lee, Thomas A. *Los códices mayas*. Tuxtla Gutiérrez: Universidad Autónoma de Chiapas, 1985

Leonard, Irving A. *Books of the Brave: Being an Account of Books and of Men in the Spanish Conquest and Settlement of the Sixteenth Century New World*. New York: Gordian, 1964

——. *Baroque Times in Old Mexico*. Ann Arbor: University of Michigan Press, 1966

León-Portilla, Miguel. *Aztec Thought and Culture*. Norman: University of Oklahoma Press, 1963

——. *Pre-Columbian literatures of Mexico*. Norman: University of Oklahoma Presss, 1969

——. *Broken Spears*. Boston: Beacon Press, 1992

——. *Códices. Los antiguos libros del Nuevo Mundo*. México DF: Aguilar, 2003

Levy, Daniel, and Gabriel Szekely. *Mexico: Paradoxes of Stability and Change*. Boulder: Westview, 1983

Lewis, Oscar. *Life in a Mexican Village*. Champaign: University of Illinois Press, 1951

——. *Five Families*. New York: Basic Books, 1959

——. *The Children o f Sánchez*. New York: Random House, 1961

——. *Pedro Martínez: A Mexican Peasant and His Family*. New York: Random House, 1964

——. *La Vida*. New York: Random House, 1966

——. *Death in the Sánchez Family*. New York: Random House, 1969

Lipski, John M. *Latin American Spanish*. London: Longman, 1994

Livermore, H. A. *The War with Mexico*. New York: Arno, 1969

Lockhart, J. *The Nahuas After the Conquest: A Social and Cultural History of the Indians of Central Mexico, Sixteenth through Eighteenth Centuries*. Stanford: Stanford University Press, 1992

——. *Nahuatl as Written*. Los Angeles, Stanford: Stanford University Press, UCLA Latin America Center Publications, 2001

Lombardo, Irma. *De la opinión a la noticia: el surgimiento de los géneros informativos en México*. México DF: Medios Utiles, 1992

Lomnitz, Claudio. *Las salidas del laberinto. Cultura e ideología en el espacio nacional mexicano*. México DF: Joaquín Mortiz, 1995

—— (ed.). *Vicios públicos, virtudes privadas: la corrupción en México*. México DF: Porrúa, 2000

——. *Deep Mexico, Silent Mexico: An Anthropology of Nationalism*. Minneapolis: University of Minnesota Press, 2001

Lope Blanch, Juan M. *El español de América*. Madrid: Alcalá, 1968

—— (ed.). *El habla de la ciudad de México*. México DF: Universidad Nacional Autónoma de México, 1971

—— (ed.). *El habla popular de la ciudad de México*. México DF: Universidad Nacional Autónoma de México, 1979

——. *Léxico indígena en el español de México*. México DF: Colegio de México, 1979

—— (ed.). *Atlas lingüístico de México*. México DF: Fondo de Cultura Económica, 1990

López Austin, *El pasado indígena*. México DF: FCE/Colegio de México, 1996

López González, Aralia *et al. Mujer y literatura mexicana y chicana: culturas en contacto*. México DF: Colegio de México, 1990

Los narradores ante el público. México DF: Joaquín Mortiz, 1967

Lowry, Malcolm. *Under the Volcano*. New York: Signet, 1965

Lozano, José Carlos. *Prensa, radiodifusión e identidad cultural en la frontera norte*. Tijuana: El Colegio de la Frontera Norte, 1991

Macías, A. *Against All Odds: The Feminist Movement in Mexico to 1940*. Westport, CT: Greenwood, 1982

Maciel, David R. and Marta Herera-Sobek (eds.). *Culture Across Borders: Mexican Immigration and Popular Culture*. Tucson: University of Arizona Press, 1998

MacLachlan, Colin M. and Jaime E. Rodriguez. *The Forging of the Cosmic Race: A Reinterpretation of Colonial Mexico*. Berkeley: University of California Press, 1980

Magaña Esquivel, Antonio. *La novela de la Revolución Mexicana*. México DF: Instituto Nacional de Estudios Históricos, 1964

——. *Medio siglo de teatro mexicano, 1900–1961*. México DF: INBA, 1964

——. *Imagen y realidad del teatro en México, 1533–1960*. México DF: CONACULTA/INBA, 2000

Malmberg, Bertil. *La América hispanohablante*. Madrid: Fundamentos, 1970

Malmström, Dan. *Introducción a la música mexicana del siglo XX*. México DF: Fondo de Cultura Económica, 1993

Martin, Michael T. (ed.). *Latin American Cinema*. Detroit: Wayne State University Press, 1997

Martínez, José Luis. *Nezahualcóyotl. Vida y obra*. México DF: Fondo de Cultura Económica, 1986

—— (ed.). *El ensayo mexicano moderno*. México DF: Fondo de Cultura Económica, 2001

Martínez, Oscar J. *Border People: Life and Society in the U.S.–Mexico Borderlands*. Tucson: University of Arizona Press, 1994

Martínez de Velasco Vélez, Patricia. *Directoras de cine: Proyección de un mundo oscuro*. México DF: IMCINE CONEICC, 1991

Martínez Rentería, Carlos. *Cultura-Contracultura*. México DF: Plaza y Janés, 2000

Matluck, Joseph. *La pronunciación en el español del valle de México*. México DF: Adrián Morales Sánchez, 1951

Mayer-Serra, Otto. *Panorama de la música mexicana: desde la independencia hasta la actualidad*. México DF: El Colegio de México, 1996

Maza, Francisco de la. *El guadalupanismo mexicano*. México DF: Fondo de Cultura Económica, 1992

McAnany, Emile G. and Kenton T. Wilkinson (eds.). *Mass Media and Free Trade: NAFTA and the Cultural Industries*. Austin: University of Texas Press, 1996

Mejía Prieto, Jorge. *Así habla el mexicano*. México DF: Editorial Panorama, 1985

Méndez Plancarte, Alfonso (ed.). *Poetas novohispanos*. México DF: UNAM, 1942 and 1945

Mendoza, Vicente. *Panorama de la música tradicional de México*. México DF: Imprenta Universitaria, 1956

——. *La canción mexicana*. México DF: Fondo de Cultura Económica, 1982

——. *El corrido mexicano*. México DF: Fondo de Cultura Económica, 1984

Mendoza López, Margarita. *Primeros renovadores del teatro en México, 1928–1941*. Mexico DF: Instituto Mexicano de Seguro Social, 1985

Merrell, Floyd. *A Sense of Culture: the Mexicans*. Boulder: Westview Press, 2003

Merrill, Tim L. and Ramón Miró. *Mexico: a Country Study*. Washington, DC: Library of Congress, 1997

Merrim, Stephanie (ed.). *Feminist Perspectives on Sor Juana Inés de la Cruz*. Detroit: Wayne State University Press, 1991

México en el Arte. (12 journal issues published, 1948–52). México DF: Instituto Nacional de Bellas Artes

Mexico: Splendors of Thirty Centuries. New York: Metropolitan Museum of Art, 1990

Meyer, Michael C. and William H. Beezley. *The Oxford History of Mexico*. Oxford: Oxford University Press, 2000

Meyer, Michael C., William L. Sherman and Susan M. Deeds. *The Course of Mexican History*. New York: Oxford University Press, 2002

Millán, María del Carmen (ed.), *Antología: poesía romántica mexicana*. México DF: Libro Mex Editores, 1957

Miller, Mary Ellen. *Maya Art and Architecture*. London and New York: Thames & Hudson, 1999

——. *The Art of Mesoamerica: From Olmec to Aztec*. London: Thames & Hudson, 2001

Miller, Robert Ryal. *Mexico: A History*. Norman: University of Oklahoma Press, 1985

Monetemayor, Carlos (ed.). *Situación actual y perspectivas de la literatura en lenguas indígenas*. México DF: CONACULTA, 1993

Monsiváis, Carlos. *Entrada Libre: Crónicas de una sociedad que se organiza*. Mexico: Era, 1987

——. *Mexican Postcards*. London: Verso, 1997

Monsiváis, Carlos and Carlos Bonfil. *A través del espejo: el cine mexicano y su público*. México DF: Ediciones el Milagro/Instituto Mexicano de Cinematografía, 1994

Montell García, Jaime. *La conquista de México Tenochtitlan*. México DF: Porrúa, 2002

Montemayor, Carlos. *Los pueblos indios de México hoy*. México DF: Planeta, 2000

——. *La literatura actual en las lenguas indígenas de México*. México DF: Universidad Iberoamericana, 2001

Monterde, Francisco. *Teatro indígena prehispánico*. México DF: UNAM, 1955

Montgomery, John. *How to Read Maya Hieroglyphs*. New York: Hippocrene Books, 2002
Mora, Carl J. *Mexican Cinema: Reflections of a Society*. Berkeley: University of California Press, 1989
Mora, Juan Miguel. *Panorama del teatro en México*. México DF: Editorial Latinoamericana, 1970
Morales, Salvador. *La música mexicana*. México DF: Universo, 1981
Moreno de Alba, José G. *El español de América*. México DF: Fondo de Cultura Económica, 1988
Moreno Rivas, Yolanda. *Historia de la música popular mexicana*. México DF: CONACULTA/Alianza/Patria, 1989
——. *La composición en México en el siglo XX*. México DF: CONACULTA, 1996
Muñoz, Fernando. *El teatro regional de Yucatán*. México DF: Gaceta, 1987
Murray, James C. *Spanish Chronicles of the Indies: The Sixteenth Century*. Boston: Twayne, 1995
Myers, Bernard S. *Mexican Painting in Our Time*. New York: Oxford University Press, 1956
Myers, I.E. *Mexico's Modern Architecture*. New York: Architectural Book Publishing Co., 1952
Navarro, Joaquina. *La novela realista mexicana*. México DF: Compañía General de Ediciones, 1955
Nelken, Margarita. *Carlos Orozco Romero*. México DF: UNAM, 1959
——. *Carlos Mérida*. México DF: UNAM, 1961
Nelson, Cynthia. *The Waiting Village: Social Change in Rural Mexico*. Boston: Little, Brown, 1971
Neuvillate, Alfonso de. *Francisco Goitia: precursor de la escuela mexicana*. México DF: UNAM, 1964
——. *Pintura actual: México 1966*. México DF: Artes de México y del Mundo, S.A., 1966
Nevares Reyes, Beatriz. *The Mexican Cinema: Interviews with Thirteen Directors*. Albuquerque: University of New Mexico Press, 1976
Nomland, John B. *Teatro mexicano contemporáneo, 1900–1950*. Translated by Paloma Gorostiza and Luis Reyes. México DF: INBA, 1967
Noriega, Chon A. and Steven Ricci (eds.). *The Mexican Cinema Project*. Los Angeles: UCLA Film and Television Archive, 1994
Noriega, Luis Antonio de and Frances Leach. *Broadcasting in Mexico*. London: Routledge & Kegan Paul, 1979
Núñez Cabeza de Vaca, Alvar. *Cabeza de Vaca's Adventures in the Unknown Interior of America*. Albuquerque: University of New Mexico Press, 1961
Nuttall, Zelia. *The Book of Life of the Ancient Mexicans*. Berkeley: University of California Press, 1983
Ocampo de Gómez, Aurora Maura. *La crítica de la novela mexicana contemporánea*. México DF: UNAM, 1981
Ochoa Campos, Moisés. *Reseña histórica del periodismo mexicano*. México DF: Porrúa, 1968
Ochoa Serrano, Alvaro. *Mitote, fandango y mariacheros*. Zamora: El Colegio de Michoacán, 1994
Olavarría y Ferrari, Enrique. *Reseña histórica del teatro en México, 1538–1911*. México DF: Porrúa, 1961

O'Malley, Ilene V. *The Myth of the Revolution: Hero Cults and the Institutionalization of the Mexican State, 1920–1940*. New York: Greenwood, 1986

Oppenheimer, Andre. *Bordering on Chaos: Mexico's Roller-Coaster Journey to Prosperity*. Boston: Little, Brown, 1998

Orme, Jr, William A. (ed.). *A Culture of Collusion: An Inside Look at the Mexican Press*. Miami: North-South Center Press, 1997

Orozco, José Clemente. *An Autobiography*. Austin: University of Texas Press, 1962

Ortiz de Zarate, Juan Manuel. *Breve historia de la música en México*. México DF: Manuel Porrúa, 1970

Oster, Patrick. *The Mexicans: A Personal Portrait of a People*. New York: William Morrow, 1989

Padúa, Alfredo Jaime. *El cine: 204 respuestas*. México DF: Editorial Alhambra Mexicana, 1994

Paranaguá, Paulo Antonio (ed.). *Mexican Cinema*. London: British Film Institute, 1995

Pastor, Beatriz. *Discursos narrativos de la conquista: mitificación y emergencia*. Hanover, NH: Ediciones del Norte, 1983

——. *Discurso narrativo de la conquista de América*. Hanover, NH: Ediciones del Norte, 1988

Pasztory, Esther. *Teotihuacan*. Norman: University of Oklahoma Press, 1997

——. *Aztec Art*. Norman: University of Oklahoma Press, 1998

Patrón Peniche, Prudencio. *Léxico yucateco*. México DF: Talleres Tipográficos Tenochtitlan, 1932

Paxton, Meredith. *The Cosmos of the Yucatec Maya*. Albuquerque: University of New Mexico Press, 2001

Paz, Octavio. *The Labyrinth of Solitude: Life and Thought in Mexico*. Translated by L. Kemp. New York: Grove, 1961

——. *Children of the Mire*. Cambridge: Harvard University Press, 1970

——. *The Other Mexico: Critique of the Pyramid*. Translated by L. Kemp. New York: Grove, 1970

——. *Sor Juana Inés de la Cruz o las trampas de la fe*. Barcelona: Seix Barral, 1982

Peña, Devon Gerardo. *The Terror of the Machine: Technology, Work, Gender and Ecology on the U.S.–Mexico Border*. Austin: University of Texas Press, 1997

Pérez Fernández, Rolando. *La música afromestiza mexicana*. Xalapa: Universidad Veracruzana, 1990

Pfandl, Ludwig. *Sor Juana Inés de la Cruz: la décima musa de México*. México DF: UNAM, 1963

Pick, Zuzana M. *The New Latin American Cinema*. Austin: University of Texas Press, 1993

Pilcher, Jeffrey M. *Cantinflas and the Chaos of Mexican Modernity*. Wilmington, DE: SR Books, 2001

Poole, Stafford. *Our Lady of Guadalupe: The Origins and Sources of a Mexican National Symbol 1531–1797*. Tucson: University of Arizona Press, 1995

Price, John A. *Tijuana: Urbanization in a Border Culture*. Notre Dame: Notre Dame University Press, 1973

Quiñones Keber, E. *Codex Telleriano-Remensis*. Austin: University of Texas Press, 1995

Quiroga, José. *Understanding Octavio Paz*. Columbia: University of South Carolina Press, 1998

Raat, W. Dirk. *The Mexican Revolution: An Annotated Guide to Recent Scholarship*. Boston: Hall, 1982

—— and William H. Beezley (eds.). *Twentieth-Century Mexico*. Lincoln: University of Nebraska Press, 1986

Rama, Angel. *The Lettered City*. Durham, NC: Duke University Press, 1996

Ramamoorthy, T.P., Robert Bye, Antonio Lot and John Fa (eds.). *Diversidad biológica de México: orígenes y distribución*. México DF: UNAM, 1998

Ramírez Berg, Charles. *Cinema of Solitude: A Critical Study of Mexican Film, 1967–1983*. Austin: University of Texas Press, 1992

Ramos, Samuel. *Profile of Man and Culture in Mexico*. Translated by P. G. Earle. Austin: University of Texas Press, 1962

Ramos Smith, Maya. *La danza en México durante la época colonial*. México DF: CONACULTA/Alianza/ Patria, 1990

——. *El ballet en México en el siglo XIX*. México DF: CONACULTA/ Alianza/Patria, 1991

Rashkin, Elissa J. *Women Filmmakers in Mexico*. Austin: University of Texas Press, 2001

Ravicz, Marilyn Ekdahl. *Early Colonial Religious Drama in Mexico*. Washington, DC: Catholic University of America Press, 1970

Reed, Alma M. *Orozco*. New York: Oxford University Press, 1956

——. *The Mexican Muralists*. New York: Crown Publishers, 1960

Reed, John. *Insurgent Mexico*. New York: International Publishers, 1969

Reed Torres, Luis and María del Carmen Ruiz Castañeda. *El periodismo en México: 500 años de historia*. México DF: Edamex, 1998

Restall, Matthew. *The Maya World: Yucatec Culture and Society, 1550–1850*. Stanford: Stanford University Press, 1997

Retablos y Exvotos. México DF: Museo Franz Mayer/Artes de México, 2000

Reyes, Alfonso. *La X en la frente*. México DF: Porrúa y Obregón, 1952

Reyes, Aurelio de los. *Orígenes del cine en México, 1896–1900*. México DF: Fondo de Cultura Económica. 1984

Reyes de la Maza, Luis. *Cien años de teatro mexicano, 1810–1910*. México DF: Sep-Setentas, 1972

Ricard, R. *The Spiritual Conquest of Mexico*. Berkeley: University of California Press, 1966

Rico, Araceli. *Frida Kahlo: fantasía de un cuerpo herido*. México DF: Plaza y Valdés, 1987

Riding, Alan. *Distant Neighbors: A Portrait of the Mexicans*. New York: Vintage, 2000

Rivera, Diego. *My Art, My Life: An Autobiography*. New York: Citadel Press, 1960

Rochfort, Desmond. *Mexican Muralists: Orozco, Rivera, Siqueiros*. New York: Universe, 1993

Rodríguez, Antonio. *A History of Mexican Mural Painting*. London: Thames & Hudson, 1969

Rodríguez, James E. (ed.) *Mexican and Mexican American Experience in the 19th Century*. Tempe, AZ: Bilingual Press/Editorial Bilingiie, 1989

——. *Common Border, Uncommon Paths: Race, Culture, and National Identity in U.S.–Mexican Relations*. Yarmouth, ME: Scholarly Resources, 1997

Rodríguez, Jeanette. *Our Lady of Guadalupe.* Austin: University of Texas Press, 1994

Rodríguez, Victoria Elizabeth. *Decentralization in Mexico.* Boulder: Westview, 1997

——. *Women's Participation in Mexican Political Life.* Boulder: Westview, 1998

Rodríguez Prampolini, Ida. *El surrealismo y el arte fantástico de México.* México DF: UNAM, Instituto de Investigaciones Estéticas, 1983

Rojas, Pedro *et al. Historia general del arte mexicano.* México DF: Hermes (numerous volumes in a series that began to be published in the 1960s)

Romo, Cristina. *Ondas, canales y mensajes: un perfil de la radio en México.* Guadalajara: ITESO, 1991

Rosario, Rubén del. *El español de América.* Sharon, CT: Troutman Press, 1970

Rotella, Sebastian. *Twilight on the Line: Underworlds and Politics at the U.S.–Mexican Border.* New York: Norton, 1998

Rouffignac, A.L. *The Contemporary Peasantry in Mexico: A Class Analysis.* New York: Praeger, 1985

Rozat, Guy. *Los orígenes de la nación. Pasado indígena e historia nacional.* México DF: Universidad Iberoamericana, 2001

Rubenstein, Anne. *Bad Language, Naked Ladies, and Other Threats to the Nation: A Political History of Comic Books in Mexico.* Durham, NC: Duke University Press, 1998

Ruiz, Ramón Eduardo. *On the Rim of Mexico: Encounters of the Rich and Poor.* Boulder: Westview, 1998

Ruiz, V.L. and S. Tiano. *Women on the U.S.–Mexico Border.* Boston: Allen & Unwin, 1987

Ruy Sánchez, Alberto. *Mitología de un cine en crisis.* México DF: La Red de Jonas, 1981

Ryan, Alan (ed.). *A Reader's Companion to Mexico.* San Diego: Harcourt Brace, 1995

Sabat de Rivers, Georgina. *El 'sueño' de Sor Juana Inés de la Cruz: tradiciones literarias y originalidad.* London: Tamesis, 1976

Sahagún, Bernardino. *Primeros memoriales.* Translated by T. Sullivan. Norman: University of Oklahoma Press, 1997

Saint-Lu, André (ed.). *Bartolomé de las Casas: Brevísima relación de la destrucción de las Indias.* Madrid: Cátedra, 1987

Salas, Elizabeth. *Soldaderas in the Mexican Military: Myth and History.* Austin: University of Texas Press, 1990

Saldívar, Gabriel. *Historia de la música en México.* México DF: Editorial Cultura, 1934

Sánchez de Armas, Miguel Angel (coordinador). *Apuntes para una historia de la televisión mexicana.* México: Revista Mexicana de Comunicación, 1998

Sanderson, Susan R. Walsh. *Land Reform in Mexico, 1910–1980.* New York: Academic Press, 1984

Santamaría, Francisco. *Diccionario de mejicanismos.* México DF: Editorial Porrúa, 1983

Sayers Peden, Margaret. *Out of the Volcano: Portraits of Contemporary Mexican Artists.* Washington, DC: Smithsonian Institution Press, 1991

Scarborough, Vernon L. and David R. Wilcox (eds.). *The Mesoamerican Ballgame.* Tucson: University of Arizona Press, 1991

Schaefer, Claudia. *Textured Lives: Women, Art, and Representation in Modern Mexico*. Tucson: University of Arizona Press, 1992

——. *Bored to Distraction: Cinema of Excess in End-of-Century Mexico and Spain*. Albany: State University of New York Press, 2003

Schechter, John Mendell. *Music in Latin American Culture: Regional Traditions*. New York: Schirmer Books, 1999

Schele, Linda and David Freidel. *A Forest of Kings: The Untold Story of the Ancient Maya*. New York: William Morrow, 1990

Schele, Linda and Mary Ellen Miller. *The Blood of Kings: Dynasty and Ritual in Maya Art*. Fort Worth, TX: Kimbell Art Museum, 1986

Schmeckebier, Laurence E. *Modern Mexican Art*. Minneapolis: University of Minnesota Press, 1939

Schmidhuber, Guillermo. *El teatro mexicano en cierne, 1922–1938*. New York: Peter Lang, 1992

Schmidt, Henry C. *The Roots of Lo Mexicano: Self and Society in Mexican Thought, 1900–1934*. College Station: Texas A and M University Press, 1978

Schroeder, Susan (ed.). *Indian Women in Early Mexico*. Norman: University of Oklahoma Press, 1997

Schwartz, Perla. *Rosario Castellanos: mujer que supo latín*. México DF: Katún, 1984

Sefchovich, Sara. *México: país de ideas, país de novelas*. México DF: Grijalbo, 1987

Séjourné, Laurette. *La Pensée des anciens américains*. Paris: F. Maspéro, 1966

Sell, Barry D. and Louise M. Burkhart (eds.). *Nahuatl Theatre*. Norman: University of Oklahoma Press, 2004

Sharer, Robert J. *The Ancient Maya*. Stanford: Stanford University Press, 1994

Sheehy, Daniel. *Mariachi Music in America*. New York: Oxford University Press, 2005

Sheridan, Guillermo. *Los Contemporáneos ayer*. México DF: Fondo de Cultura Económica, 1985

Siade, Giorgiana Paulín de. *Los indígenas bilingües de México frente a la castellanización*. México DF: Universidad Nacional Autónoma de México, 1974

Simpson, Lesley Byrd. *Many Mexicos*. Berkeley: University of California Press, 1967

Siqueiros, David Alfaro. *Siqueiros*. México DF: Ediciones Galería de Misrachi, 1965

——. *Art and Revolution*. London: Lawrence & Wishart, 1975

Smith, Bradley. *Mexico: A History of Art*. New York: Harper & Row, 1968

Smith, Clive B. *Builders in the Sun: Five Mexican Architects*. New York: Architectural Book Publishing Company, Inc., 1967

Smith, J.B. *The Image of Guadalupe: Myth or Miracle?* New York: Doubleday, 1983

Smith, Lois Elwyn. *Mexico and the Spanish Republicans*. Berkeley: University of California Press, 1955.

Smith, Michael E. *The Aztecs*. Oxford: Blackwell, 2003

Smith, Verity (ed.). *The Encyclopaedia of Latin American Literature*. London: Fitzroy Dearborn, 1997

Sommers, Joseph. *After the Storm: Landmarks of the Modern Mexican Novel*. Albuquerque: University of New Mexico Press, 1968

Sosa Pedroza, Laura *et al. Diccionario del español usual en México*. México DF: Colegio de Mexico, 2001

Soto, Shirlene Ann. *Emergence of the Modern Mexican Woman*. New York: Arden, 1990

Soustelle, Jacques. *Daily Life of the Aztecs*. Stanford: Stanford University Press, 1961

——. *Los olmecas*. México DF: Fondo de Cultura Económica, 2000

Stabb, Martin. *In Quest of Indentity: Patterns in the Spanish American Essay of Ideas, 1890–1960*. Chapel Hill: University of North Carolina Press, 1967

Standish, Peter and Steven M. Bell. *Culture and Customs of Mexico*. Westport and London: Greenwood Press, 2004

Stavenhagen Gruenbaum, Rodolfo. *La cuestión étnica*. México DF: El Colegio de México, 2001

Steele, Cynthia. *Politics, Gender, and the Mexican Novel, 1968–88: Beyond the Pyramid.* Austin: University of Texas Press, 1992

Stein, Philip. *Siqueiros: His Life and His Works*. New York: International, 1994

Stevens, Donald F. *Based on a True Story: Latin American History at the Movies*. Wilmington, DE: Scholarly Resources, 1997

Stevenson, Robert. *Music in México: a Historical Survey*. New York: Thomas Crowell, 1952

——. *Music in Aztec and Inca Territory*. Berkeley: University of California Press, 1968

——. *Christmas Music from Baroque Mexico*. Berkeley: University of California Press, 1974

Suárez, Víctor. *El español que se habla en Yucatán*. Mérida: Universidad de Yucatán, 1980

Suárez Radillo, Carlos Miguel. *El teatro neoclásico y costumbrista hispanoamericano*. Madrid: Ediciones Cultura Hispánica, 1984

——. *El teatro romántico hispanoamericano*. Madrid: Ediciones Cultura Hispánica, 1993

Suchlicki, Jaime. *Mexico: From Montezuma to Nafta, Chiapas, and Beyond.* New York: Brasseys, 1996

Sullivan, Edward J. *et al. Latin American Art in the Twentieth Century*. London: Phaidon, 2000

Sullivan, Edward J. and Clayton C. Kirking. *Nahum B. Zenil: Witness to the Self\ Testigo del Ser*. San Francisco: The Mexican Museum, 1996

Sullivan, Thelma. *Compendium of Nahuatl Grammar.* Salt Lake City: University of Utah Press, 1988

Szanto, George. *Inside the Statues of Saints: Mexican Writers on Culture and Corruption, Politics and Daily Life.* New York: Vehicle, 1997

Tangeman, Michael. *Mexico at the Crossroads: Politics, the Church, and the Poor.* Maryknoll, N.Y.: Orbis, 1995

Tatum, Charles. *Chicano Literature*. Boston: Twayne, 1982

Taylor, Kathy. *The New Narrative of Mexico*. Lewisburg, IA: Bucknell University Press, 1994

Taylor, W.B. 'The Virgin of Guadalupe in New Spain: An Inquiry into the Social History of Marian Devotion'. *American Ethnologist*, 14/1, 1987, 9–33

Tedlock, Dennis. *Popol Vuh: The Mayan Book of the Dawn of Life*. New York: Simon & Schuster, 1996

——. *Rabinal Achí: A Mayan Drama of War and Sacrifice*. New York: Oxford University Press, 2003

Teichman, Judith A. *Policymaking in Mexico: From Boom to Crisis*. Boston: Allen & Unwin, 1988

Teichmann, Reinhardt. *Esta narrativa mexicana: Ensayos y entrevistas*. México DF: Leega, 1991

Thomas, Hugh. *Conquest: Moctezuma, Cortés, and the Fall of Old Mexico*. New York: Touchstone, 1995

Tibol, Raquel. *Frida Kahlo: una vida abierta*. México DF: Oasis, 1983

Todorov, Tzvetan. *The Conquest of America*. New York: Harper & Row, 1984

Toor, Frances. *A Treasury of Mexican Folkways*. New York: Crown Publishers, 1947

Torres, Vicente Francisco. *Narradores mexicanos de fin de siglo*. México DF: Universidad Autónoma Metropolitana, 1989

Toscano, Salvador. *Arte precolombino de México y de la América Central*. México DF: UNAM, 1984

Toussaint, Manuel. *Pintura colonial en México*. México DF: Imprenta Universitaria, 1965 (translated and edited by E. Wilder Weismann as *Colonial Art in Mexico*. Austin: University of Texas Press, 1967)

Tovar de Teresa, Guillermo, *Pintura y escultura en Nueva España (1551–1640)*. México DF: Azabache, 1992

Trejo Delarbe, Raúl, (coordinador). *Televisa: el quinto poder*. México, DF: Claves Latinoamericanas, 1985

——. *La sociedad ausente*. México DF: Cal y arena, 1992

——. *Ver, pero también leer. Televisión y prensa: del consumo a la democracia*, México DF: Instituto Nacional del Consumidos, n.d.

Trueblood, Alan S. *A Sor Juana Anthology*. Cambridge: Harvard University Press, 1988

Tuñón, Julia. *Mujeres de luz y sombra en el cine mexicano: la construcción de una imagen (1939–1952)*. México DF: Colegio de México, IMCINE, 1998

Turner, F.C. *The Dynamic of Mexican Nationalism*. Chapel Hill: University of North Carolina Press, 1968

Unger, Roni. *Poesía en voz alta in the Theater of Mexico*. Columbia: University of Missouri Press, 1981

Uriarte, María Teresa (ed.). *El juego de pelota en Mesoamérica. Raíces y supervivencias*. México DF: Siglo XXI, 1992

Usigli, Rodolfo. *Mexico in the Theatre*. Translated by W.P. Scott. Mississippi: University of Mississippi Romance Monographs, 1976

Vaillant, George C. *The Aztecs of Mexico*. Harmondsworth: Penguin, 1961

Valenzuela Arce, José Manuel. *Nuestros piensos: culturas populares en la frontera México–Estados Unidos*. México DF: CONACULTA, 1998

—— (ed.). *Por las fronteras del norte. Una aproximación cultural a la frontera México-Estados Unidos*. México DF: Fondo de Cultura Económica, 2003

Vallens, V.M. *Working Women in Mexico During the Porfiriato, 1880–1910*. San Francisco: R. & E. Research Associates, 1978

Van Young, Eric (ed.). *Mexico's Regions: Comparative History and Development*. San Diego: UCSD Center for U.S.–Mexican Studies, 1992

Vázquez, Josefina Zoraida and Lorenzo Meyer. *The United States and Mexico*. Chicago: University of Chicago Press, 1985

Vásquez, Josefina Zoraida (ed.). *Gran historia de México ilustrada*. México DF: Planeta DeAgostini, 2001

Vaughan, Mary Kay. *La política cultural en la Revolución. Maestros, campesinos y escuelas en México, 1930–1940*. México DF: Fondo de Cultura Económica, 2001

Velazco, Salvador. *Visiones de Anáhuac*. Guadalajara: Universidad de Guadalajara, 2003

Vila, Pablo. *Crossing Borders, Reinforcing Borders: Social categories, Metaphors and Narrative Identities on the U.S.–Mexico Frontier*. Austin: University of Texas Press, 2000

Villanueva, Tino (ed.). *Chicanos: Antología histórica y literaria*. México DF: Fondo de Cultura Económica, 1980

Villarello Vélez, Ildefonso. *El habla de Coahuila*. México: Ediciones Mastil, 1970

Villegas, Abelardo. *Filosofía de lo mexicano*. México DF: Fondo de Cultura Económica, 1960

——. *El pensamiento mexicano en el siglo XX*. México DF: Fondo de Cultura Económica, 1993

Villoro, Luis. *Estado plural, pluralidad de culturas*. México DF: Paidós, 1998

Viqueira Montalbán, Juan Pedro. *¿Relajados o reprimidos? Diversiones públicas y vida social en la Ciudad de México durante el Siglo de las Luces*. México DF: Fondo de Cultura Económica, 2001

Warman, Arturo. *Los indios mexicanos en el umbral del milenio*. México DF: Fondo de Cultura Económica, 2003

Warner, Ralph E. *Historia de la novela mexicana en el siglo XIX*. México DF: Antigua Librería Robredo, 1953

Warnock, John W. *The Other Mexico: The North American Triangle Completed*. Montreal: Black Rose, 1995

Weismann, Elizabeth Wilder. *Mexican Art and the Academia de San Carlos*. Austin: University of Texas Press, 1962

——. *Art and Time in Mexico: From the Conquest to the Revolution*. New York: Harper & Row, 1985

Weiss, Judith A. *Latin American Popular Theatre: The First Five Centuries*. Albuquerque: University of New Mexico Press, 1993

Westheim, Paul. *Tamayo*. Mexico DF: Ediciones Artes de México, 1957

Widdifield, Stacie G. *The Embodiment of the National in Late Nineteenth-Century Mexican Painting*. Tucson: University of Arizona Press, 1996

Wilkie, James W. and Albert I. Michaels. *Revolution in Mexico: Years of Upheaval, 1910–1940*. Tucson: University of Arizona Press, 1984

Williams, Jerry. *El teatro del México colonial. Época misionera*. New York: Peter Lang, 1992

Williamson, Rodney. *El habla de Tabasco: estudio lingüístico*. México DF: Colegio de México, 1986

Wolf, Eric. *Sons of the Shaking Earth*. Chicago: University of Chicago Press, 1959

——. *Pueblos y culturas de Mesoamérica*. Mexico DF: Era, 1997

Wolfe, Bertram David. *The Fabulous Life of Diego Rivera*. New York: Stein & Day, 1963

Womack, John. *Zapata and the Mexican Revolution*. New York: Vintage, 1970

Wood, Stephanie. *Transcending Conquest*. Norman: University of Oklahoma Press, 2003

Zamora, Martha. *Frida Kahlo: the Brush of Anguish*. San Francisco: Chronicle, 1990

Zarauz López, Héctor L. *La fiesta de la muerte*. México: CONACULTA, 2000

——. *México: Fiestas cívicas, familiares, laborales y nuevos festejos*. México DF: CONACULTA, 2000

Zea, Leopoldo. *Apogeo y decadencia del positivimo en México*. México DF: Colegio de México, 1944

—— (ed.). *Características de la cultura nacional*. México DF: UNAM, 1969

Zorita, Alonso de. *Life and Labor in Ancient Mexico*. Translated by B. Keen. New Brunswick, NJ: Rutgers University Press, 1963

WEBSITES

Websites are notoriously unstable and often unreliable in content. The few that have been identified here are thought likely to provide sound information and to last for some time

Lanic.utexas.edu/la/mexico/ *LANIC is the richest source of information on the web for information on Latin America and has links of all sorts*

Mexonline.com/culture.htm *General information*

Mexconnect.com/mex_/ *General information and photos, links*

Mexico.com/index.html *General information*

Inegi.gob.wx/ *Good for official statistics*

Mexico.web.com.mx/ *Provides links to a wide variety of sources*

Cinemexicano.mty.itesm.mx/front.html *For cinema*

Unam.mx//filmoteca/ *Information on cinema from the National Autonomous University*

Imcine.gob.mx/ *The official site of the Mexican Film Institute*

Wam.umd.edu/ ?dwilt/mfb.html *On cinema*

Lonestar.utsa.edu/rlwilson/pio.html *Links to sites on music and cinema*

En.wikipedia.org/wiki/Music_of_Mexico *Basic information on a variety of musical genres*

Newslink.org/nonus.mex.html *Access to the Mexican news media*

Lib.utsa.edu/Instruction/helpsheets/mexstates2.html *For online access to Mexican newspapers*

Lib.nmsu.edu/subject/bord/laguia *Covers U.S. border culture*

Utep.edu/border/ *Another site rich with information on the U.S. border culture*

Cnca.gob.mx/index_content.html *The official site of CONACULTA, Mexico's National Council for Culture and the arts*

Artcyclopedia.com/nationalities/Mexican.html *For art*

Museoblaisten.com *A virtual museum that gives very good representative samples of Mexican painting*

Interamericaninstitute.org *A research-oriented site dealing with cultural history*

e-local.gob.mx *Official regional information.*

Azteca.net/Aztec/nahuatl/index.shtml *For the Aztecs and Nahua culture*

Mexico.udg.mx/principal/index.html *Site run by the University of Guadalajara, with information on a number of cultural subjects*

INDEX

www.ingramcontent.com/pod-product-compliance
Lightning Source LLC
LaVergne TN
LVHW050525100826
845148LV00002B/440